Space Regulations Library

Volume 11

The *Space Regulations Library* is a long-standing series of cutting-edge research written by practitioners and academics and addressing novel and emerging issues relating to the national and international regulation of space activities. The series covers key topics relating to, among other topics of significance, various approaches to the regulation of national space activities, the privatisation and commercialisation of space activities, NewSpace applications and developments, the role of cybersecurity and Artificial Intelligence in space activities, military uses of outer space, the exploration, exploitation and utilisation of space natural resources, and the settlement of space disputes. Through a rigorous selection and peer-review process, the *Space Regulations Library* aims to publish innovative works that highlight legal and policies issues of interest and concern for actors and stakeholders in the competitive and congested domain of outer space. In a shared global commons where various socio-economic, scientific, security, and commercial interests intersect, it is vital for industry professionals, government officials and academics worldwide to take note of existing rules as well as the challenges and trends in the formulation and implementation of regulations and policies governing space activities. With the practical insights and recommendations offered by the authors on a variety of topics in a domain where developments often outpace existing rules and policies, the *Space Regulations Library* aims to contribute to the continued dialogue on how to safeguard and promote the long-term sustainability, safety and security of outer space.

Ian Grosner
Editor

Space Regulation in Latin America

Past, Present, and Future

Springer

Editor
Ian Grosner
Legal Department
Brazilian Space Agency
Brasilia, DF, Brazil

ISSN 1572-6134 ISSN 2542-9558 (electronic)
Space Regulations Library
ISBN 978-3-032-05827-0 ISBN 978-3-032-05828-7 (eBook)
https://doi.org/10.1007/978-3-032-05828-7

This Springer imprint is published by the registered company Springer Nature Switzerland AG
The registered company address is: Gewerbestrasse 11, 6330 Cham, Switzerland

Foreword

This book provides timely evidence of the progress being made in the field of space activities in Latin America and the Caribbean. In this respect, a very well-thought-out selection has been made, conducted by Ian Grosner as editor, on different visions from a national and regional perspective. Issues related to the national analysis have been addressed by Carolina Catani (Argentina), Ian Grosner (Brazil), Victoria F. Valdivia Cerda (Chile), Fermín Romero Vázquez (Mexico), Hebe Romero (Paraguay), and Mariana García (Uruguay). In addition, the book is enriched with studies from a regional perspective, where Latin American and Caribbean Network of institutions and universities work on issues related to outer space technology, science, policy, and law (ReLaCa Espacio), by Marta Gaggero and the development of spatial issues in Central America studied by Alina Nassar.

The authors face the challenge of analyzing outer space activities in detail, indicating which international space treaties have been signed by each of the states surveyed, if the state in question is a member of COPUOS, or to what extent their space activities can be classified as dual use or are for defense or civilian purposes only. It also indicates whether there is a UN-controlled registry of space objects or the state under review has a specific national space law. Moreover, it discusses if a state has created a space agency or, where appropriate, which is the main regulatory body responsible for overseeing space activities. It also studies to what extent the state under review conducts space regulation activities and how it authorizes, controls, and supervises private companies carrying out space activities. How is the state involved in international cooperation in the space sector, both in aspects related to new technologies and in their representation in international organizations? It discusses whether partnerships exist with other Latin American countries and also indicates what prospects the state has regarding regulation related to space debris, militarization and weaponization of space, or the exploitation of natural space resources.

The wealth of reflections in this study makes this work an essential reference to know the state of the matter of space activities in Latin America and the Caribbean. Let us keep in mind that the development of effective laws and policies on national and regional space activities depends on the presence of appropriate professionals who are able to disseminate information and knowledge on the legal framework governing outer space activities and promote the need to ratify the UN treaties on outer space.

Above all, the current and future development of national and regional space law will depend on the ability to pass on the experience and effort put into practice by the actors concerned in promoting cooperation in the Latin American and Caribbean regions in matters that directly affect the economic, technological, and social interests of the states in the region.

Currently, there are a number of challenges that should not go unnoticed, as they directly impact the development of the states in the region and the possibility of not being displaced from international competition compared to other regions of the world. Latin American and Caribbean states have a lot to contribute in issues related to space activities, as can be deduced from the reflections in this book.

The international community is confronted with a series of new models of spatial activities that, as a result of the development of technology, are positioning themselves as novel fields of activity that require detailed legal regulation. The aim is to prevent future problems, where space becomes a chaotic environment in which the law of the economically more powerful prevails to the detriment of humanity's interests. As the Preamble to the Outer Space Treaty reminds us, "their exploration and utilisation should be carried out for the benefit of all peoples, regardless of their level of economic and scientific development."

Indeed, issues related to the commercial exploration of outer space arise, since, in the face of the claims of some states or private companies that have expressed their intention to appropriate certain areas of the Moon or Mars or asteroid resources, there is an urgent need to clarify the basis and limits of commercial uses in space. Let us remember that Article 11 of the Moon Agreement tells us that the Moon and its natural resources are the common heritage of mankind and that, although few states have ratified it, this does not preclude customary law from developing over time that Latin American and Caribbean countries should consider. This is especially significant when limited resources benefit developing countries, rather than only major powers or multinational companies..

It is important to note that private companies are now involved in activities that were once the sole responsibility of governments. As a result, they must comply with the legal regulations. It is crucial for governments to remember their obligations under Article VI of the Outer Space Treaty, which clearly states that nongovernmental entities intending to carry out activities in outer space must obtain authorization and be continuously supervised by the state. Therefore, it is recommended for governments to incorporate appropriate requirements into their national laws to ensure that any activities conducted by private entities are properly authorized and continually monitored.

Another theme that is making headway in the context of space activities is related to space tourism, since private companies and entities have started to make flights to space. Consider the aggravating circumstance that in the absence of specific regulations, these companies are using part of the airspace and part of outer space and that, as specified in the Convention on International Liability for damage caused by space objects, we are faced with different legal regimes in liability matters. It should be remembered that in Article II, it states that when the damage is caused in the airspace or on the Earth's surface, the responsibility is absolute. In contrast, in Article III, it should be noted that when the damage occurs outside the Earth's surface and outside of airspace, the liability in outer space shall be relative, based on guilt alone. We might deduce that it would be timely to consider that these types of activities are claiming to delineate exact responsibilities of the companies dedicated to this type of tourism, regulating the notions of responsibility and registration considering air law and space law.

Therefore, it becomes obvious that the development of space law as a whole calls for an appropriate legal regime regulating trade activities in the use, exploration, and exploitation of space and its resources. The specificity of space activities must be considered in order to not only respect the principles that have been approved by all states in the five space treaties but also, in the shaping of new principles, take account of technological advances and the emergence of new actors that were not planned in the 1970s when the five treaties were developed.

We are in the twenty-first century, facing a paradigm shift where, as a consequence of the globalization of economic activities, we noted that the public sector builds partnerships with the private sector in the framework of their public policies. This implies the need to develop new strategies in the field of space activities, because states alone will not be able to withstand international competition, and it will be appropriate that, in the Latin American context, projects such as Latin American and Caribbean Space Agency (ALCE) and *Red Latinoamericana y del Caribe del Espacio* (ReLaCa Espacio) are encouraged, in order to generate the appropriate synergy to unite and empower national agencies.

The Latin American and Caribbean states should take into consideration specific project types, such as the need for integration, at a national level, with the different sectors interested in developing space activities to achieve the unification of civilian and military interests at the government level, including consultation with academic and business circles, in order to generate projects and programs to expand its national and regional outreach. This must be done without forgetting to declare, from the government spheres, the willingness of the state to use space for peaceful purposes in accordance with what is specified in the space treaties, as well as develop and enhance scientific programs to strive for the application of new technologies that help to promote the economy and a well-coordinated spatial policy and with a positive impact on the population, since space is intimately linked to the interests of society.

In the context of these reflections, the importance of promoting "space culture" should be noted in the Latin American and Caribbean countries. To do so, we should enhance linked education to issues related to space law and policy as one of the basic pillars of "space culture." Let us remember that, in 2002, at the IV Space Conference of the Americas, it was suggested the creation of a Regional Education Center in the areas of space science, technology, and legislation. Let us keep in mind that the importance a state attaches to space law education is intimately related to the technological and scientific development of a country.

In the framework of the COPUOS Subcommittee on Scientific and Technical Matters, in its report of the 61st session in 2024, it was recommended that the Year 2029 be proclaimed as the international year on raising awareness about asteroids and planetary defense. During the session, it was pointed out that it would be an excellent opportunity to carry out an educational campaign on the danger posed by near-Earth objects (NEO), in order to raise awareness among states and the public opinion on the potential danger posed by the impact of an asteroid hitting our planet.

However, conflicts do not only come from space, for we also have them on Earth. The international community lives in uncertain times where wars rage against their peoples, whereby, from our perspective of Latin American jurists and experts on space affairs, we have the responsibility to foster international relations and cooperation, as well as the peaceful settlement of disputes in the field of space activities. We must not forget that in the Permanent Court of Arbitration, we have a section for conflict resolution in matters related to outer space with a list of expert arbitrators. Lastly, it should be noted that Latin American and Caribbean states have, in the United Nations Committee on the Peaceful Uses of Space (COPUOS) and in its Office for Outer Space Affairs (UNOOSA), the best-case scenario to claim their rights before the international community. For that reason, those countries in the area that are already members of COPUOS are to be congratulated and should encourage those that are not yet members to join its ranks.

Jaen, Spain Juan Manuel de Faramiñán Gilbert

Contents

RELACA and the Latin American Round of the Manfred Lachs Space Law Moot Court Competition Aim to Expand the Knowledge of Space Law in the Latin American and Caribbean Region by Promoting Its Development in the Educational Area

Marta Gaggero

Contents

Abstract The Latin American and Caribbean Network of Universities and Institutions that Research on Space Technology, Policy and Law, ReLaCa Espacio (RELACA), is an academic institution created thanks to the impulse given by the European Center for Space Law, which proposed to create something similar in the Latin American and Caribbean region. The objective of the Network is to bring

---

M. Gaggero (✉)
Red Latinoamericana y del Caribe del Espacio, RELACA Espacio, Montevideo, Uruguay

I. Grosner (ed.), *Space Regulation in Latin America*, Space Regulations Library 11, https://doi.org/10.1007/978-3-032-05828-7_1

together all those institutions and people interested in space in order to achieve greater development of this subject in the region. The legal framework governing RELACA is made up of the Commitment Act signed in Buenos Aires in 2017 and the Statute that establishes the aims and purposes of the institution and its structure. Since its first meeting at the Sergio Arboleda University in Bogotá, Colombia, in 2016, which was the starting point of the Network, RELACA has organized ten annual international meetings. Another important milestone in RELACA's development was the recognition, in 2020, by the International Institute of Space Law (IISL), of Latin America as the fifth region represented in the Manfred Lachs Space Law Moot Court Competition. The Latin American round would take place during the annual RELACA Meetings.

1 Introduction

The Latin American and Caribbean Network of Universities and Institutions that Research on Technology, Policy and Law of Outer Space, ReLaCa Espacio (RELACA), was born under the impetus given by the European Centre for Space Law (ECSL)[1] of the European Space Agency (ESA). The ECSL expressed the importance of bringing together universities and institutions that research issues related to technology, policy, science, and law of outer space. It underlined how useful it would be to transfer the European experience to the area of Latin America and the Caribbean, taking into account the developments in the space sector, which have taken place in this region in recent decades.

Taking into consideration this impulse and this initiative, the implementation of the Network began to be devised. This took into account the importance—which has been increasing in recent decades—of research relating to activities in outer space; the development of space technology; the planning of space policies; and the legal support provided by the corpus juris spatialis generated within the framework of the United Nations with the support of the majority of the states of the international community.

In addition, as already indicated, consideration was given to the increase in outer space-related activities by states in Latin America and the Caribbean.

[1] ECSL, created in 1987, has a consolidated historical trajectory through which it has managed to transmit at the European level a whole philosophy of understanding the branch considered as the most creative of public international law, "trendsetting."

Based on previous collaborations with Latin America and faithfully following the mandate stipulated in UNISPACE III and the foundations of Public International Law and its most illustrious creators, ECSL chose to share/extend its experience with/to other subjects located in South America and the Caribbean. Through this initiative, ECSL intends to materialize the principles of international solidarity, cooperation between states, common benefit, peace, freedom, etc., all this to make space law a legal tool at the service of society and states. www.esa.int/About_Us/Space_Law_virtual_network_with_Latin_American_countries/Description.

2 The Creation of RELACA

In view of the above, and in order to materialize the project of creating an institution dedicated to studies and research in the area of Latin America and the Caribbean, the Seminar "Space Activities: Legal Perspective" was organized by the Sergio Arboleda University of Colombia in 2016, an event considered the starting point for the creation of RELACA.

The mentors and ideologues of RELACA were present at the event: Dr. Marco Ferrazzani, legal advisor of the European Space Agency (ESA) and member of the ECSL Board of Directors, and Dr. Juan Manuel de Faramiñan Gilbert, professor of public international law and international relations at the University of Jaén, Spain. Eng. Raúl Joya from the Sergio Arboleda University joined them. Mr. Joya was part of the university's research team that developed the first Colombian satellite, the microsatellite Libertad 1, launched in 2007, a project in which Joya participated as mission director.[2] Engineer Joya then became the link between this continent and the promoters of the creation of the RELACA.

After this meeting in Colombia, plans began to organize the next one, thus beginning a series of meetings or congresses that meant the development and growth of RELACA.

The next meeting took place at the University of El Salvador, Buenos Aires, Argentina, in March 2017, an event that was organized by Dr. Mercedes Esquivel de Cocca, professor of air and space law at the university, who afterwards became the National Contact Point (NCP) of Argentine. The Argentine Space Agency (CONAE), ESA, the University of Jaén, and the Sergio Arboleda University supported the congress.

2.1 *Commitment Act*

At the 2017 Buenos Aires Meeting, a Commitment Act was signed on March 21. The signatories adhered to the purpose of expanding the culture of outer space through the study and dissemination of technology, politics, and law as fundamental factors of scientific and human progress.

On that occasion, inspired by the ECSL experience, the need to draw up an annual plan and draft a Statute that would govern the operation of RELACA was pointed out. It was highlighted in the document that humanity faces an important challenge that was embodied in the five space treaties developed within the framework of the United Nations and emphasized the transcendental work carried out by the Committee on the Peaceful Uses of Outer Space (COPUOS) in order to preserve outer space as a common good.

---

[2] El primer satélite colombiano. https://www.usergioarboleda.edu.co/el-primer-satelite-colombiano/.

The Commitment Act included a special thanks to the Head of ESA's legal service, Marco Ferrazzani, and the work of its commissioner, Juan Manuel de Faramiñán Gilbert, who marked the way forward. This would consist of bringing together all those universities, agencies, and research centers that promote knowledge in matters related to outer space.

The Statutes, together with the Commitment Act, constituted the legal structure of the Network.

It was agreed on that occasion that Dr. Juan Manuel de Faramiñán Gilbert would act as international director of RELACA, together with the National Point of Contacts (NPOCs) that had signed the Act, the International Secretary, and the Academic Council.

2.2 *Statute of Operation*

In accordance with the provisions of the Statute, the Network is an international academic organization, composed of natural or legal persons, administered and governed by an International Board of Directors, whose purpose will be to coordinate and encourage the study of space activities in Latin America and the Caribbean through academic institutions, official entities, and individuals.

The possibility of implementing cooperation agreements that allow the establishment of scientific research programs and the training of researchers and professionals in the scientific and technological field is considered.

It is also provided that international meetings will be held annually for the dissemination, proposal, and discussion of projects, news, and prospects of the different aspects of space activity.

3 National Points of Contact

In order to generate an effective infrastructure, the Network encouraged the creation of National Points of Contact (NPOCs) in each of the countries where the Network's activities were formalized. The NPOCs will be specialists and/or representatives of universities, institutions, or bodies of recognized prestige and national professional qualification in matters related to outer space technology, policy, and law.

Each NPOC shall assume the purposes and objectives of the Network and, as far as possible, promote research on all topics related to the exploration, use, and research of outer space from the legal, political, sociological, communicational, scientific, and technological point of view, for which the following objectives shall be taken into account:

- To take advantage of and complement the efforts made and the resources available in Latin America and the Caribbean in the field of research related to outer

space and to promote the development of these efforts and resources, including documentation in a coordinated manner
- To promote knowledge and support research activities, including the dissemination of information and the organization of workshops and professional exchanges
- To promote exchanges, through the organization of national and international colloquiums and congresses in all disciplines related to outer space

In each country where an NPOC formalizes, there will be a national director who will direct it, forming afterwards a work team at the national level that will act with the national director (vice director, secretary, treasurer, members).

In the beginning, RELACA had NPOCs in Colombia, Argentina, Uruguay, Chile, and Spain, later joined by the NPOCs of Paraguay, Mexico, Brazil, the Dominican Republic, Guatemala, Peru, Ecuador, and Honduras.

4 "Dr. Aldo Armando Cocca" Award

In 2022, the Board of Directors of RELACA decided to confer an award to the best research paper presented at the annual meetings. It would bear the name Dr. Aldo Armando Cocca, and its purpose was to develop vocations in the younger generations.

The award ceremony would take place during the annual meetings.

Aldo Armando Cocca was a professor, ambassador, jurist, and researcher internationally recognized as a pioneer in space matters. In reference to his background, it is worth mentioning, among other outstanding achievements, that Dr. Cocca was the one who presented the first doctoral thesis in space law at the University of Buenos Aires, Argentina. He was also the one who upheld in the COPUOS his doctrine of space as a Common Heritage of Mankind.

He is considered one of the creators of space law.

5 Manfred Lachs Space Law Moot Court Competition

In 1992, the International Institute of Space Law (IISL) introduced the Manfred Lachs Space Law Moot Court Competition (MLSLMCC). This competition is a simulated oral argument in which a case must be resolved by applying the rules of space law. The teams participating in the competition have to present before a court the legal arguments regarding a dispute between States in the framework of space law, where the parties must defend each of the positions. The first stage consists of presenting in writing the arguments to defend each of the opposing positions, and the second stage consists of presenting the arguments orally before a panel of judges who are experts in the field and who ask questions and evaluate aspects such as the quality of each team's analysis, their knowledge, their advocacy skills, and their understanding of the problem.

The MLSLMCC offers law students participating in the competition the opportunity to deepen their knowledge and experience in public international law and outer space law.

Since its creation, different regions of the world (Africa, Asia-Pacific, North America, and Europe) have joined the competition, carrying out regional rounds in which different universities have participated and the winners of each round have competed in the international final that takes place during the annual congress of the International Astronautical Federation (IAF). The winning teams, in addition to receiving recognition and prizes, would be financially supported, both in terms of travel to the country where the world final is held, accommodation, and food.

Usually, three judges of the International Court of Justice score the MLSLMCC World Final.

Latin America was not included as a region. In view of this, Dr. Jairo Becerra, member of the Board of RELACA, belonging to the Catholic University of Colombia, had the initiative, together with a collaborating team of the University, to summon students from universities in the region to participate in the MLSLMCC.

In 2018, the challenge of opening the Latin American round was taken on, and in 2019, the first edition of the competition was held as a test, with a view to forming the fifth region that would participate in the world rounds. The event was held at the Catholic University of Colombia.

Finally, in 2020, the IISL unanimously recognized Latin America as the fifth region.[3] This recognition meant a great satisfaction for the promoters of the initiative.

Dr. Becerra and Prof. Laura Gamarra from the Catholic University of Colombia became the regional organizers of the Latin American Round of the Moot Court.

RELACA considered that the acknowledgment by the IISL of the Latin American round as the fifth region of the MLSLMCC was a very important issue, so it supported the proposal of those who had achieved this objective, to hold the final round of the Latin American competition during the celebration of the annual RELACA meetings. This would involve the participation of universities in the region and would allow those attending the annual meetings of RELACA to observe such an important competition. The teams that participate in the competition could also attend the sessions of the RELACA meetings.

In 2020, the second edition of tests was held, but due to the beginning of the COVID-19 pandemic, the competition had to be held virtually.

By 2021, Latin America was already officially included as the fifth region in the world organization, and the first Latin American Round of the MLSLMCC took place in Lima, Peru, at the Peruvian University of Applied Sciences UPC. In 2022, the Latin American round was successfully held, in person, in Punta Cana, Dominican Republic. That year it had the support of the Dominican Aerospace Association and the Technological Institute of Santo Domingo. In 2023, the round was held in Mexico City, with the support of the Mexican government's Ministry of

[3]Latin America | Manfred Lachs Space Law Moot Court Competition - International Institute of Space Law | IISL. https://iisl.space/index.php/latin-america-manfred-lachs-space-law-moot-court-competition/.

Foreign Affairs, RELACA NPOC in Mexico, and UNAM. Finally, in 2024, the Latin American round was held in Jaén, Spain. On this occasion, RELACA had the support of the organizers of the meeting and specifically, with regard to the competition, obtained the valuable contribution of the Kinnamon editorial.[4] The company donated a significant amount of money to cover the cost of the winners' trip to Milan, where the Moot Court final would take place.

In short, the joining of forces between the Catholic University of Colombia and RELACA further hierarchized the international meetings while adding more interest for the participants. Students from several universities in the region[5] had the opportunity to demonstrate their vast knowledge in the field of space law and aspire to be finalists in the Latin American round of the competition. The winning team will have the opportunity to represent the Latin American region in the final round of the competition, which takes place during the annual International Congress of Astronautics (IAC) of the International Astronautical Federation (IAF).

6 Annual Meetings of RELACA

In accordance with the provisions of its Statutes, the Network agreed to hold annual meetings in the countries where NPOCs operate. The organization of these meetings would be in charge of RELACA together with the local organizers.

It should be remembered that, since 2020, the space competition, MLSLMCC, was held during the annual RELACA meetings.

The seminar held at the Sergio Arboleda University of Colombia in 2016, as was pointed out *ut supra*, was considered as the first congress or meeting of RELACA.

6.1 Second International Meeting, Buenos Aires, March 21–22, 2017

During the second international meeting of RELACA in Buenos Aires in 2017, a Commitment Act was signed, giving birth to the Network. It was established that there was a need for a Statute to define the purposes and principles of the organization.

[4] The editorial Kinnamon, based in Spain, was founded in 2015. It has published titles ranging from novels to the study of space, science fiction, comics, the study of Macaronesia, and legal books. The editorial is presided by José Javier Soto, a notary who, 10 years ago, finally settled in Santa Cruz de Tenerife.

[5] Universities participating since 2019 include, among others, Universidad Católica de Colombia, Universidad Andes de Colombia, Universidad Católica de Asunción, Paraguay, Universidad Sergio Arboleda de Colombia, Pontificia Universidad Católica de Chile, Universidad Peruana de Ciencias Aplicadas (UPC), Universidad Autónoma de México (UNAM), Universidad La Salle de México, and Universidad de Santos, Brazil.

As for the academic part, during 2 days of work, papers that dealt with the topics of space resources, climate change, the international space station, space liability, protocol on prevention and assistance in case of natural disasters, law and engineering, unmanned systems, academic proposals on remote sensing, and postgraduate careers and international cooperation were presented.

6.2 *Third International Meeting, Montevideo, May 25, 2018*

In 2018, the third international meeting took place in Montevideo, organized by the Aeronautics and Space Research and Information Center (CIDA-E) together with the faculty of law of the University of the Republic (Udelar), venue of the event.

Experts from Latin America and ESA participated in this meeting, where issues of space law and policy, communication, and space cooperation were discussed.

Dr. Hebe Romero from Paraguay expressed her interest in joining RELACA as NPOC of Paraguay. Once her candidacy was accepted, Dr. Romero offered Asunción to hold the next meeting.

6.3 *Fourth International Meeting, Asunción, May 24, 2019*

The Paraguayan Space Agency (AEP) and the Paraguayan Aerospace Research Center (CIAP) supported the meeting that was organized by the national director of the NPOC in Paraguay, Dr. Hebe Romero Talavera, from the AEP.

The theme of the meeting was "The new challenges of outer space in a globalized world," and the venue was the Universidad San Carlos.

Four panels took place, which dealt with the following topics: space policy, space technology, space law, and space social communication.

6.3.1 Authorities of the Board of Directors of RELACA

During the fourth meeting, the Academic Council of the RELACA, led by Dr. Juan Manuel de Faramiñán as International Director, met. Its members unanimously approved the formalization of the Network through the creation of a nonprofit association, a task in charge of the International Legal Advisor of the Network, Dr. Mercedes Esquivel.

The Board authorities were formed as follows:

- International Director: Dr. Marta Gaggero Montaner (Uruguay)
- International Director Emeritus: Dr. Juan Manuel de Faramiñán Gilbert (Argentina–Spain)
- International Deputy Director: Dr. Hebe L. Romero Talavera (Paraguay)

- International Legal Advisor: Dr. María de las Mercedes Esquivel (Argentina)
- Academia, Research and Development R+D: Prof. Jairo Becerra (Colombia–Spain)
- Science and Technology: Prof. Mg. Alejandro J. Román M. (Paraguay)
- International Secretary: TUP María de las Victorias Cocca y Esquivel (Argentina)

6.4 *Fifth International Meeting, 2020 (Virtual)*

RELACA held the fifth meeting virtually, due to the global pandemic and in order to give continuity to the annual meetings. The Peruvian University of Applied Sciences (UPC), with the support of the Catholic University of Colombia and the Latin American Network of International Law Journals (RELAREDI), organized it.

On that occasion, the theme of the congress was "The space sector as an engine of national development."

Given that the number of people interested in participating in the RELACA Meetings was increasing, the Board decided that, starting in 2021, a call for papers would be issued to those interested to submit papers on the topics to be covered (space policy, space technology, space law, and space society). This call established that those interested had to present previously an abstract on the topic that they will develop in the presentation, which must be approved by the Board of Directors of RELACA. Papers may be written in English, Spanish, and Portuguese. At the fifth meeting 392 people registered, and 54 papers were presented.

6.5 *Sixth International Meeting, Lima, June 18, 2021*

Taking into account that the problem of the pandemic persisted, the sixth meeting was held in an online format through the platform of the Peruvian University of Applied Sciences (UPC).

Under the title "Space at the service of society," as in previous meetings, topics treated related to space politics, technology, law, and society. There were presented more than 50 papers.

6.6 *Seventh International Meeting, Punta Cana, Dominican Republic, May 12–14, 2022*

The seventh meeting, whose title was "Space Renaissance: commercial opening of space for the benefit of humanity," was held simultaneously, in face-to-face and virtual formats.

The Technological Institute of Santo Domingo (Intec) and the Dominican Aerospace Association collaborated with the organization of the meeting.

In addition to the topics that were discussed in the previous meetings (space law, society, and policy), issues related to space commerce and STEAM were added, and more than 40 papers were presented.

6.7 Eighth International Meeting, Mexico City, April 11–14, 2023

The Mexican Foreign Ministry hosted the meeting, and the thematic axis was "Strengthening Latin American integration from the space field." The eighth meeting was organized by the Ministry of Foreign Affairs, the Latin American and Caribbean Space Agency (ALCE), the Mexican Space Agency (AEM), and the Mexican House of Representatives, with the support of academic institutions, commercial enterprises, communicators, and others.

The meeting had three keynote speakers, Dr. Salvador Landeros (AEM), Dr. Gustavo Medina Tanco (LINX-ICN-UNAM), and Dr. Sergio Camacho Lara (CRECTEALC-Mexico), and held six sessions: diplomacy and space policy; STEM; economy, space activity, and telecommunications; space law; space weather; and miscellaneous. The dissertations addressed, from various perspectives, Latin American and Caribbean integration through space activities.

The speakers (face-to-face or virtual) presented 47 papers, and 360 attendees were registered (160 face-to-face and 200 virtual).

In a special ceremony, the Dr. Aldo Armando Cocca Award was presented for the first time to Dr. Tatiana Viana from Brazil, secretary general of the Italian-Latin American international organization (IILA). The research paper Dr. Viana presented at the VII Punta Cana Meeting related to "The space policy of IILA as a factor of socioeconomic development and strengthening of scientific diplomacy in Latin America and the Caribbean" was found to be well deserving of the award.

One of the most outstanding results of the eighth meeting, derived from a proposal by Dr. Tatiana Viana and outlined by RELACA's Mexico NPOC, was the creation of two action teams, which would allow RELACA to work intersessionally between each meeting. The integrated teams were (1) towards a global space traffic management system, with the participation of experts from Argentina, Brazil, Chile, Spain, and Mexico, and (2) human settlements in outer space, made up of experts from Argentina, Spain, and Mexico.[6]

---

[6] A21México.a21.com.mx/café-espacial/2023/04/21/fortalecer-la-unidad-e-integracion-de-america-latina-y-el-caribe-traves-de.

6.8 Ninth International Meeting, Jaén, May 8–10, 2024

The ninth meeting addressed the theme of "New space activities: challenges and expectations," exploring the advances, challenges, and opportunities in the space field at a global level.

The University of Jaén (venue of the meeting), AstroAndalus, and the AstroAndalus University Chair in Aerospace and Astronomical Studies were the organizers of the event.

Six thematic sessions were held, which considered aspects related to space law, education and dissemination of science, night sky policies and management, astrotourism, aerospace sector, and science and technology.

For the second time, the Dr. Aldo Armando Cocca Award was given to the best paper presented at the eighth meeting held in Mexico City in 2023. The award was given to Dr. Álvaro Erices Bravo of Argentina, for his paper on "*The legal status of astroblems in Argentina and the need to create an integrated regulation in the Americas and the world.*" The subject matter was considered very interesting, rarely dealt with, and analyzed in depth.

It is worth noting that this was the first time that RELACA's annual meeting took place outside the Latin American continent. Dr. Juan Manuel de Faramiñán commented in a note published in the Jaén newspaper:

> It happened that this year, in view of the political problems and alterations in some Latin American countries, they proposed that we hold it in Spain, at the University of Jaén, since Carmen Muñoz, a professor at this institution, is the one who is in charge of the national point of contact for RELACA Espacio in Europe. In addition, we decided to join it with the Chair of Aerospace and Astronomical Studies that we created two years ago at the University of Jaén, called AstroÁndalus, by the Jaén-based company of the same name. Together with them we have set up this IX RELACA Espacio Meeting.[7]

The result of the congress was very successful. There were 400 registered participants (in person and virtual), and 49 papers were presented. It was an extremely positive meeting for RELACA and for the University of Jaén in particular, since it placed it on the global map of the spatial discussion.

7 Conclusions

The creation of RELACA as an academic institution means a great contribution to the Latin American and Caribbean region. Its main objective is to study and do researches on space issues from all points of view: scientific, technological, political, academic, legal, and others. In the region, a significant development of space

[7] Juan Manuel de Faramiñán, de la Cátedra AstroÁndalus de la UJA: "La provincia se convierte en unreferenteespacial."https://www.diariojaen.es/jaen/juan-manuel-de-faraminan-de-la-catedra-astroandalus-de-la-uja-la-provincia-se-convierte-en-un-referente-espacial-YA9882357.

activities can be perceived in many states. The Network, which brings together representatives of universities and institutions of the region linked to space matters, allows learning about the different existing realities. It is a means through which cooperation mechanisms can be sought or the carrying out of joint work on certain topics can be coordinated. This allows for progress in spatial development in any of the areas of study of the Network.

Eight years after the birth of RELACA, we can say that the Network has grown a lot, evidenced by, among other things, the number of people and institutions that demonstrate their interest in joining the Network, many of which are already part of it; by the increase in the number of NPC's; by the large number of attendees at the annual meetings; by the number of papers presented; and by the recognition it receives from people and public and private institutions. This has resulted in RELACA now occupying an important place in the international space community.

The awarding of the Dr. Aldo Armando Cocca prize is undoubtedly an incentive for young participants to present papers on the various topics discussed at the annual meetings.

The linking of RELACA's activities with the Moot Court Competition, as already mentioned, has redoubled interest in participating in the annual meetings and has made it possible to demonstrate to the international space community the solid knowledge of space law that students from universities and educational institutions in the region have.

In addition to all this advances, papers presented at the last international meetings will soon be published through agreements reached with prestigious editorials.

Undoubtedly, RELACA's main interest is to continue advancing along this path in which it puts all its effort and enthusiasm.

References

A21 México (2023). a21.com.mx/café-espacial/2023/04/21/fortalecer-la-unidad-e-integracion-de-america-latina-y-el-caribe-traves-de

Becerra J (2023) "The RELACA Espacio network and the Latin American round of the Manfred Lachs Space Law Moot Court Competition". UN/IAF 30th. Workshop on Space Technology for Socio Economic Benefits "Challenges and Capacity-building Opportunities for Emerging Space Nations". University-level education in Space policy and law. Baku, Azerbaihan, 30 September 2023. https://www.unoosa.org/documents/pdf/psa/activities/2023/UN-IAF2023/Presentations/Session_9_Becerra_23Sep2023.pdf

De Faramiñán Gilbert JM (2024) De Faramiñán Gilbert, Juan Manuel de la Cátedra AstroÁndalus de la UJA: "La provincia se convierte en un referente espacial". https://www.diariojaen.es/jaen/juan-manuel-de-faraminan-de-la-catedra-astroandalus-de-la-uja-la-provincia-se-convierte-en-un-referente-espacial-YA9882357

De Faramiñán Gilbert JM. Red Latino Americana y del Caribe de Universidades e Instituciones que investigan sobre la Tecnología, la Política y el Derecho del Espacio Ultraterrestre. http://www.juanmanueldefaraminangilbert.es/videos/

El primer satélite colombiano. https://www.usergioarboleda.edu.co/el-primer-satelite-colombiano/

European Space Agency (ESA). https://www.esa.int/About_Us/Space_Law_virtual_network_with_Latin_American_countries/Description

Gaggero M (2021) "Latin American Space Initiatives-Latin American and Caribbean Space Network-RELACA Space Network". APSCO/ESA/CISL Space Law Workshop 2021. Regional Cooperation schemes on Space Law and Policy. 6–8 September, 2021. Sanya, China. Proceedings, pp 192–198

International Institute of Space Law (IISL). Latin America Manfred Lachs Space Law Moot Court Competition. https://iisl.space/index.php/latin-america-manfred-lachs-space-law-moot-court-competition/

Challenges and Opportunities of Non-spacefaring Nations in Seeking to Establish in Today's Space Economy

Alina Nassar and Jessy Aguilar

Contents

Abstract The early years of space exploration were driven by geopolitical interests, the prevalence of military objectives, and national security reasons, in parallel with scientific goals. During this era, the USA and the former Union of Soviet Socialist Republics (USSR) dominated the field. Today, we are living in an era of space development. Governments' priorities of defense, exploration, and science continue to be the basis for space programs; however, private corporations are getting more involved, driven by commercial interests. The current space ecosystem offers multiplicity of participants from the public and private sectors and a variety of commercial applications and uses of space technologies and services. Technological advancements have lowered launch costs, making space more accessible. Our lives on Earth rely on space technologies and services. Nations have

---

A. Nassar (✉)
San José, Costa Rica

J. Aguilar
Prairieville, LA, USA

I. Grosner (ed.), *Space Regulation in Latin America*, Space Regulations Library 11, https://doi.org/10.1007/978-3-032-05828-7_2

recognized the value that space brings to societies and its convergence with the sustainability and development goals. Developing economies of non-spacefaring nations should aspire to establish a strong national space sector; their success depends on social, political, technological, and other aspects. To determine if it is a national goal worth pursuing, countries should examine the current space ecosystem and assess their own opportunities and challenges.

1 Introduction

Over the years, more than 70 space agencies have been established across the world, and a significant number of start-ups and legacy companies are delivering new technologies, providing services, and making innovations in the space sector. A field that used to be dominated by a few powerful spacefaring nations has been "democratized" by the entrance of a multiplicity of public and private actors and the introduction of commercial space activities. These dynamics are positively impacting the economies of the space-participant States, allowing them to create new jobs, boost innovation, increase competitivity, and develop infrastructure and capability to serve those States' science, social, and technology programs.[1] Those benefits are mostly reaching nations with robust space programs and with the financial resources to heavily invest in them. However, nations with less developed space sectors are aspiring to become active participants in the space economy. This chapter addresses how developing nations may establish themselves in today's space setting.

2 Understanding the Space Sector

2.1 The Beginnings of Space in the Governments' Agenda

The space race began in the middle of the twentieth century, driven by geopolitical interests and the Cold War's fierce enmity between the former Union of Soviet Socialist Republics (USSR) and the USA. Military objectives and national security reasons have prevailed since the early ages of space exploration, with a parallel interest in the pursuit of scientific objectives and benefits to society. For the USA, the former USSR, and other countries that were early involved in space activities, this has been a strategic target for defense and an opportunity to develop and display their military prowess[2] and leadership. By the late 1950s, the USSR had developed the first intercontinental ballistic missile (R-7 Semyorka) and sent the first satellite

[1] Nassar Jorge et al. (2022), p.5.

[2] Nassar Jorge et al. (2022), p.6.

to orbit, the "Sputnik," both in 1957. This event not only marked the beginning of space exploration but also intensified the Cold War rivalry, prompting the USA to create NASA in 1958 and accelerate its own space program.

The USSR also successfully completed the first manned mission to space in 1961, with Yuri Gagarin orbiting Earth once and returning safely, and sent the first woman into outer space, Valentina Tereshkova, in 1963. The USA strengthened its focus to win the space competition, and between 1960 and 1973, it spent a budget of approximately 25 billion dollars under the Apollo program (approximately, over 200 billion dollars in today's value). Unsurprisingly, on July 21, 1969, astronaut Neil Armstrong set foot on the Moon for the first time in human history.

In the decades of 1950s, 1960s, and 1970s, other States such as Japan, China, and European countries were also engaged in space activities, developing and testing technologies for that purpose and establishing their national goals. Japan, for instance, established its National Space Development Agency in 1969,[3] while China launched its first satellite, Dong Fang Hong 1, in 1970. Multiple European nations began collaborating, eventually forming the European Space Agency (ESA) in 1975. Their goal was to advance space technologies for a variety of purposes, including military applications, enhancing national prestige, promoting scientific research, and fostering economic growth. Gradually, States have been initiating and implementing space programs, helped by improved technologies and appropriate legal frameworks. The space race was no longer a two-player contest but a global endeavor. National defense, space exploration, and science continued to prevail in the elaboration of national space agendas. Research, development, and technological evolution were oriented toward these objectives, with the public sector playing a leading role. As procurement from the governments and space agencies grew higher, it allowed for the growth of aerospace companies, which developed key technologies, products, and services required to serve national space programs. These companies became integral partners in the government's efforts to push the boundaries of space technology.

In addition to national efforts, international cooperation increased as well, reaching top levels with endeavors like the International Space Station (ISS), a multinational cooperative program venture of the USA, Japan, Canada, Russia, Belgium, Denmark, France, Germany, Italy, the Netherlands, Norway, Spain, Sweden, Switzerland, and Great Britain, which started operations in 1998. Initially, space development was dominated by the geopolitical interests of the nations with the greatest military and economic power. Progressively, more States around the world joined the space race, individually or in collaboration with others, pursuing national defense, exploration, and scientific experimentation. Given the existing preponderance of the public agenda for space, the participation of the private sector was initially limited to the possibilities of contracting with space agencies to provide specific products or services necessary for the development of those agencies' programs[4]. Today, space exploration is no

[3] Japan Aerospace Exploration Agency (n.d.). The National Space Development Agency of Japan (NASDA). https://global.jaxa.jp/about/history/nasda/index_e.html.

[4] Nassar Jorge et al. (2022), p.7.

longer exclusively under government control. More than ever, private companies are entering the space arena, helping advance space innovation through their projects, such as developing reusable rockets and suborbital space tourism, among many other revolutions.

2.2 *The Current Landscape of Space*

The space system has evolved to its current state of almost endless opportunities and applications on Earth and beyond, both at the public and private levels. We are living in what is considered a new era in space development, sometimes referred to as the "New Space" age, where the commercialization and democratization of space are key features. While government priorities of defense, exploration, and science continue to drive funding for major space programs, the space sector is witnessing rapid geographic expansion, a broader impact across industries, and increased collaboration between the public and private sectors. Initiatives like NASA's Commercial Crew Program, which hires private businesses to transport people to the ISS, are a prime example of this change. Indeed, public-private partnerships are becoming an important tool for encouraging creativity and increasing access to space. With a significant focus on profitability, a robust ecosystem of entrepreneurs supported by equity and venture capital has evolved.

The business is vibrant, as evidenced by the fact that, as of 2021, there were over 12,000 space tech start-ups and 4000 investors, according to SpaceTech Analytics.[5] Globally, governments are utilizing public-private partnerships to capitalize on private sector innovation and guarantee the achievement of national space goals. In today's trends, space agencies are defining their needs, and the industry now enjoys greater freedom to determine how those capabilities are going to be built for the agency client. This represents a marked shift from earlier models, where governments had more control over the technical and managerial aspects of space projects. Activities that have existed since the early phases of space in the 1960s and 1970s, such as space exploration and research, as well as commercial services in telecommunications and satellite imaging, are now accompanied by novel uses of space resulting from improved technologies. Moreover, the pursuit of profitability has become the primary driver for new companies and start-ups participating in commercial space.[6] By 2025, the commercial space business is estimated at USD $415 billion, of which approximately 71% of the revenue is made by the private sector with applications on-Earth and in-orbit.[7] These innovations include satellite-based Internet services, Earth observation for climate monitoring, and space resource

[5] https://www.spacetech.global/dashboard.

[6] Golkar et al. (2021), pp. 2–9.

[7] Amadeus Capital: Space Tech Stack 2025: Mapping Value from Ground to Orbit and Back available online https://www.amadeuscapital.com/space-tech-stack-2025-mapping-value-from-ground-to-orbit-and-back/.

utilization, all powered by technological breakthroughs like artificial intelligence, miniaturization, and advanced propulsion systems. Private enterprises seek to provide long-term business plans for space-based services that quickly turn into profitable operations, such as active debris removal, in-orbit refueling, space tourism, and microgravity experimentation and manufacturing. Innovation in the sector is, in parallel, motivated by the ambitious goals that participants from the public and private sectors are setting, among them, becoming permanent inhabitants of the Moon and frequent travelers into deep space, exploiting and using space resources, and creating a market for in-orbit commercial services (manufacturing, active space debris collection, spacecraft refueling and satellite reparation, and space tourism).[8]

To support the new and future developments, some companies are working on what will be private permanent stations in the low Earth orbit (LEO).[9] These infrastructures will provide in-space services to governments, corporations, and other entities and will be fundamental for the development of a LEO economy,[10] propelled by those prospected new markets. For example, companies like Axiom Space and Blue Origin are working on private LEO space stations that aim to offer a wide range of services, from manufacturing to space tourism, potentially creating a thriving commercial market in the coming decades.[11] The multiple possibilities being offered beyond Earth's atmosphere are driving an interest that is incomparable in history, according to the Organization for Economic Cooperation and Development (OECD). Per an OECD's 2019 report, this is a pivotal moment for spacefaring nations, both established and emerging, to capitalize on the expanding space economy.[12] Nations that might not have had the means to participate in the initial space race can now carve out positions in the sector, frequently by focusing on technological innovation and research or by working with more developed spacefaring countries through international cooperation. In this context, aspirant space nations must navigate the characteristics of the current space ecosystem to identify where the gains are and consolidate a position. First, today's space ecosystem presents a growing variety of stakeholders at both public and private levels. The number of nations engaging in space activities, issuing public space policies, and creating formal structures to implement space programs has increased in the past decades. From the perspective of the governments, there are over 70 space agencies worldwide and more countries launching initiatives to create them or participating in the space sector without a formal space agency.[13]

[8] Nassar Jorge et al. (2022), p.9.

[9] A low Earth orbit is one that is relatively close to Earth's surface, at an altitude of approximately 160 km and up to 1000 km above Earth's surface.

[10] The concept of a "LEO economy" refers to the in-orbit trade, manufacturing of products, and provision of services by private companies instead of government space agencies. ESA and NASA foresee a future scenario in which most of their needs in space will be covered by third-party providers, from which the agencies will purchase the services and products.

[11] Howell (2021).

[12] OECD (2019).

[13] Brukardt et al. (2022a, b).

Spacefaring nations have different levels of approach to and involvement in the subject. Accordingly, they structure their policies and programs based on their targeted goals and capabilities. Some of them manufacture their own spacecrafts and have launching facilities and robust space programs backed by significant public funding. Other countries, with smaller budgets or different strategies, focus on research, development, and technological innovation, creating payloads for in-space experimentation and testing. The USA, Russia, Japan, India, China, the UK, Member States of the European Union, and, more recently, Luxembourg, New Zealand, and the United Arab Emirates (UAE) are among the nations with intense activity in the space sector, at individual and multilateral planes.[14] Nonetheless, emerging countries in Africa, Asia, and Latin America are also taking bold steps to insert themselves into the space sector and benefit from a space economy, securing access to space and procuring collaboration with the spacefaring powers to develop their own capabilities. Indeed, close to 100 non-spacefaring countries have at least 1 satellite in orbit.[15] The multiplicity of participants has amplified international cooperation through the development of joint projects among national space agencies, under bilateral or multilateral agreements, with ESA being the classical and most relevant and successful case of multilateralism in space. More recent examples are the Artemis Accords[16] for lunar exploration promoted by the USA and with over 50 countries thus far parties to it;[17] its counterpart from China, the International Lunar Research Station, has so far been subscribed by 16 countries;[18] and the Latin American and Caribbean Space Agency (ALCE, as is the acronym in Spanish), whose charter has been signed and ratified by 11 countries, the necessary number to enter into force.[19]

Given space missions are very expensive and highly hazardous, allocation of risks and costs among States (and even between States and companies) makes more complex and sophisticated missions possible. It also allows States to specialize in and contribute unique innovations, technologies, or expertise for the development of

---

[14] Scatteia et al. (2020), p. 4.

[15] OECD (2023).

[16] An initiative of the United States of America to promote and create a safe and transparent environment of Principles for International Cooperation in the Civil Exploration and Use of the Moon, Mars, Comets, and Asteroids for Peaceful Purposes.

[17] Angola, Argentina, Armenia, Australia, Austria, Bahrain, Bangladesh, Belgium, Brazil, Bulgaria, Canada, Chile, Colombia, Cyprus, the Czech Republic, Denmark, Dominican Republic, Ecuador, Estonia, Finland, France, Germany, Greece, Iceland, India, Israel, Italy, Japan, Liechtenstein, Lithuania, Luxembourg, Mexico, the Netherlands, New Zealand, Nigeria, Norway, Panama, Peru, Poland, the Republic of Korea (South Korea), Romania, Rwanda, Saudi Arabia, Senegal, Singapore, Slovakia, Slovenia, Spain, Sweden, Switzerland, Thailand, Ukraine, the United Arab Emirates, the UK, the USA, and Uruguay.

[18] Venezuela, Belarus, Pakistan, Azerbaijan, South Africa, Egypt, Nicaragua, Thailand, Serbia, Kazakhstan, Senegal, Djibouti, Ethiopia, Russia, Bolivia, and China.

[19] Antigua and Barbuda, Belize, Cuba, Dominica, Mexico, Nicaragua, Paraguay, the Dominican Republic, Saint Vincent and the Grenadines, Saint Lucia, and Venezuela have formally ratified the ALCE's Charter. It entered into force on October 27, 2024.

missions of other nations, sharing the mission's benefits altogether. In the private sector, legacy companies continue to be fundamental in today's space, joined by a crescent number of start-ups. This robust base of newcomers accelerates progress in space, but their inventions oftentimes have spillover effects on other industries that apply them into their own processes. The development of new technologies, new production systems, miniaturization of satellites, components off the shelf, standardization, and new commercial launching services have lowered launching costs.[20] A functional satellite can now be small and successfully accomplish specific missions. These changes make space accessible to others beyond traditional space agencies with huge budgets and backed by public funding. Indeed, mass production of small and microsatellites, smaller and reusable launch vehicles, and mega-constellations of satellites expanding broadband Internet from space are some of the disruptions seen in the current landscape. There have been, too, paradigm shifts in space agencies which boost participation of other parties. National space agencies have designed programs with financial and other incentives to support innovation in the private sector. Financial resources for space businesses have also come in recent years from private equity investors and venture capital, as well as wealthy individuals entering the industry. Authors also recognize a change in how space ventures and their products and services are conceived, given that private equity and venture capital are primarily driven by economic profit.[21]

Finally, the exponential growth of the space sector will be evident downstream and upstream. The services provided from space, such as satellite broadband Internet, telecommunications, geospatial services, global positioning systems, weather predictions, and Earth observation, enhance our lives on Earth. At the same time, space spin-offs or technology transfers from space to other industries have a huge impact on products and services on Earth, permitting significant advances in science, medicine, agriculture, food production, and other areas that are valuable to all countries. Indeed, in a recent study[22] released in 2023, the OECD reiterated the potential of space technologies and space-based infrastructure to help manage and solve global challenges. This study expanded the OECD's prior study of 2019, where it created a non-exhaustive list[23] of space technologies and uses that it considers could become fully operational by 2030, including entertainment, meteorology and climate change, distance learning and telemedicine, E-commerce, location-based consumer services, and disaster prevention and management, among others. The list includes OECD's "outsiders" or services beyond Earth such as adventure space tourism (suborbital and orbital), in-orbit servicing, and power relay satellites. The dynamics of the current space environment are both promising and challenging for global development. The participation of multiple and nontraditional stakeholders, the creation of new businesses,

[20] Scatteia (2020), p. 2.

[21] Golkar et al. (2021), pp. 2–9.

[22] OECD (2023), p. 86.

[23] OECD (2019), p. 86.

and the spillover effects of space on other industries are positively impacting growth for those States with clear goals, programs, and policies. They are seeing internal growth, job creation, innovation, and capacity building to serve their own objectives and to collaborate with other nations.[24] Others, with different levels of progress, are, too, pursuing their own space ambitions from political and economic perspectives. Space is fundamental for governments' achievement of developmental goals.[25]

2.3 A Nation's Diverse Approaches to Space

As space evolved from a bipolar born to a multipolar sector, the multiplicity of States participating has coined the concepts of "non-spacefaring" and "emerging space" nations. In essence, "non-spacefaring" States had not been traditionally or historically involved in space and do not possess launch capabilities or space assets, often lacking a national space policy or the institutional or legal framework to participate in the space economy. "Emerging space nations" are more advanced in the process by having a declared interest and objective to participate in the space economy and are in the process of developing or intending to develop their institutional, policy, or technical capabilities to participate in space. Many countries, therefore, have joined the space sector in the past decades or are pursuing it now, motivated still by geopolitical reasons but mainly by the aspiration of accomplishing economic and social goals:

> Increasingly, states as varied as Indonesia, Nigeria, Colombia, and Tunisia have invested in space assets primarily as a vehicle to promote socio-economic growth through better natural resource management and improved communications or even to inspire their youth to study science. (…) Brazil and Argentina, have invested in and produced prototype space launchers for future domestic and commercial applications, especially for low Earth orbit placement. Many other developing countries from Mexico to Egypt and Malaysia, while lacking independent launching capabilities, have nonetheless invested in space-based assets (…), which have been dedicated to everything from remote sensing and communications to military reconnaissance.[26]

Luxembourg and New Zealand are among the countries that are leveraging their strengths in the space industry to make a mark alongside emerging space players like Brazil and South Korea by aligning with their existing capabilities and resources. These countries demonstrate how smaller nations can shape the space economy by positioning themselves strategically. They highlight the significant contributions that well-positioned smaller countries can make to the space industry. Luxembourg

[24] Nassar Jorge et al. (2022), p.15.

[25] United Nations Office of Outer Space Affairs. See https://www.unoosa.org/res/oosadoc/data/documents/2023/stspace/stspace85_0_html/st_space_085E.pdf.

[26] Harding (2016a, b), pp. 1–2.

has developed laws for space mining activities.[27] At the same time, Rocket Lab in New Zealand is known for its expertise in launching satellites into orbit, proving that tailored strategies can pave the way for dominance in specialized sectors.[28] Space activities add immense value and advantages to societies;[29] therefore, it is not surprising to see governments' incremental interest in the field. Moreover, it has been recognized by States that:

> the level of development and technological autonomy of a country contribute to the strengthening of its sovereignty and greater economic and social growth. Space is considered a strategic asset and also a potential focus for investments. The space sector is considered to be of high technological intensity and, as such, it is capable of generating increasing returns for the economy.[30]

With a more advanced and pioneering space career in the region, Brazil and Argentina are both leaders in Latin America in space exploration and have focused their efforts on LEO satellites that play a role in various applications such as climate monitoring technology, communications, and keeping track of agricultural activities.[31] By investing in satellite deployment projects, these countries are not only advancing their capabilities but also tapping into the commercial space industry. Another regional space leader, Chile, aims at strengthening its national space capabilities of design, construction, and operation of space systems and ground infrastructure.[32] It recognizes Earth observation, geo-localization, and space infrastructure as essential for the attainment of SDGs. Smaller countries without launch capabilities or space assets opt for more conservative projects focused on innovation, education, and attraction of investment and cooperation. To continue in Latin America, the Technical University of Costa Rica (TEC, by its acronym in Spanish) in collaboration with the Central American Space Association (ACAE, its acronym in Spanish) spearheaded a groundbreaking project that brought unprecedented visibility and impulse to Costa Rica's space industry: the Irazu Project. It consisted of the production of the first satellite made in Central America, manufactured utilizing the CubeSat technology. The satellite's mission was to monitor carbon emissions and was successfully launched in April 2018, with the cooperation of the Japanese Space Agency (JAXA), and released in May 2018, from the Japanese ISS module. The Irazu Project[33] demonstrated Costa Rica's capabilities to design and build a small satellite and to perform on all stages of the mission, launching excepted. Other developing nations in Central America such as Honduras and Guatemala are cultivating research, innovation, and entrepreneurship as a mean to enter the space arena. Indeed, a second CubeSat mission in the region is in progress as a result of

---

[27] https://legilux.public.lu/eli/etat/leg/loi/2017/07/20/a674/jo/en.

[28] Gibbs (2012), pp. 279–332.

[29] Patel (2019).

[30] Brazil Space Agency. See https://www.gov.br/aeb/pt-br.

[31] Gibbs (2012), pp. 279–332.

[32] Chile's National Space Policy, published on July 22, 2025.

[33] Gomez-Jenkins (2023), pp. 217–225.

the work of the National Autonomous University of Honduras (UNAH) and other educational institutions across Central America, a milestone of regional cooperation in space.

Since the 1990s and 2000s, we have witnessed a significant increase in the number of spacefaring nations, resulting from emerging commercial and national space programs in the Middle East, Asia, and Africa,[34] as well as some nations in Latin America. In addition, advancement in the private sector and the lowered costs in many aspects of the design and production of space technologies have allowed access to space to nations with reduced budgets; and while these countries are unlikely to soon match the levels of investment and progress of the most powerful spacefaring ones, they should aim at finding a differentiator, something they can do extremely well in the commercial space environment.[35] Luxembourg's emphasis on space mining and Rocket Lab's specialization in satellite launches in New Zealand demonstrate how nontraditional spacefaring countries can excel in global space technology advancement. The progress made by private sector companies has also made it easier for small countries to get involved in space activities by reducing the entry barriers to access technology.[36] In 2018, Kenya launched its first CubeSat, developed in partnership with Japan, marking its first significant step into space.[37] The miniaturization of satellite technologies and commercial launch services like Rocket Lab and SpaceX has created more opportunities for emerging space nations to engage in space exploration, research, and telecommunications. With the decrease in launch capability costs, smaller countries can now concentrate on developing their satellite technologies instead of purchasing costly launch vehicles. Countries from emerging economies strive to create the right conditions to build a solid space sector and access the spillover from space technology and the wealth creation. International cooperation to access space expertise and resources is becoming increasingly important. For example, the ALCE unites smaller nations to access resources and knowledge and play a role in space activities. Smaller countries can also succeed by specializing in space niches such as CubeSat manufacturing, data analytics, and satellite servicing rather than competing with the giants in the large space launch market. There is no formula or prescribed process for a country to become a spacefaring nation or consolidate spacefaring involvement. There is no one size fits all. Social, political, and technological variables influence how and when a nation can enter space and successfully sustain that participation. Issues of cost constraints, technological output, the political will to maintain long-term space programs, and multilateral agreements, such as the Artemis Accords or the Outer Space Treaty, give smaller countries a platform to participate in space activities through international cooperation.

[34] Aganaba-Jeanty (2016), pp. 3–11.

[35] Patel (2019).

[36] Ospina (2019), pp. 253–266.

[37] Mwakilishi (2018, May 12). *First Kenyan-made satellite deployed into space from Japan.* Retrieved October 8, 2024, from https://www.mwakilishi.com/article/kenya-news/2018-05-12/first-kenyan-made-satellite-deployed-into-space-from-japan#google_vignette.

3 Relevant Aspects of Becoming an Aspirant Space Nation

The impact of space on societal development has become increasingly clear, with nations across the globe pursuing participation in this strategic sector. Space continues to be a symbol of strength and superiority, and for many countries, it has also become a mandate to ensure long-term national progress and national security and to guarantee that all relevant space actors make a sustainable and peaceful use of this domain. Every day, small and emerging economies strive to position themselves within the competitive and fast-evolving space sector. The question then becomes how can these nations take full advantage of the space sector and its economy? Furthermore, is it a valid and worth pursuing goal for countries where there seem to be higher and more significant priorities for their populations? The global trends of investment in space and the sector's overall influence on societal and economic progress are, undoubtedly, an attractive prospect that developing nations may explore for that push to economic growth and sustainable advancement.

Despite the recognized relevance of space in advancing the SDGs, entering the sector remains a costly endeavor, and aspiring countries must adopt a strategic approach on how to do it. Those that have successfully entered and participated in the space sector exhibit certain characteristics that are worth mentioning. First, have an industry with high-quality standards and reliability which is ready to engage in global supply chains for the space industry. Brazil's space industry, for example, has successfully positioned itself as a regional leader in space technology.[38] At a smaller scale, the Costa Rica Aerospace Cluster (CRAC) created in 2015 is composed of over 40 Tier 3 and Tier 4 companies[39] that participate in the global supply chain of the aerospace community and are well known for their high standards and for holding internationally recognized certifications specifically required for the industry, such as the Quality Management System standards for Aviation, Space and Defence (ISO AS9001) and the accreditation for specific processes granted by the United States National Aerospace and Defence Contractor Accreditation Program (NADCAP) to serve in the supply chain of original equipment manufacturers (OEMs).

Second, these countries develop programs to attract foreign direct investment (FDI) that allow technology and know-how transfers, in addition to the fact that establishing high-tech space companies within a country can generate new job opportunities and enhance a country's overall infrastructure and focus on specific products. For example, developing small satellites and Earth observation systems can contribute to the growing global demand for satellite services, such as climate

[38] Gibbs (2012), pp. 279–332.

[39] There are four tiers in the aerospace supply chain, based on the suppliers' products and capabilities. Tier 4 entities provide raw materials and processing, while Tier 3 suppliers produce components and structural parts. At the top of the chain are Tier 2 suppliers who design components and parts. Tier 1 providers, meanwhile, work on large systems and the assembly of structures, also with design capabilities.

monitoring and geospatial data for natural resource management. This growing sector has the potential to complement other industries with further developments in telecommunications, Earth observation, and climate monitoring, which are aligned with global trends of achieving sustainability goals. However, relevant FDI for the development of the space sector can only go hand in hand with education and the building of the required capabilities. Indeed, a country's space ambition is nothing without academia and science. Another area of opportunity is space situational awareness services in LEO as well as debris tracking services, two fundamental activities in today's congested space. Chile is another example of a country that takes advantage of its capabilities and characteristics to position itself in the space economy. The Chilean Space Policy of 2025 has recognized its comparative advantages, such as its privileged geographic location in the southern hemisphere, favorable climatic conditions, the presence of strategic resources, and growing investment in scientific and technological infrastructure related to astronomy and space activities. To stimulate the space sector, emerging nations must address academic, commercial, technological, legal, institutional, and financial issues, and governments must support the development of capabilities, technologies, and skilled talent, to identifying national problems that can be tackled with space solutions and attract FDI. The space sector has the potential to be one of the drivers of economic growth.

As the space sector evolves, emerging space nations must focus on the laws and regulations necessary to support the development of the field. The domestic legal framework must be adapted and developed to address new challenges, such as private sector involvement in space innovations to support ambitious space aspirations fully. A well-established legal framework, along with a space policy and program, protects the interests and rights of the different stakeholders involved and sets their obligations. Indeed, the establishment of a space agency as part of a country's strategy to participate in space positions emerging nations in the international arena and allows the use of the diplomatic means and channels to influence international space discussions, protect its interests as an aspirant space nation, and foster cooperation with other nations, which often require a competent agency to establish collaboration and enter into formal agreements. Authors have recognized that:

> the implementation of space projects of most developing countries very much relies on international cooperation with major space-faring nations and foreign commercial sectors. Without national space laws and a stable legal environment, it is difficult to persuade the major space-faring nations and foreign commercial sectors to take part in collaborative space programs. It provides a predictable legal environment for international investment and cooperation.[40]

A national space agency is also crucial to maintaining sovereignty in space. Establishing such an agency promotes the transition from a spacefaring nation that depends on foreign service to one that provides essential services to its population, such as satellite telecommunication services. Lacking autonomy in these areas threatens national security and economic viability. A strong and fully functional

[40] Zhao (2016), pp. 12–18.

agency makes a country an international contender for space-related research and international cooperation in the field. It also attracts private investments and lets the country form global partnerships, especially with those nations with aligned interests in the space economy. More immediately, the agency could also yield a domestic space industry with high-skill jobs and innovation derived from building the necessary capabilities.

3.1 Crafting a National Space Policy and Strategy

Designing and implementing a national space policy are by no means a simple task. It requires a careful and strategic balancing of stakeholders' interests, determining the scope of activities, and planning the allocation of resources. A well-crafted public policy is meant to address a targeted goal in a specific context and within a determined time frame. However, it should also be wise enough to endure and push for advancement, at least in the short and midterm. Moreover, a compelling national space policy requires effective communication, dissemination, and engagement across all sectors of society. A well-formulated space policy leads to prioritization, effective programming, and the subsequent decisions on the required regulations, the amount of budget to be allocated, and the actions to be taken. When the USA President John F. Kennedy committed to sending a man to the Moon and returning him safely, he was making more than a promise. He was deciding on a public policy that the USA carefully deployed with the engagement of all sectors of society. Politicians, academia, the industry, and the rest of the population embraced President Kennedy's vision of the nation as a space superpower and supported it.[41] The same has occurred with Russia, China, Japan, and the European Union; all big players in the space arena have seen space as a national priority. However, for emerging space nations the motivations may be different. To advance their space policies and programs and move from simple aspirants to real space actors, new spacefaring countries must make firm decisions about what role to play in space and about the role space will play in their development, considering the vast evidence on the impact of space technologies and applications in industrial, societal, and economic progress. These nations need to construct a shared vision of public priorities and how space fits in those priorities, considering the strengths, opportunities available, and the challenges they must face to accomplish a coherent approach to space. The importance of having a strong space agency and solid space policies is undisputed. Both are essential for protecting sovereignty and developing independent activities within the space sector. We have already seen how nations like the United Arab Emirates (UAE) and Luxembourg have achieved innovation through dedicated agencies and frameworks and opened new economic opportunities.

[41] Nassar Jorge et al. (2022), p.47.

A successful space policy shall also include a functional space agency as a main step toward strong participation in the space economy. Indeed, in the long term, a space agency may help the nation to become independent of foreign companies and take control of vital services like satellite communications, disaster management, and climate monitoring. Because space operations support industries like agriculture, telecommunications, and environmental management, they are becoming increasingly significant in accomplishing sustainable development goals (SDGs). A well-defined, visionary, and long-term planned space policy would enable to fully utilize these technologies to address domestic issues while promoting international collaboration. Such investments, as in the Nigerian, Chilean, and Mexican space programs, for example, indicate the possibility of achieving the development goals and their feasibility. These agencies should be guided by national policies to position themselves considering changing trends in the space economy, use foreign direct investment, and stimulate public-private partnerships. It is fundamental that, by creating a space agency, the country may be integrated into international relations within the field of space exploration, international cooperation in the field of sustainable practices of outer space, prevention of space debris, and active participation in the regulatory process at the international level. A fully functioning agency would also be responsible for advancing science and technology and developing skills for those industries related to space exploration. Emerging spacefaring nations are on the rise; these nations need space agencies and space policies to help build the capacity to compete in fields such as satellite manufacture and data provision.

A good national space policy encourages the growth of more professionals like scientists, engineers, and entrepreneurs who will, in turn, help transform space ambitions. In addition to the above, effective and strategic space policies could provide a proper basis for long-term strategic planning that makes space activities sustainable and aligned with the nation's interests. Only then would these nations be in the right position to develop a clear roadmap with clear and achievable objectives that ensure the proper allocation of resources and provide guidelines for participation by all relevant sectors. This could help decrease the risks of space activities, such as further proliferating space debris or even the collision of satellites, and it would also be in line with international law and treaties. Policies could also entice space companies with tax breaks, research grants, or other funding options, which could, in turn, help establish a sound space industry to attract talent and capital. In fact, such measures trigger economic growth and technological progress, not only in space but also in renewable energy, agriculture, health, and so forth.

Transparency in space policy guarantees clarity and regulatory certainty, which private companies need to make investment decisions on specific space initiatives. It speaks to potential partners and investors that the country is serious about developing an enabling environment and recognizing space as a stable, growth-oriented industry. This will attract FDI and improve trust among potential partners. It opens avenues for technology transfer and joint ventures that spur innovation and capacity building.

Finally, space policy plays a very fundamental role in developing standards for ethics and principles concerning the responsible use of space. Policies of sustainability, mitigation of space debris, and principles of peaceful use of space and equitable access to the resources of space enable non-spacefaring nations to take pivotal roles in the global conversation on the future of space governance. Indeed, their contribution to the shaping of global space policy makes such policy and the international legal framework more effective and fully representative of the interests of smaller nations.

3.2 *The Strengths and Opportunities*

Having a proven track record on attraction and retention of FDI, accrued experience, and an installed capacity that can benefit space companies desiring to expand to jurisdictions with the competitive advantages is fundamental to grow the space sector of an emerging space nation, as well as having the capacity to host advanced operations on space technology, research, development, and manufacturing. A good strategy for smaller nations is to consider FDI as an opportunity to attract space companies that further develop the industry. Smaller nations may benefit from the trends in nearshoring and friendshoring and establish international cooperation with nearby spacefaring nations. This is fully supported by the shift in the organization of supply chains brought by the COVID-19 crisis but is subject to the influence of other global crises. The COVID-19 pandemic and war conflicts exposed the vulnerabilities of globalized supply chains and severely disrupted the continuity of many businesses due to border closures, quarantines, and government-imposed lockdowns. Industries with suppliers spread across continents suffered shortages, increased costs, and difficulties to deliver their products and services because of the lack of raw materials. As said, a global pandemic is not the only disruptor that can collapse supply chains; other events, such as severe weather conditions due to climate change, trade wars, and armed conflicts, can cause the same devastating effects.[42] Corporations around the world have been forced to rethink their supply chains to avoid the repetition of the disruptions lived with the pandemic by applying a series of measures. By nearshoring, firms are relocating business units closer to their main facilities and markets in nearby countries, where logistics are less complicated and distortions are less likely to jeopardize the business continuity. For countries in Latin America, for example, their location in the vicinity of the USA can be a platform to attract some of the space business that is burgeoning within the territory, offering to ensure business continuity for manufacturing companies while leveraging trade agreements with their partners.

The OECD has indicated that changes in space manufacturing processes and increased development of small satellite and CubeSat constellations influence the management of space manufacturing supply chains, with trends such as vertical

[42] Nassar Jorge et al. (2022), p.49.

integration of production and increased internationalization of supply chains.[43] Indeed, Google and Amazon, two technology giants with ambitious initiatives to compete in the mega-constellations business, have a presence in several countries in Latin America, and these nations may leverage this to attract those lines of their businesses.

There is also a relevant geopolitical component behind nearshoring that cannot be left unnoticed because it deals with the security and protection of supply chains. The world is living again times of Eastern-Western polarization that, in a globalized world, jeopardize the supply of goods and fundamental materials for production. Nearshoring not only focuses on easing the logistics of transportation of goods and provision of services but also on protecting the supply chains to guarantee resources under all circumstances. There is a tendency to consider the scope of political affinity and shared democratic values between the country purchasing the goods or services and the country from which those are sent or provided. Certainly, this is an opportunity in which emerging space nations shall assess their political standpoint to strategically position in a market formed by strong geopolitical blocks.[44]

Countries with educated multilingual and skilled human talent and a better position to successfully launch themselves into space must ensure that their public education policies support science, research, and development. Indeed, maintaining and improving the quality of education by developing strong STEM education shall be a national priority to provide future generations with the necessary skills to thrive in high-tech industries, including space.

From the political perspective, stability and the certainty and reliability of a legal framework, respect for the rule of law and due process of law, as well as abiding by the international commitments acquired by the State are fundamental. The protection of intellectual property is especially critical in a sector like space, where intellectual property protection can be essential for a company's success.

In the area of international collaboration, cooperation, and partnerships, for aspiring space nations—likely more than any others—it plays a fundamental role in the development of those countries' space capabilities. These alliances are necessary not only to gain access to space through traditional spacefaring nations' launching facilities but also for transfers of know-how and technologies, talent formation, and even for financing of entrepreneurship and innovation. Indeed:

> major spacefaring countries are now using space as a political tool to reach non-traditional partners in order to build trusting relationships across political borders, illustrating that foreign policy and space are now increasingly overlapping, and therefore reinforcing the radical restructuring that started in the 1990s. Furthermore, recent geopolitical developments, combined with the funding constraints of the various space-faring countries, have made it clear that greater international cooperation is the way forward for major space activities.[45]

---

[43] OECD (2019).

[44] Nassar Jorge et al. (2022), p.49–50.

[45] Peter (2016), pp. 145–153. https://doi.org/10.1016/j.spacepol.2016.11.004.

Among examples of regional cooperation in Latin America is the treaty that recently created the Latin American and Caribbean Space Agency (ALCE, by its acronym in Spanish), together with Antigua and Barbuda, Argentina, Bolivia, Cuba, Dominica, Ecuador, Guatemala, Haiti, Honduras, Mexico, Nicaragua, Panama, Paraguay, Peru, the Dominican Republic, Santa Lucia, San Vicente and the Grenadines, and Venezuela. For less space-experienced nations, participation in a forum along with countries that have longer space experience and more robust capabilities enables exchanges of information, knowledge, and other forms of collaboration on space projects. To maximize participation and ensure an efficient allocation of resources, Member States to ALCE must first define a space strategy and assess whether ALCE's direction is in alignment with the objectives pursued by each of them individually. That is, to make further international cooperation truly effective and impactful on the development of the space sector, the definition of the nation's space policy and the operation of a space agency or a special office of the government dedicated to space are a fundamental step. Finally, boosting the space sector should not be seen as one isolated objective but as an opportunity to generate growth and innovation in other areas. Space technology has countless applications on the ground and convergences with many other industries and sectors. Therefore, a space policy should define how space technology and the related capabilities will assist in other areas pursued to accomplish sustainable development goals. For example, Earth observation can help in the fight against drug trafficking, the prevention and mitigation of natural disasters, the conservation and management of the country's natural resources, fishing policies and monitoring of fishing activities, and the provision of satellite Internet to rural areas that improves connectivity and thus education and health services. A national space strategy must align priorities to build a thriving space sector that benefits its people and strengthens a nation's position in the global space economy.

3.3 *The Challenges*

Given the unique characteristics of the space sector, there is a need for a careful assessment and balance of expectations within a national space policy. The space sector is amid a new development cycle, with better and less costly technologies that can be accessed by many and not only the powerful and resourceful space agencies. There are also new commercial space-to-Earth activities derived from satellite signals and data and governments' programs supporting the development of the space economy. However, "available data on the space economy show that the growth of commercial space activities remains modest overall and should not be overestimated".[46] Indeed, government objectives of defense and space exploration still prevail as drivers of a space economy. For aspiring countries, the consideration

[46] OECD (2019).

of those aspects is fundamental given that defense and exploration are domains reserved to national enterprises; thus, the possibilities to attract foreign investment or business opportunities in that field are certainly very limited.[47]

In addition, with many countries around the world entering the space sector, competition is higher. States, in particular, aspiring space nations, must carefully plan their space policies and programs in ways that are strategic not only to fulfil internal needs but also to allow commercialization in the international market.

The OECD's recommendation is for governments to map national and foreign space economies (including actors and activities), in cooperation with national statistical offices, industry associations, and private contractors. That way, aspiring nations can make strategic investments in space programs and policies that effectively insert them in the space sector's global value chains and bring benefits to their societies.

Space—in orbit and on Earth—is highly competitive, barriers to entry are high, talent is highly specialized, and investment is required in the order of large sums even for the small projects. Strategic differentiation is crucial for countries with limited budgets to invest, even more so when such a budget comes from taxpayers who want to see the return of their investment as a condition to continue supporting a public policy, just as Luxembourg did.

In the area of education, one of the most relevant issues that traditional spacefaring and aspiring nations are facing is talent formation. With the current and expected growth of the space sector, more skilled and specialized talent is required to keep up with the pace of innovation and development. Without the human capital, namely, experts, technicians, researchers, scientists, and students, there is no space project that can be successful.[48]

To have skilled and well-formed talent, the quality of education in areas related to space and its applications, that is, sciences, engineering, technology, and mathematics (STEM), must be of the highest levels. By bringing space closer to students in the early ages of development (primary and early ages of secondary school), a nation is planting the seeds of future students of the so-called STEM careers. According to OECD's recommended practices, there must be centralized and independent external evaluation mechanisms, performance-based and competitive funding, and a connection with the business sector to increase incentives for universities to raise the quality and relevance of their research and innovation. Indeed, more innovation helps improve efficiency and performance at the industry levels, making the country more competitive. Talent capabilities can also be enhanced by international cooperation via training, internships, and technology transfers:

> space faring nations and established space institutions have both for-profit and non-profit incentive to contribute to basic space technology and human resource development in emerging countries (…) The personnel and workforce [of emerging space countries] must be adequately equipped to propagate sustainable space activities within their home countries (…) for emerging countries striving to achieve self-sustainable space programs with

---

[47] Nassar Jorge et al. (2022), p.54–55.

[48] Nassar Jorge et al. (2022), p.55.

> limited resources, as a first step we recommend a university-based fostering environment in conjunction with an external university-based training environment.[49]

To be successful, emerging space nations must articulate between academia, the education system, and the industry, to strategically prepare the talent needed to progress innovation and a national space sector. Finally, the financial component in space also presents a challenge for developing nations. Space activities demand high capital investment, and the return of it is either not guaranteed or happens after a long cycle of research, development, and implementation. In the current space environment, there is a low availability of funds for start-ups, particularly in aspiring space nations. Governments' procurements and grants are still the main direct financing instruments for space technology, research, and development.[50] However, according to the OECD, other financing instruments are important, such as loans, loan guarantees, seed grants, and similar instruments for small and young enterprises, that at the same time are sources of new employment and economic growth through innovation.[51] Tax incentives for research and development activities are a way to promote financing and investment in the space sector, as well as the OECD's recommendation of performance-based funding structures.[52]

The government, academia, and industry players must work together to build a comprehensive national space policy to prosper in the space sector. Key obstacles that need to be addressed by this strategy include the development of talent, financial constraints, and escalating global rivalry. It should support international collaboration to improve talent creation through training and technology transfer, as well as financial initiatives from the public and private sectors, including tax breaks for research and development. By coordinating these efforts, an aspirant space nation can ensure the long-term viability of its space objectives and develop a competitive presence in the international space economy.

4 Conclusion

Space has become closer to societies than we could ever imagine. Once a faraway domain used by a few nations for geopolitical purposes and to display power and leadership, it is now a common place for several States and actors from different fields, including science, academia, and private corporations. Furthermore, life on Earth—as we know it today—has become heavily dependent on many space technologies, services, and applications.

It has then come to be evident that no nation can ignore the impact of space on the daily lives of its population. Deciding not to engage in the growing space sector

[49] Polansky et al. (2016), pp. 19–23.

[50] De Freitas (2015), pp. 32–38.

[51] OECD (2019).

[52] Nassar Jorge et al. (2022), p.57.

as an avenue to improve social and economic development would be a policy mistake.

There are certain conditions that, under the appropriate direction and policies, would favor a nation's participation in the space arena and bring benefits to its society: a good talent base, the presence of space-related companies, political and economic stability, and respect for the rule of law and intellectual property are appealing to foreign investors.

Many countries are ahead of others in the space race. But far from discouraging the entrance of the latter into a competitive field, their experiences should serve to feed a national strategy based on internal needs and goals and the international role the country decides to play in space. To move forward in this direction, the following main areas of focus are suggested.

Ratification of International Space Treaties. The development of the space sector in emerging countries demands the incorporation into their domestic legal framework of the international treaties that govern matters related to outer space. The ratification of these agreements sends a strong signal of the State's commitment to abide by the common understandings and agreements of the international community and provides legal certainty to the different national and foreign stakeholders participating in the space sector.

Committed Leadership. There is a need for clear leadership and direction. Initiatives and efforts for the development of the space sector have not been absent; however, further cohesion is required. To advance the space sector, a leader is needed, a champion who identifies convergent points between space and other policy goals and can amalgamate a multidimensional space policy, balancing stakeholders' interests. Engaging with the different stakeholders across government, academia, and the industry to understand their goals and how space can further support their achievement.

Capability Building. To establish the coalitions to build the additional capabilities, an aspirant space nation needs for a successful and strategic journey into the space sector. Capabilities must be supported by the necessary human capital, infrastructure, industrial base, and appropriate research and development activities in both the public and private sectors. In the process of building those capabilities, international cooperation, alliances, and partnerships are fundamental. In seeking such cooperation, nations should make sure that it serves the outlined goals. The current landscape is competitive, with limited resources and more nations seeking the same strategic partnerships to develop their own space capabilities. Successful nations are those smart enough to move fast. The recently created Latin American and Caribbean Space Agency (ALCE) will also serve as a forum to establish alliances with the region's well-established spacefaring nations, such as Mexico, Argentina, and Chile, to the extent that it carefully balances the resources it puts into ALCE and how much it can contribute to and boost the country's own space agenda.

Competitive Advantages. Competitive advantages shall be enhanced to continue to differentiate an aspirant space nation. Knowing its strengths, it shall put in place an innovative and specialized approach to space that also fosters internal development. It shall find that niche that has long-term validity and that would enhance the country's competitiveness and global position. This conversation requires the engagement of all relevant stakeholders, and an analysis of data on the value of the space sector and its value chains informs investment decisions.

Formulation of a National Space Vision, Policy, and Strategy. A national space policy must begin with a commonly recognized and shared vision: the horizon where it wants to position itself in the future and which responds to a convergence of interests and objectives of the different stakeholders. The strategy dictates the set of guidelines, the actions to reach the policy goals, and who is in charge.

The formulation and implementation of a public space policy imply efforts in several fronts: finance, education, science, innovation, technology, industry, legal, and regulatory. In each of them, policymakers should identify the challenges faced, the existing capabilities, and the priorities going forward, with the respective budget allocations, implementation, and monitoring.

A national space policy should not be abstracted from the State's other policy objectives; to the contrary, it should serve as a vehicle to achieve them. A space policy can only be successful if it considers multi-sectoral needs within its own programs that unite several initiatives to enhance the country's capabilities.

Finally, as technology advances faster than the speed of space agencies and policies, short-, mid-, and long-term planning, as well as flexibility in the programs, are fundamental to keep up with the changing environment.

References

Aganaba-Jeanty T (2016) Introducing the Cosmopolitan Approaches to International Law (CAIL) lens to analyze governance issues as they affect emerging and aspirant space actors, Space Policy 37, Part 1. https://doi.org/10.1016/j.spacepol.2016.05.007

Amadeus Capital: Space Tech Stack 2025: Mapping Value from Ground to Orbit and Back available online https://www.amadeuscapital.com/space-tech-stack-2025-mapping-value-from-ground-to-orbit-and-back/

Brukardt R et al (2022a) Mckinsey Space around the Globe. https://www.mckinsey.com/industries/aerospace-and-defense/our-insights/space-around-the-globe

Brukardt R et al (2022b) The role of space in driving sustainability, security, and development on earth. McKinsey & Company. https://www.mckinsey.com/industries/aerospace-and-defense/our-insights/the-role-of-space-in-driving-sustainability-security-and-development-on-earth#

Challenges and Opportunities at the Dawn of the New Space Age [PDF document]. Perry World House. University of Pennsylvania. https://global.upenn.edu/sites/default/files/perry-world-house/pwh-new-space-age-2022.pdf

Colombian Space Commission. http://cce.gov.co/Paginas/cce.aspx

De Freitas M et al (2015) Innovation policies in Brazilian and Dutch aerospace industries: how sectors driven by national procurement are influenced by its S&T environment. Space Policy 34. https://doi.org/10.1016/j.spacepol.2015.08.003

Gibbs G (2012) An analysis of the space policies of the major space faring nations and selected emerging space faring nations. Ann Air Space Law 37:279–332

Golkar A et al (2021) Definition of new space—expert survey results and key technology trends. IEEE J Miniat Air Space Syst (Online) 2(1). https://doi.org/10.1109/JMASS.2020.3045851. https://ieeexplore.ieee.org/document/9298818

Gomez-Jenkins M et al (2023) Project Irazú: space and ground systems engineering of a 1U CubeSat Store and Forward Mission for Environmental Monitoring. Trans Jpn Soc Aeronaut Space Sci 66(6):217–225. https://doi.org/10.2322/tjsass.66.217
Harding RC (2016a) Conclusions: space policy in developing countries. Space Policy 37, Part 1. https://doi.org/10.1016/j.spacepol.2016.10.001
Harding RC (2016b) Introduction: space policy in developing countries. Space Policy 37, Part 1. https://doi.org/10.1016/j.spacepol.2016.05.006
Howell E (2021) India launches Amazonia-1 satellite for Brazil and 18 others into space. Space.com. https://www.space.com/india-launches-amazonia-1-satellite-18-others
Japan Aerospace Exploration Agency (n.d.) The National Space Development Agency of Japan (NASDA). https://global.jaxa.jp/about/history/nasda/index_e.html
Jones H (2018) The recent large reduction in space launch cost. NASA Ames Research Center. International Conference on Environmental Systems. https://ttu-ir.tdl.org/handle/2346/74082
Mwakilishi (2018, May 12) First Kenyan-made satellite deployed into space from Japan. Retrieved October 8, 2024, from https://www.mwakilishi.com/article/kenya-news/2018-05-12/first-kenyan-made-satellite-deployed-into-space-from-japan#google_vignette
NASA. https://www.nasa.gov/humans-in-space/commercial-space/commercial-crew-program/
Nassar Jorge, A., De Man, P., Madders, K., & KU Leuven. Faculteit Wetenschappen. Opleiding Master of Space Studies degree granting institution. (2022). Costa Rica into Space: a case study of the policy challenges, opportunities and options for an aspirant space nation seeking to esta blish itself in today's setting. KU Leuven. Faculteit Wetenschappen. Unpublished.
OECD (2019) The space economy in figures: how space contributes to the global economy. OECD Publishing, Paris. https://doi.org/10.1787/c5996201-en
OECD (2023) The space economy in figures: responding to global challenges. OECD Publishing, Paris. https://doi.org/10.1787/fa5494aa-en
Ospina S (2019) Emerging economies' contributions to space activities and legislation. Proc Int Inst Space Law 62:253–266
Patel NV (2019) There has never been a better time to start a small space agency. MIT Technology Review. https://www.technologyreview.com/2019/11/26/131822/why-its-now-the-perfect-time-to-start-a-small-space-agency/
Peter N (2016) The changing geopolitics of space activities. Space Policy 37, Part 3. https://doi.org/10.1016/j.spacepol.2016.11.004
Polansky JL et al (2016) A university-based model for space-related capacity building in emerging countries. Space Policy 36. https://doi.org/10.1016/j.spacepol.2016.01.001
Private Companies, Not Governments, Are Shaping the Future of Space Exploration. Futurism. https://futurism.com/private-companies-not-governments-are-shaping-the-future-of-space-exploration
Property Rights Alliance, International Property Rights Index 2023. https://www.international-propertyrightsindex.org/#compare-container
Scatteia L et al (2020) The role of emerging space nations in supporting sustainable development and economic growth. Pricewaterhouse Coppers. https://www.pwc.fr/fr/assets/files/pdf/2020/03/en-france-pwc-space-practice-emerging-space-nations-paper.pdf
Space Tech Analytics (2022) Space Tech Industry 2021, Year Overview. (Online). Available at https://www.spacetech.global/dashboard
United Nations (2023) Office for Outer Space Affairs Contribution to the "Space2030" Agenda, EU Space Supporting a World of 8 Billion People. https://www.unoosa.org/res/oosadoc/data/documents/2023/stspace/stspace85_0_html/st_space_085E.pdf
World Intellectual Property Organization, Global Innovation Index 2024. https://www.wipo.int/gii-ranking/en/costa-rica
Zhao Y (2016) The role of bilateral and multilateral agreements in international space cooperation. Space Policy 36. https://doi.org/10.1016/j.spacepol.2016.02.007

Argentine

Carolina E. Catani

Contents

The contents of this chapter are written for academic purposes and personal capacity. It should not be interpreted as the position of CONAE nor of the Argentine Nation.

C. E. Catani (✉)
Director and Professor on Legal and Technical Posgraduate, University of Salvador (USAL), Buenos Aires, Argentina

Responsible on Space Law at National Commission for Space Activities (CONAE), Buenos Aires, Argentina

Director of the Group on International Affairs of Outer Space. Argentine Council for International Relations (CARI), Ciudad Autónoma de Buenos Aires, Buenos Aires, Argentina
e-mail: ccatani@conae.gob.ar

I. Grosner (ed.), *Space Regulation in Latin America*, Space Regulations Library 11, https://doi.org/10.1007/978-3-032-05828-7_3

Abstract The Argentine Republic's history in space activities dates back to the origins of the space age. First under the Air Force and then separating it from the military sphere with the creation of the National Commission for Space Activities (CONAE), Argentina has developed and launched several satellites, moving forward among the nations that have their own capabilities for the development, testing, and construction of their own missions for Earth observation and communications, and has also generated capabilities in the private sector that is beginning to emerge. Now, having made great progress in human resources capabilities, technologies and infrastructure development, National Space Plans, and international cooperation agreements, an update of the national regulations is seen as necessary to harmonize the regulatory dispersion to accompany this growth, such as strengthening the authorization and licensing procedures for space operators, among others, in line with the most modern global space laws.

1 Introduction

Space activities have grown exponentially. More and new actors from both the governmental and nongovernmental sectors are taking part. A recent report from the World Economy Forum in knowledge partnership with McKinsey & Co. (April, 2024) entitled "Space: The $1.8 trillion opportunity for global economic growth" concludes that the global space economy estimated at $630 billion in 2023 will be worth $1.8 trillion by 2035.[1]

This implies that the capabilities of the space sector will increase. That is why the space sector in Latin America and the Caribbean must prepare to be a regional player in the global space economy, based on the development of its individual

[1] World Economy Forum and McKinsey & Co. (April, 2024) *"Space: The $1.8 trillion opportunity for global economic growth"*, p. 2. Available at: https://www.weforum.org/publications/space-the-1-8-trillion-opportunity-for-global-economic-growth/.

capabilities, but in a regional understanding in order to provide socio-productive benefits to its population.

In this sense, this chapter offers a look at Argentina's past and present in space matters, particularly in its segments of institutional development, technologies, human resources, and scientific-technological and regulatory capabilities, in view of the opportunities that this ecosystem proposes. In this way, the reader will be able to have a first approximation on some of the topics mentioned above.

2 Topics

This chapter will address an analysis of space activities in the Argentine Republic. Among the topics to be discussed are the legal framework in which these are carried out, both for governmental and nongovernmental entities, which treaties have been ratified by this nation, and whether it has a space agency and space missions and, therefore, if there is a National Registry in accordance with international legal frameworks.

On the other hand, current issues such as space debris and weaponization and exploitation of space resources are also part of the topics developed.

As space activity is a favorable environment for international cooperation, contributions will be introduced that allow us to learn about the existence of national agreements and projects and collaborations with other countries and/or space agencies. These and other topics are developed below.

2.1 Which International Space Treaties Has the Argentine Republic Signed as a Party?

Argentina has signed four of the five space treaties.

The first one is the *Treaty on Principles Governing the Activities of States in the Exploration and Use of Outer Space, including the Moon and Other Celestial Bodie*s (Outers Space Treaty).[2] It was adopted by the General Assembly in its resolution 2222 (XXI), signed by the country on January 27, 1967, and approved by Law No. 17.989 on December 4, 1968.[3]

The second one is the *Agreement on the Rescue of Astronauts, the Return of Astronauts and Return of Objects Launched into Outer Space* (Rescue Agreement). It

[2] *OST:* Adopted by the General Assembly in its resolution 2222 (XXI), opened for signature on January 27, 1967, entered into force on October 10, 1967. https://www.unoosa.org/oosa/en/ourwork/spacelaw/treaties/introouterspacetreaty.html.

[3] *Law No. 17.989 (Outer Space Treaty and Rescue Agreement).* http://servicios.infoleg.gob.ar/infolegInternet/anexos/205000-209999/208688/norma.htm.

was adopted by the General Assembly in its resolution 2345 (XXII),[4] signed by the country on May 28, 1968, and also approved by Law No. 17.989 on December 4, 1968.[5]

The next one is the *Convention on International Liability for Damage Caused by Space Objects* (Liability Convention). It was adopted by the General Assembly in its resolution 2777 (XXVI),[6] signed by the Argentine Republic on March 29, 1972, and approved by Law No. 23.335 on July 30, 1986.[7]

Finally, the fourth and the last one is the *Convention on Registration of Objects Launched into Outer Space* (Registration Convention). It was adopted by the General Assembly in its resolution 3235 (XXIX),[8] adopted by the Argentine Republic on January 14, 1975, and approved by Law No. 24.158 on September 30, 1992.[9] Regarding the "Moon Agreement,"[10] Argentina is not a party to it, and, therefore, it was neither ratified nor incorporated into the national legislation.

It is important to mention the outstanding legal hierarchical status granted to international treaties and conventions. In 1994 the Argentine Republic approved a reform to the National Constitution (C.N.),[11] in which the members of the Constituent Assembly agreed to give special recognition to international treaties and conventions. Thus, in the reformed National Constitution, in Chapter Four on the powers of the Congress, the new Article 75 (ap. 22) states that it is incumbent upon the Congress: "To approve or reject treaties concluded with other nations and with international organizations and concordats with the Holy See." Adding the following: "Treaties and concordats have hierarchy superior to laws."

In this way, it assigns to international treaties and conventions a hierarchical level superior to other laws issued by Congress. Consequently, the aforementioned space treaties and conventions have been included in this higher hierarchical level.

---

[4] *Rescue Agreement:* Adopted by the General Assembly in its resolution 2345 (XXII), opened for signature on April 22, 1968, entered into force on December 3, 1968 [https://www.unoosa.org/oosa/en/ourwork/spacelaw/treaties/introrescueagreement.html].

[5] *Law No. 17.989 (Outer Space Treaty & Rescue Agreement).* http://servicios.infoleg.gob.ar/infolegInternet/anexos/205000-209999/208688/norma.htm.

[6] *Liability Convention:* Adopted by the General Assembly in its resolution 2777 (XXVI), opened for signature on March 29, 1972, entered into force on September 1, 1972 [https://www.unoosa.org/oosa/en/ourwork/spacelaw/treaties/introliability-convention.html].

[7] *Law No. 23.335* (Convention on International Liability for Damage). http://servicios.infoleg.gob.ar/infolegInternet/anexos/20000-24999/23571/norma.htm.

[8] *Registration Convention*: Adopted by the General Assembly in its resolution 3235 (XXIX), opened for signature on January 14, 1975, entered into force on September 15, 1976. https://www.unoosa.org/oosa/en/ourwork/spacelaw/treaties/introregistration-convention.html.

[9] *Law No. 24.158 (Convention on Registration of Objects Launched into Outer Space) https://servicios.infoleg.gob.ar/infolegInternet/verNorma.do?id=556.*

[10] *"Moon Agreement"* Agreement Governing the Activities of States on the Moon and Other Celestial Bodies. Adopted by the General Assembly in its resolution 34/68, opened for signature on December 18, 1979, entered into force on July 11, 1984. https://www.unoosa.org/oosa/en/ourwork/spacelaw/treaties/intromoon-agreement.html.

[11] National Constitution Law No. 24,430. Orders the publication of the official text of the National Constitution (sanctioned in 1853 with the reforms of 1860, 1866, 1898, 1957, and 1994). http://servicios.infoleg.gob.ar/infolegInternet/anexos/0-4999/804/norma.htm.

In fact, this is one of the significant reforms introduced, taking into account that other treaties related to human rights, which are listed in an exhaustive manner, are now directly considered to have constitutional hierarchy (a level even higher than the other treaties and conventions). However, since this is not the subject of the present point, we will not go further into this matter.

2.2 *Is the Argentine Republic a Member of COPUOS?*

Argentine is a member of the Committee on the Peaceful Uses of Outer Space (COPUOS) since December 13, 1958, when the General Assembly Resolution 1348 (XIII) of the United Nation established an *ad hoc* Committee on the Peaceful Uses of Outer Space.

At this moment there were only 18 members: Argentina, Australia, Belgium, Brazil, Canada, Czechoslovakia (now Czech Republic and Slovakia), France, India, Iran, Italy, Japan, Mexico, Poland, Sweden, the Union of Soviet Socialist Republics (now Russian Federation), the United Arab Republic (now Egypt), the United Kingdom of Great Britain and Northern Ireland, and the USA.

Since then, our nation has participated in the sessions of the Committee and both Subcommittees without interruption, every year.

2.3 *Has the Argentine Republic Signed the Artemis Accords?*

On July 27 of 2023 Argentine became the 28th nation to sign the Artemis Accords in a ceremony at the Casa Rosada, in Buenos Aires, by the minister of Science, Technology and Innovation Daniel Filmus on behalf of Argentina and with the presence of the NASA administrator Bill Nelson.

This sign was in the framework of two centuries of diplomacy relationship between both countries and a long relationship in space activities since 1991. An example of that mutual cooperation on space matters an on-Earth observation (among others) is the SAC satellite series and specially the SAC-D Aquarius.

Argentine President Fernández and the ambassador of the USA, Marc Stanley, with other officials and representatives, also attended in the signing meeting.

2.4 *Can Space Activities Be Classified as Dual Use, or Are They Only for Defense or Civil Purposes?*

When the "Treaty on Principles Governing the Activities of States in the Exploration and Use of Outer Space, including the Moon and Other Celestial Bodies" (Outer Space Treaty-OST) was adopted in 1967, it was definitely established that the access, use, and exploration of outer space, as well as the technologies to be used in this field, would be for peaceful purposes. That spirit had previously been incorporated in the "Declaration of Legal Principles Governing the Activities of States in the Exploration and Use of Outer Space"[12] (Declaration of Legal Principles) and in the recitals of General Assembly resolution 1962 (XVIII) of December 13, 1963 "*Recognizing* the common interest of all mankind in the progress of the exploration and use of outer space for peaceful purposes," adopting the Declaration of Principles. As member of that treaty, the Argentine Republic recognizes and reaffirms the principle of the peaceful purposes of use of space and space activities.

It should be noted that this was a legal construction through which the States agreed and accepted that space activities would be carried out, for peaceful purposes. This taking into account the prevailing context in those times of Cold War and the origin or basis of the technologies coming from the domain and knowledge of the military field and fundamentally missile. On the other hand, it was also expected that in some way this definition of "exclusively for peaceful uses" (Article IV del OST),[13] agreed upon by the nations, could act as a way to avoid transferring the effects of wars on Earth to the new field of outer space, mainly taking into account the ruinous consequences derived from nuclear bomb attacks. Definition that must be analyzed in an integral interpretation, considering not only Article IV of the OST but also Article IX,[14] among others.

This implies that Article IV of the OST expressly includes a direct prohibition on the deployment of nuclear weapons, but a legal loophole remained with respect to other weapons.

At the same time, there is some discussion regarding the wording of the second paragraph of the aforementioned article, which reads: "The Moon and other celestial bodies shall be used by all States Parties to the Treaty exclusively for peaceful purposes." As can be seen, this sentence does not include the reference to "outer space" as is usually the wording in the context of the OST, which refers to outer space, the Moon, and other celestial bodies. It is argued in doctrine that this omission was intentional, allowing certain States to carry out military activities, such as the USA and the Union of Soviet Socialist Republics, which by the time the OST was drafted had already launched military satellites.[15] Nevertheless, as interpreted

---

[12] General Assembly Resolution 1962 (XVIII) of December 13, 1963 https://www.unoosa.org/oosa/en/ourwork/spacelaw/principles/legal-principles.html.

[13] Article IV*: "States Parties to the Treaty undertake not to place in orbit around the Earth any objects carrying nuclear weapons or any other kinds of weapons of mass destruction, install such weapons on celestial bodies, or station such weapons in outer space in any other manner.*

The Moon and other celestial bodies shall be used by all States Parties to the Treaty exclusively for peaceful purposes. The establishment of military bases, installations and fortifications, the testing of any type of weapons and the conduct of military manoeuvres on celestial bodies shall be forbidden. The use of military personnel for scientific research or for any other peaceful purposes shall not be prohibited. The use of any equipment or facility necessary for peaceful exploration of the Moon and other celestial bodies shall also not be prohibited."

[14] See art. IX OST.

[15] Stephan et al. (2021). *Cologne Commentary on Space Law. Outer Space Treaty*. pp. 144–145.

in the framework of the Vienna Convention Treaty, Article 31 indicates that "any subsequent practice followed in the application of the treaty"[16] shall be taken into account for the purposes of interpretation. The reference to peaceful use may therefore be interpreted as including "outer space." And considering that the space activities shall conduct for peaceful purposes, the technologies should follow the same purposes in the outer space.

Despite that stipulation, over the years it has not been possible to reach a clear and unequivocal concept as to what is meant by "peaceful purposes" as referred to the Outer Space Treaty. This has also led to consider the concept of defense and nonaggressive or non-offensive use for the interpretation of what is understood by "use for peaceful purposes".[17]

Facing that difficulty, and the centrality for years analyzing the issue of peaceful use and purposes from the point of view of technologies without reaching an agreement on its definition, a new look puts the focus on the behaviors of States in their deployment of space activities. Thus, we are faced with the dichotomous situation of referring to dual use or dual purpose in a thin line or "blurred line" between civilian and military dual-use capabilities in space.

This is a reminder that technologies are not neutral. Or better said, they themselves depend on the behavior adopted with them or on the behavior or purpose that the human being ultimately assigns to them. As stated in the International Seminar '60 years of the first human being in space. Exploration, use and exploitation of outer space' organized by the Mexican Space Agency, the Institute of Legal Research of the UNAM, and the Mexican Secretary of Foreign Affairs on May 12, 2021, the author of this chapter has already argued that: technology, far from being neutral, reflects the plans, purposes and values of our society, giving "real content to the space of life in which they are applied, increasing certain purposes, denying and even destroying others" (Winner, 1977:38 in Osorio, 2003:2).[18] It is a system of actions where social, economic and political interests of those who design, develop, finance and control a technology are embodied. (Osorio: 2003:2).[19] That is why the events that took place before the first launch, but mainly since the beginning of the space race, also put in the same scenario the interests of the actors of the time, considering that space technology could not be accepted as neutral per se, and that it should be understood as a system that "integrates knowledge, organizational processes, values and cultural representations, as well as technical elements" (Osorio:2003), applying to both material and social systems".[20]

Hence, with the advent of the first satellite orbiting in space, States understood the need to promptly establish an international legal regime that assigns a peaceful

[16] See Art. 31 of Vienna Convention on the Law of Treaties, approved by Law No. 19.865 of Argentina. http://servicios.infoleg.gob.ar/infolegInternet/anexos/215000-219999/217116/norma.htm.

[17] Stephan et al. (2021), pp. 145–146.

[18] Osorio (2003).

[19] Osorio (2003).

[20] See the full paragraph in: Catani (2024).

meaning to space activities and the technologies to be used therein. Despite this, in view of current developments, this concept and peaceful spirit is gradually being threatened by the increased dependence on the use of space and space activities and the growth of destructive and nondestructive counter-space measures deployed by several nations to "enhance their military and national security capabilities through the use of space".[21] Thus, according to the study conducted by the Secure World Foundation in 2023 based on open sources, we find nations such as the USA, Russia, China, India, Australia, France, Iran Japan, North Korea, South Korea, and the UK have already in some way advanced the development of "their own counterspace capabilities that can be used to mock, disrupt, interrupt, deny, degrade or destroy space systems".[22]

This has been clearly analyzed in the treatment given during the United Nations "Open-ended working group (OEWG) on reducing space threats through norms, rules and principles of responsible behaviors," approved by General Assembly resolution 76/231,[23] in the framework of the Prevention of Armed Race in the Outer Space (PAROS) and the Disarmament Commission. Challenges are posed not only by the definition of the concept of peaceful purposes but also by the dual-use capabilities of many space technologies that were conceived for peaceful use but which could change that meaning. Such is the case of co-orbital approaches, an intentional collision of two satellites ("hit to kill"), or an intentional interference in radio frequencies, to cite just some examples. So they could change depending on whether the capabilities are to be used for peaceful or non-peaceful purposes.

As Azcárate and Lagos (2023) argue, "the desire to approach PAROS from a behavioral point of view is partly due to the challenges posed to arms control by the dual-use and dual-purpose nature of space-based infrastructure and technical capabilities".[24,25] This prevents a clear definition of the concept of a weapon (despite efforts to do so, as can be seen even in the treaty proposal offered by China and Russia). In this sense, Lagos (chair of the OEWG referred to above) is also in favor of working on an approach focused on behaviors rather than capabilities, as this "may be more effective in ensuring space security".[26]

Unfortunately, back to analyzing if space activities be classified as dual-use, or are they only for defense or civil purposes, places us almost back to the times before the Space Treaty, where this instrument supposed was a clear tool to prevent an arms

---

[21] Secure World Foundation (2023), p. Vi.

[22] Secure World Foundation (2023), p. vi.

[23] See *United Nation General Assembly resolution 76/231* https://undocs.org/Home/Mobile?FinalSymbol=a%2Fres%2F76%2F231&Language=E&DeviceType=Desktop&LangRequested=False.

[24] See Azcárate Ortega and Lagos Koller (2023), p. 26.

[25] Azcárate, makes a distinction between dual-use and dual-purpose objects: "*A distinction between dual-use and dual-purpose objects highlights that threats to space security do not stem merely from the capabilities of space systems but also from the manner in which they are utilized and the intent behind their use. This is particularly relevant when assessing the threat perception of dual-purpose objects…*" See Azcárate Ortega (2023).

[26] See Azcárate Ortega and Lagos Koller (2023), p. 27.

race in space. For although it has been agreed that space activities should be carried out for peaceful purposes, mankind does not seem to be close to this will actually happen.

2.5 *Is There a Registry of Space Objects Maintained by the United Nations?*

The Argentine Republic, by ratifying in 1986 the Convention on Registration of Objects Launched into Outer Space of 1975,[27] incorporated it into its national legislation and assumed the commitment to register space objects launched into space.

Subsequently, by means of Presidential Decree No. 125 of 1995 (published in the Official Gazette [Boletín Oficial] No. 28,192 of July 25, 1995),[28] it implemented such treaty, by providing for the creation of the National Registry of Objects Launched into Outer Space. This Registry not only guarantees the identification of the objects but also, among other stipulations, grants Argentina the status of State of Registry, thus complying with international obligations regarding space activities. This legal framework is fundamental for the development and regulation of space activities in the country. Indeed, its Article 1° provides for the creation of the National Registry and places it under the orbit of the National Commission on Space Activities (CONAE), the Argentine space agency, which is the implementing authority. By placing it under the authority of CONAE, it is guaranteed that there will be a specialized agency in charge of its implementation and supervision.

In its only ten articles the general guidelines are established, entrusting CONAE with the regulation of its operation and determination of the fees to be paid (Article 4).

Substantively, it provides that the National Registry shall receive from the owners and operators the registration of space objects. Likewise, other annotations of rights, resolutions, contracts, acts, and legal facts referring to the object will be registered (conf. Art. 2°). This allows us to foresee that, almost concomitantly with the creation of the civil space agency, a projection toward the participation of the private sector in the future was taken into account. Events that combine with the successive National Space Plans, envisioning the generation of local nongovernmental capacities, beyond those that the National State may develop by itself and for itself.

On the other hand, it is decreed that the registration of the objects is mandatory (Art. 3°), which grants the National State the jurisdiction and control of such objects in accordance with the international standards in force and wherever it is located.

---

[27] See supra n. 9 y 10.

[28] See Presidential Decree No. 125 of 1995 (published in the Official Gazette No. 28,192 of July 25, (1995). Available on line at https://www.boletinoficial.gov.ar/detalleAviso/primera/7152296/19950725?busqueda=1.

The basic information required for entry in the Registry is as follows:

- Date and territory or place of expected launching. [This indicates that the registration application process must be carried out prior to the launch.][29]
- Appropriate designation of the space object and identifying mark in non-disintegrable parts. [Such a measure is not only in accordance with the registration itself but also imposes on the applicant the obligation to place identifying marks on the object, which must be informed in the application for registration of the object.]
- International conventions agreed in case the object to be launched is carried out jointly with other launching State(s).
- General function envisaged for the object.
- Name(s) and address(es) of the owner(s) and/or operator(s) of the object. [In practice, according to the regulations defined by CONAE, both are registered.]
- Basic predicted orbital parameters, which include nodal period, inclination, apogee, and perigee.
- Launch service provider.
- Companies involved in the construction of the object to be launched and its launch vector.
- Identification of who is to execute the control of the object.
- Location and characteristics of the telemetry, remote control, satellite control, and control stations (TTC), and of the master and tracking station, as applicable.
- Frequencies and transmission powers of the space station on board.
- Mass of the space object.
- Expected lifetime of the space object.
- Expected date of disintegration, recovery, or loss of contact with the space object.
- Precautions taken regarding non-contamination of outer space including celestial bodies and whether mechanisms are foreseen for delivery to a transfer orbit at the end of the object's lifetime.
- Information on insurance policies.

In addition to those listed above, any event that leads to the end of the useful life and accident or that renders it unusable for its operational mission shall also be recorded.

From the list of items stipulated, the requirement to indicate the measures adopted in relation to the non-pollution of outer space and its celestial bodies, as well as those measures planned to be adopted after the end of the useful life of the object launched into space (such as sending it to a transfer orbit), stands out as consistent with the vision of the COPUOS Space Debris Mitigation Guidelines and the Long-Term Sustainability Guidelines[30] (considering that the National Registry dates from 1995).

---

[29] Hereinafter, what is written between [ ] is the author's own writing and not a verbatim transcription of the source involved.

[30] See *Space Debris Mitigation Guidelines of the Committee on the Peaceful Uses of Outer Space* (2010), available online at https://www.unoosa.org/pdf/publications/st_space_49E.pdf. & Long-

Finally, in order to comply with Article IV of the Registration Convention, the Ministry of Foreign Affairs, International Trade, and Worship, through the Office of the General Director for International Security, Nuclear, and Space Affairs, will notify to the secretary-general of the United Nations of all registrations and entries made in the National Registry. It should be added that in accordance with the "Declaration on the practices of States and international organizations in registering space objects" adopted by Resolution A/62/101[31] of the General Assembly on December 17, 2007, the Argentine National Registry has adopted the use of the form proposed in that resolution, thus facilitating the harmonization of the information to be provided. https://www.unoosa.org/oosa/documents-and-resolutions/search.jspx?view=documents&f=oosaDocument.series_s1%3AUNOOSA/%2FREG/%2FFRM/%2F

As established in Article 4 of Presidential Decree No. 125/95[32] previously analyzed, CONAE proceeded to regulate the operation of the National Registry, first through Resolution No. 252/96 and later by Resolution No. 260[33] of 1999 of CONAE, which is still in force today. CONAE's resolution also approved the registration procedure of objects launched into outer space (see Annex Resolution) along with a set of forms that are attached as annexes to the resolution (Articles 2 and 3) to be completed by the registrant with all the required information.

Expanding on what is defined in the Presidential Decree, the procedure regulation provides that "registrations, annotations and acknowledgments before the Registry may be requested, as the case may be: a) By the owner or operator of the space object, or their legal representatives. b) By the National State, or any of the agencies under the National State. c) By whoever has a legitimate interest in securing the right to be registered. d) By the International Organizations to which the National State is a party. e) By competent judicial or administrative authority" (Art. 12).

In turn, is defined that it must be registered in the National Registry: a) "any space object launched or whose launch is promoted by the National State, or which is launched from the national territory or facilities belonging to the National State, provided that the object has not been previously registered in another launching State" (Article 1).

As can be seen, the definition of Launching State of the Registration Convention of Article 1 is maintained, as well as the definition of space object, which, far from

Term Sustainability Guidelines approved in the report of the Committee on the Peaceful Uses of Outer Space on the work of its 62nd Session (adopted by A/RES/74/82) https://www.unoosa.org/res/oosadoc/data/documents/2021/stspace/stspace79_0_html/st_space79S.pdf.

[31] See UNOOSA, A/RES/62/101 *Recommendations on enhancing the practice of States and international intergovernmental organizations in registering space objects* (2007) Available online at https://www.unoosa.org/oosa/oosadoc/data/resolutions/2007/general_assembly_62nd_session/ares62101.html.

[32] See supra n. 30.

[33] See at CONAE's web page *"Registro de satélites"*. Available online https://www.argentina.gob.ar/ciencia/conae/institucional/registro-de-satelites.

expanding or clarifying the concept, reiterates that a space object is understood as "any physical object, manned or unmanned, launched into space for the purpose of exploration and use of outer space, including the Moon and other celestial bodies." It includes the launch or transport vehicle (regardless of whether it is recoverable or not), "as well as the payload or artificial satellite to be placed in orbit."

On the other hand, the procedure regulation established the remaining facts and legal acts that will also be in charge of the National Registry of Objects Launched into Outer Space (conf. Art. 1) in addition to the registration of the object to be launched. They are:

- To take note of any document that constitutes, transmits, declares, modifies, or extinguishes rights in rem relating to the registered objects
- To take note of any document that provides for seizures and interdictions or that in any way affects the domain or availability of the registered objects
- To note any other fact or legal act that in any way affects the legal status of the registered object, including the conclusion of its useful life, as well as any accident or fact that renders it useless to fulfill its purpose, its disintegration, recovery, or loss of contact
- To record any fact or legal act that deprives the owner, operator, or who for any reason has rights over the registered object of the free availability of its assets
- To issue all the certifications that correspond to the entries contained in its records
- To provide the information related to the registered objects that must be provided in accordance with the international treaties and/or conventions subscribed by the Argentine Republic or those resulting from the laws in force

That is to say, it is a Registry in which an object to be launched into space is recorded, through which it will remain under the jurisdiction and control of the Argentine National State when it becomes a State of Registry (provided that no transfer takes place). But other legal facts and acts that go beyond the Registry information provided for in the International Convention will also be recorded therein. Such is the case of paragraphs b) and c), which significantly resemble this Registry in some of its scope to Argentine real estate or aircraft registries, especially with regard to real rights, seizures, interdictions, or any other affectation to the domain and availability of the registered objects, which CONAE included, based on delegated powers. From the survey carried out, as the National Registry is public, no annotation of any of the cases foreseen in paragraphs b) and c) on the registered objects has been noted.

Objects in the National Registry of Objects Launched into Outer Space shall be identified with the letters RA plus a number, which must coincide with the number of the original folio in which it is registered. Such identification shall correspond to the effects provided for in Article 5, paragraph 17, of PEN Decree No. 125/95 (identification mark located on non-disintegrable parts), without prejudice to the identification that the owner grants to its space object.

In order to avoid duplicity, see the full Resolution CONAE No. 260/99 approving the "Organic Regulations of the National Registry of Objects Launched into Outer Space" (the procedure regulation of the National Registry of Objects Launched into

Outer Space) and the respective annexes (forms) to be completed by the applicant of the registration.[34] All the information submitted through the forms must always be accompanied by supporting documentation, including those of the owner (whether a legal or natural person). Likewise, after the analysis carried out by the application authority, the application for registration, or the required annotation, could be approved or rejected.

Finally, the procedure must be in writing. However, given the time elapsed and the updating of the procedures in the National Public Administration—under which the Registry is located—they have turned to the electronic file processing (digital way).

2.6 Does the Argentine Republic Have a National Specific Space Act or Regulations?

The legal system that regulates the Argentine space activities includes laws, norms, and regulations of different hierarchical level. Nevertheless, currently Argentina does not have a single and specific "space law" that covers all or at least the main topics, as other nations around the world.

The basic norms that give rise to national commitments in space matters are the four international space law treaties previously listed,[35] which, since their ratification by Argentina, are already part of the body of national laws. These treaties are at the highest hierarchical level. As from their local incorporation and entry into force, the nation, as mentioned above, deployed its spatial development and began the consequent regulatory deployment through other rules of different hierarchical level and subject matter that regulate them and operationalize their articles.

From there on, it could be said that the first and most relevant space regulation issued to govern space activities was the Presidential Decree No. 995/1991 ratified by Law No. 24.061[36] by which CONAE was created as a civil space agency and which is still in force today. In addition to the division of space activities from military orbit, this Presidential Decree defines at the same time regulations for the agency itself as well as for the development of space activities at the national level both with respect to the governmental public sector and the private sector as will be described below.

[34] *CONAE's Resolution n. 260/99* in the Official Gazette of the Nation No. 29.153 (1st Section of Monday, May 24, 1999 pages 11 to 14), is available in the following link https://www.boletinoficial.gob.ar/detalleAviso/primera/7195327/19990524.

[35] Outer Space Treaty, Rescue Agreement, Convention on International Liability for Damage, and the Convention on Registration of Objects Launched into Space. See supra Sect. 2.1.

[36] *Presidential Decree No. 995/1991 ratified by Law No. 24.061* is available on line at https://servicios.infoleg.gob.ar/infolegInternet/anexos/5000-9999/6295/texact.htm.

Virtue of the powers assigned to CONAE by Article 2 of the Decree No. 995/91,[37] the space activities are deployed under the framework of National Space Plan. CONAE proposes to the president the National Space Plan, who approves them by Presidential Decrees which turns out to be the National Public Policy on space matters.

By *Decree No. 2076/94*,[38] the 1st National Space Plan was approved, declaring space activity as an area of scientific-technological activity and as a national priority and CONAE's strategic plan.

The following Decree No. 1330/99[39] updates Decree No. 2076/94 and establishes the National Space Plan for the period 1997–2008, as well as that the actions foreseen therein have the character of Strategic Plan of the National Commission of Space Activities.

The next National Space Plan was approved by Decree No. 532/05[40] and declares the development of space activity as a state policy and a national priority. It establishes that this Plan and also the actions planned for the period have the character of Strategic Plan of the National Commission for Space Activities.

A new revision of the National Space Plan for the period 2017–2030 was approved by the Board of Directors of CONAE and submitted for the consideration of the National Executive Power (president of the nation); but at this moment, it has not been yet approved by such authority. In light of the presidential elections in December 2023, this proposed plan may be under review. This has brought concern to the entire space sector, given that after its update, it is expected to be known by the entire national and international space ecosystem, taking into account the impact it has on the socioeconomic space system of our country in the short, medium, and long term. However, the strategic guidelines of the plan approved by Decree No. 532/05 could be interpreted as remaining in force until the new update. However, the absence of a "space law" does not imply the absence of space regulations, since, as mentioned above, the implementation of the treaties has been carried out progressively, articulated through specific norms of different hierarchy, as related to the registration of operators, satellite activities, Earth observation, telecommunications, authorizations for the use of the spectrum, and assignment of frequencies or registration of objects launched into space, among others. Some of these will be explained as the chapter progresses.

At the same time, it should be noted that until not so long ago, space activity was practically concentrated in the hands of the government sector. However, since the generation of national capacities toward the private sector in the implementation of the Space Plan, new actors have emerged. For this reason, it is advisable to move

---

[37] See supra n. 37.

[38] *Presidential Decree No. 2076/94* Available on line at http://servicios.infoleg.gob.ar/infolegInternet/anexos/10000-14999/14118/norma.htm.

[39] *Presidential Decree No. 1330/99*. Available on line in the following link: http://servicios.infoleg.gob.ar/infolegInternet/verNorma.do?id=61059.

[40] *Presidential Decree No. 532/05*. Available on line in the following link: http://servicios.infoleg.gob.ar/infolegInternet/anexos/105000-109999/106502/norma.htm.

toward an updating and modernization of the current regulation that allows, on the one hand, to reorder the entire regulatory framework given its dispersion and at the same time strengthen it with the inclusion of new standards and requirements that are taking place at the international level at the request of COPUOS and the United Nations Resolutions that are being adopted.

In this way, it will be possible to harmonize with the regulatory updates that are emerging at a global level, but mainly at a regional level in Latin America and the Caribbean, which will undoubtedly foster the flow of cooperation and the opening of new markets for the national production of both technologies and services.

2.7 *Does the Argentine Republic Have a Space Agency?*

Since 1991 the Argentine Republic approved the creation of its national civil space agency by means of Presidential Decree No. 995/1991 ratified by Law No. 24.061.[41] Since then, the National Commission for Space Activities (CONAE)[42] is the space agency of the Argentine Republic, to which several functions and competences have been assigned, as we will see below.

It should be noted that the Argentine Republic created CONAE on the basis of preexisting experience and capabilities in the space field. Its institutional predecessor was the National Commission for Space Research (CNIE) existing since 1960, under the orbit of the Argentine Air Force. From that CNIE, studies were carried out with rocket launches and stratospheric balloons, in scientific collaboration with the Institute of Astronomy and Space Physics (IAFE). The first antenna for downloading data from the Landsat satellites of the USA was also installed in the country, and progress was made in missile developments, among others (Groetzner et al. 2021, p. 21).[43]

Therefore, when the decision was made to establish a national space agency, outside the military orbit, it was appropriate to take advantage of that knowledge and experience to put it at the service of the nation in a peaceful sense. "The technical complexity of space activities" made it necessary to establish an entity that could coordinate such activities at the national level, including the private sector as well as the public and governmental sectors, in order to "avoid dispersion and overlapping of efforts." Hence, it was "necessary to establish a national authority that centralizes, organizes, administers and executes a global space policy" (PEN Decree No.995/91, recitals[44]).

Thus, by means of the aforementioned PEN Decree No. 995/91, CONAE was created as a decentralized organism of the National State "competent to understand,

[41] See supra n. 38.

[42] CONAE'S official web page: https://www.argentina.gob.ar/ciencia/conae.

[43] Groetzner et al. (2021).

[44] *Presidential Decree No. 995/1991 ratified by Law No. 24.061.* See supra n. 38.

design, execute, control, manage and administer space projects and undertakings" for peaceful purposes "with the capacity to act publicly and privately, in the scientific, technical, industrial, commercial, administrative and financial fields, with full administrative and financial autonomy" (Art. 2).

Its original dependence was directly assigned to the president of the nation. But over the years, because of restructuring of the administrative structures and management of the National Public Administration, it was placed under the orbit of the National Foreign Ministry, then under the Ministry of Federal Planning, Public Investment, and Services, later under the Ministry of Science, Technology and Innovation, and currently under the orbit of the Chief of Cabinet of Ministers, at the Secretary of Science and Technology, according to the distribution of ministerial areas and government structures (Law No. 22.250, Law of Ministries).

As stated by the former Secretary General of CONAE Felix Menicocci, "The creation of CONAE meant an opportunity to develop space activity even more intensely and to promote the projects that the country had had until then".[45,46]

CONAE is in charge of "proposing the National Space Plan for the use and exploitation of space science and technology for peaceful purposes," which must be submitted to the National Executive Power (president of the nation) for its approval. This is the fundamental tool for the deployments of the nation's space policy, which covers action courses among which are those related to Earth remote sensing, the generation of capabilities, the development of the space access vector (national launcher), the training of highly qualified and specialized human resources, and the deployment of international cooperation, among others.

For its part as already mentioned, it also has among its main responsibilities those of "centralizing, organizing, administering and executing the National Space Plan" for peaceful purposes and coordinating all activities of the National Space System, whether they are carried out directly or indirectly by public or private institutions.

Its functions beyond those foreseen in the National Space Plan also include research, training for human resources and researchers, professionals, technicians, and qualified personnel through courses, scholarships, and interaction with universities, government agencies, and other institutions in the country or abroad in space disciplines and their applications, and the development of advanced engineering in national space technologies.

It is also empowered to execute and contribute to the integral development of national space projects and to transfer space technology for uses in different fields like agronomy, cartography, mining, meteorology, geology, environment, medicine, communications, defense, industry or other areas, to State entities, and, especially,

---

[45] Groetzner et al. (2021), pp. 21–22.

[46] To learn about CONAE in its most outstanding milestones, you can access the following link where, on the occasion of the Anniversary of its 30 years of life since its creation, the most outstanding are compiled in a work. https://www.argentina.gob.ar/sites/default/files/mirarlatierradesdeelespacio-conae-30aniversario.pdf.

under license, to the private sector, providing technical assistance to achieve the quality standards it determines (conf. Art. 3 Decree PEN N° 995/91).

Cooperation is a fundamental principle of space activity. CONAE may enter into agreements with other agencies or private entities of the country, in order to transfer or cooperate in the development of space activities and promote cooperation agreements with public and private entities of other countries, in accordance with the foreign policy of the republic and with the due intervention of the Ministry of Foreign Affairs and Worship. Finally, among its faculties is that of providing technical assistance to the National State in the participation in congresses, conventions, conferences, meetings, and international organizations devoted to space matters (conf. Art. 3).

Regarding the management and administration of the space agency, it may act in a public and private capacity, may enter into agreements with public or private entities, and enter into contracts necessary for the fulfilment of its purposes. To carry out its mission, it may in turn carry out acts of commerce and perform all the legal acts necessary for its normal operation that allow it to obtain the financial resources necessary for its activities (Arts. 3 and 4).

Regarding the control and transfer abroad of space equipment and technology and arms control, it may propose a regime in accordance with nonproliferation criteria and parameters with the prior authorization of a commission composed of different ministries, including at least the Ministries of Defense, Economy, and Foreign Affairs, and Worship (Art. 4).

Its organizational structure is made up of a board of nine members, of which eight are political members representing different ministerial areas (such as foreign affairs, defense, communications, science and technology, economy, education) and one is executive-technical. Its presidency and vice presidency are exercised by members of a political nature and the executive and technical management by a professional of the space agency's own staff, who is appointed by the members of the Board of Directors to perform executive functions (conf. Art. 6). Directors of a political nature shall serve for a term of 4 years.

2.8 What Is the Primary Regulatory Body Responsible for Overseeing Space Activities?

First of all, a distinction must be made between regulatory body from the authority of supervision and control, which are not always under the same authority.

In federal matters, according to the National Constitution, the National Congress has the primary competence in regulatory matters at the national level through the enactment of laws, which may include spatial matters.

On the other hand, the national legal system assigns to the National Executive Power (president) certain faculties regarding the regulation of laws, either through Decrees of Necessity and Urgency (DNU) or Presidential Decrees (Decrees), as appropriate. Likewise, as a result of powers delegated from norms that so provide (laws, Presidential Decrees, etc.), these may be assigned to certain governmental structures and autarchic entities or agencies. Such is the case of the Argentine space agency, which is precisely an autonomous entity of the National Public Administration with legal personality.

In space matters, as regards control powers, in principle it should be noted that national space projects and undertakings, in their general conception, have been entrusted to the national space agency, CONAE, as can be seen from the powers assigned in Article 2 of Decree No. 995/91, which states the following: "The National Commission on Space Activities is the only agency of the National State competent to understand, design, execute, control, manage and administer space projects and undertakings." Two words stand out there. First, "understand," which, as already interpreted by the National Treasury Procurator's Office, corresponds to the assignment of the primary competence to a governmental body. And on the other hand, "control," where, from the term itself, there is no doubt about the express assignment to CONAE in relation to the supervision of space projects and undertakings.

And although CONAE has been expressly assigned control powers, there is no express assignment of regulatory powers. However, as the case may be, nothing prevents it from being granted such powers by virtue of delegated powers or, as the case may be, as a consequence of the implementation of those powers granted. An example of the aforementioned is the case of Presidential Decree No. 125 of 1995 for the creation of the Registry of Objects Launched into Outer Space, where such delegation is clearly seen by entrusting it to carry out the implementation and the procedure to that effect.

On the other hand, it should be noted that with the development of space activities and the incursion of the nongovernmental sector or of actors participating in the national space market, the National State has also entrusted other areas of government with control and/or, as the case may be, regulatory functions, either because of their specificity or because of complementarity within the framework of the National Space System, which CONAE is the authority in charge of coordinating. This is the case, for example, in matters of telecommunications and management and administration of the orbit-spectrum resource as provided by Law No. 27.078,[47] among others, and as will be developed ahead.

On the other hand, in terms of supervision, other entities are also involved, depending on the case, which, although they are not authorities in space matters, such as the Customs, may be linked to the space sector due to their competences or by virtue of international commitments assumed by the Argentine Republic. An example of the latter is Presidential Decree No. 603/92 and its amendments on the "Regime for the Control of Sensitive Exports and War (bellicose) Materiel." By means of this export control regulation, a National Commission for the Control of Sensitive Exports and War Materiel was created, which evaluates requests for prior export licenses on a

[47] Law No. 27.078 Information and Communications Technologies. Digital Argentina. Updated version available on line at: https://servicios.infoleg.gob.ar/infolegInternet/verNorma.do?id=239771.

case-by-case basis. In its national commitments, Argentina has maintained that "the proliferation of weapons of mass destruction is a serious threat to international peace and security, for which all States must act firmly and unitedly to stop it." And it is in this context that Argentina "supports the exclusively peaceful development of space activities and reaffirms its willingness to work in this field with a high sense of responsibility and transparency" (conf. recitals of Presidential Decree N° 603/92[48]). For this purpose, the lists of products and recommended criteria are included in different Annexes of the Decree as amended. More information available at: https://www.argentina.gob.ar/defensa/comision-nacional-de-control-de-exportaciones-sensitivas-y-material-belico-concesymb.

At the provincial or municipal level, there may be complementary regulations depending on the activity to be developed, such as those related to the installation of infrastructures or stations, for example, which require authorization or environmental impact studies.

The National Civil Aviation Authority (ANAC) also exercises supervision and control within the framework and scope of its competences and in relation to the passage through airspace, as has occurred during the tests carried out during the development process of the satellite launcher, in the program executed by CONAE in relation to the course of action "Access to Space."

2.9 What Are the Primary Regulations Governing Space Activities, and How Are Private Companies Performing Space Activities Authorized, Monitored, and Supervised?

Without prejudice to the aforementioned, the most relevant ones are listed below.

The primary regulatory authority for the control of space activities is CONAE, the Argentine civil space agency. This is defined in Article 2 of Presidential Decree No. 995/91: "The NATIONAL COMMISSION FOR SPACE ACTIVITIES is the only agency of the National State competent to understand, design, execute, control, manage and administer projects and undertakings in space matters, and it has the following functions..."

It should be noted that the Presential Decree dates back to 1991 and that the evolutionary process of both spatial activities and the dynamism of the State's structures since then has led to the sharing or complementarity of authorization and supervision functions between different levels of the National State.

Notwithstanding the above, and getting back to the functions in charge of CONAE, by its creation decree it was also imposed the function of "coordinating all the activities of the National Space System, including all the public and private institutions that perform, directly or indirectly, space activities" (conf. Art. 3 inc. h).

[48] Presidential Decree N° 603/92 (Control regime for sensitive and war material exports). Available on line at https://servicios.infoleg.gob.ar/infolegInternet/verNorma.do?id=12381.

And although this rule is in full force and effect, it has not been possible to find a rule that regulates the processes or procedures for that purpose. Therefore, in view of the growth of new private sector actors involved in spatial matters, it is advisable to promote an organizing mechanism to provide clarity to such coordination processes.

It could be considered that, in such absence, the articulation occurs in fact through actions promoted by CONAE itself, since its governance structure includes a Board of Directors made up of representatives from different ministerial levels (see Presidential Decree No. 995/91, Article 5)[49]. This could in some way promote coordination actions under this framework, in order to involve other national and/or local areas at the time of authorization or control processes. However, given that the coordination includes private institutions that directly or indirectly carry out space activities, a procedure should be approved, as mentioned above, to provide legal certainty, order, and transparency to all the actors involved, so that those who seek to carry out space activities in the civilian field can clearly conduct themselves in the indicated field. This, considering in turn the need to articulate the national space activity, within the framework of the National Space Plan, thus allowing the fulfillment of the strategic guidelines designed for the nation, in a harmonious whole of public-private action for the socioeconomic development of the country.

Related to this, as time went by, some resolutions were issued by CONAE, establishing complementary guidelines by virtue of the assigned competences. Some of these are as follows.

§ **CONAE Resolution No. 330/96.**[50] ***"It establishes that any organization or public or private entity*** *that projects, initiates or develops, by itself or through third parties, activities associated with satellites, including feasibility and design tasks, as well as their construction, launching and subsequent operation, must notify CONAE. The tasks to be performed for the use of the same in the scientific field or for the application of remote sensing and communications shall also be notified"* (Section 1).

This is a regulation of administrative rank, issued by CONAE, based on the need to operationalize and comply with the provisions of Article VI of the Space Treaty ratified by Argentina and incorporated into its national legislation, taking into consideration that, according to its creation regulation, it was assigned control powers.

Although this is the first regulatory step taken in terms of authorization and control, this regulation focuses on satellite-related activities, is not sufficient to exercise a broader control over other activities related to space activities (directly or indirectly, as stated in Presidential Decree PEN No. 995/91), such as the development of launchers.

[49] See full text available on line at: https://servicios.infoleg.gob.ar/infolegInternet/anexos/5000-9999/6295/texact.htm.

[50] CONAE Resolution No. 330/96. Published in the Official Gazette of 22-Aug-1996 Number: 28462 Page: 3. Available on line at: https://www.boletinoficial.gov.ar/detalleAviso/primera/7161462/19960822?busqueda=1.

The mechanism defined is that of notifying the authority, without it being clear from the text that it is a request for authorization and the consequent granting of a license under preestablished terms and conditions. Notwithstanding the foregoing, it is stipulated that, as a result of the information provided by the notifying party, CONAE may make observations in order to comply with national and international laws and regulations on the matter, including space treaties.

As for the sanctioning measures, Article 5 of the Resolution provides that CONAE may not recognize or authorize any application for registration in the Registry of Objects Launched into Outer Space, if this prior notification has not been complied with, adding that it may even not authorize the export of the object or its launching. Now, in order to do so, CONAE should be informed about the infringing activity, otherwise any of these proposed measures could not be effective.

In this regard, a certain degree of weakness may be noted with respect to this resolution, since although CONAE has management, administration, and control powers over space projects, it has not been granted regulatory attributions. Therefore, it could be debatable whether the issuance of such Resolution is within the scope of its competences. It should be noted that it has been possible to learn about the interest in updating the rules on the granting of authorizations and licenses, in order to bring them to international standards, compatible with the rules and laws of other nations, based on the issuance of a higher-ranking rule and with an appropriate sanctioning program, associated with a licensing scheme for the development of space activities. In the opinion of this author, first of all, it is necessary to define for Argentina what is space activity. This would make it possible to clearly establish which are the space activities and which are those associated with these activities, in order to be able to delimit the scope of what is under the jurisdiction of the space domain with respect to the aeronautical domain at the national level, in order to harmonize them, if necessary. Likewise, achieving this adequate harmonization framework with the most modern international legislative models would facilitate the adequate compliance with the obligations of Argentina, CONAE, and space operators, providing CONAE as enforcement authority with tools for the adequate fulfillment of its functions.

This would also allow private sector actors to be in line with other nations, thus providing better opportunities for their participation in the space sector market. The more harmonized the rules governing space activities at the international and national levels, the greater the possibilities of keeping space safe and sustainable in the long term and of having greater international or transnational business opportunities for the Argentine space sector.

§ **CONAE Resolution No. 303/97 on Satellite Systems.**[51] "*It establishes that any action by public or private entities aimed at the establishment of satellite systems under national jurisdiction must be initiated by CONAE, which, after*

[51] *CONAE Resolution No. 303/97 on Management for Satellite Systems.* Published in the Official Gazette of Aug 22, 1997 Number: 28714 Page: 5. Also available on line at https://servicios.infoleg.gob.ar/infolegInternet/anexos/45000-49999/45234/norma.htm.

*analyzing it, will channel it to other National Agencies if its intervention is necessary" (*Art. 1*)*. Again, this is a measure more oriented to coordination within the framework of the execution and inclusion within the framework of the National Space Plan, than to the adoption of licensing regimes for the authorization at national level of a space operator, whatever the activity in which it is to be deployed. It proposes that the first step should be taken before CONAE, and then, if necessary, other government agencies should be involved through the latter. It should be recalled that this measure was issued prior to the law creating ARSAT S.A. (Empresa Argentina de Soluciones Satelitales Sociedad Anónima AR-SAT), which grants to this national company powers over geostationary satellite communications systems. Hence, the importance of coordinating with the other State agencies.

§ **CONAE Resolution No. 463/97.**[52] **It creates a Registry of Space Operators**, under CONAE, based on the fact that it coordinates the National Space System. "The aforementioned Registry shall register any individual or legal entity, whether public or private, that performs or intends to perform space activities" (Section 2). The registration will be processed through a model note requesting the registration in the Registry of Space Operators, indicating the name or corporate name, depending on whether it is a company or a natural person and whether it is a public or private entity, the commercial and legal domicile, and the area of activity (communications, remote sensing, navigation, research, ground station, satellite systems). It must also inform the type of activity (service provision, commercialization, manufacture, import, export, others) and the person authorized to represent it.

In relation to the previous resolutions, it does not arise taxatively that an authorization license is issued. In a way, they are for the reception of general information, with an organizing vision of knowledge of the spatial ecosystem, since it collects information from both public and private sector operators. Perhaps the one analyzed in the first term resembles this, but in concrete terms, it does not conclude the process with the granting of a license.

From the early 1990s to the present, CONAE's functions have been complemented by other government areas and autonomous entities, which also intervene as appropriate in the process of authorization and/or supervision of space activities or activities related to them, such as those related to observatories, deep space stations, radars, and, in particular, telecommunications for the authorization and assignment of frequencies and orbit-spectrum and the provision of satellite communications services. The latter functions are currently in charge of the National Communications Entity (ENACOM) and the Secretariat of Innovation, Science, and Technology.

The main regulations governing space telecommunications activities are summarized below:

---

[52] *CONAE Resolution No. 463/97.* Registry of Space Operators. Published in the Official Gazette of 11-Nov-1997 Number: 28771 Page: 4. It is also available on line at the following link: https://servicios.infoleg.gob.ar/infolegInternet/anexos/45000-49999/47215/norma.htm.

§ **Law No. 26.092: "Creates the Argentine Company of Satellite Solutions Sociedad Anónima AR-SAT.**[53] Grant said company the authorization to use the orbital position 81° West Longitude and its associated frequency bands."

According to the provisions of Article 4, the company's corporate purpose *is "to carry out by itself, or on behalf of third parties or associated with third parties: a) the design, development, construction in the country, launch and/or commissioning of geostationary telecommunications satellites in orbital positions that result or result from international coordination procedures before the International Telecommunication Union (ITU) and frequency bands and b) the corresponding exploitation, use, provision of satellite facilities and/or commercialization of satellite and/or related services."* Likewise, a special regime of shares is established, kept in the hands of the State, at least 51% of the share capital, with decision-making power.

§ **Law No. 27.208**[54] **"Declares the development of the satellite industry as a state policy and a national priority regarding geostationary telecommunications satellites, and approves the Argentine Geostationary Satellite Plan 2015-2035 to be executed by the company AR-SAT."** It is recommended to read it because it contains the vision of the Argentine Republic in terms of geostationary satellites and communications services raised in 2015, in an environment of its socioeconomic, political, and industrial context, incorporating the latter as a source for national development.

§ **Law No. 27.078**[55] **Argentina Digital. Information technology and communications.** This law declares "the development of Information and Communications Technologies, Telecommunications, and their associated resources to be of public interest, establishing and guaranteeing complete network neutrality." Its purpose is also "to enable access by all inhabitants of the Argentine Republic to information and communications services under equitable social and geographic conditions, with the highest quality parameters." It is "a public order rule and excludes any type of regulation of content, regardless of its transmission medium" (conf. Article 1). It also aims to guarantee the human right to communications and telecommunications and recognizes information and communications technologies (ICT) as a preponderant factor in the technological and productive independence of the nation, under clear and transparent guidelines that favor the sustainable development of the sector and seeking the accessibility and affordability of ICT and communications for the population. It assigns a role to the State as a planner (conf. Article 2).

Regarding satellite communications, it establishes that the administration, management, and control of orbit-spectrum resources corresponding to satellite networks are in the hands of the National State through the Ministry of Communications,

---

[53] *Law No. 26.092:* See the updated version at http://servicios.infoleg.gob.ar/infolegInternet/anexos/115000-119999/115886/texact.htm.

[54] *Law No. 27.208 Satellite Industry Development Law Argentine. Geo-Stationary Satellite Plan* https://servicios.infoleg.gob.ar/infolegInternet/anexos/250000-254999/254823/texact.htm.

[55] *Law No. 27.078:* Available on line at https://servicios.infoleg.gob.ar/infolegInternet/verNorma.do?id=239771.

in accordance with the international treaties signed and ratified by the Argentine State. In order to exploit this resource, both by public and private entities, authorization is required for this purpose and in accordance with the provisions applicable to the matter (conf. Article 33).

The principle of freedom applies to the provision of facilities for satellite communications systems; however, a registration must be processed for their operation by the owners of such systems, for the sole purpose of coordinating the use of radio frequencies and avoiding interference on other systems in accordance with the regulations issued by the Enforcement Authority (conf. Article 44), which fell to the Secretariat of Innovation, Science, and Technology, which by Resolution No. 12/2024[56] creates the "Registry for the provision of satellite facilities through geostationary systems" within the scope of the National Communications Entity (ENACOM). That is, the Registry is assigned to ENACOM. It is a decentralized governmental entity of the National Public Administration with jurisdiction in telecommunications. As was also entrusted to the Secretariat of Innovation, Science, and Technology, the preparation of an ordered text of the General Regulations for Satellite Management and Services was also arranged but, in this case, for the "Provision of Global Satellite Communications Services through Non-Geostationary Orbit Satellite Constellations" (NGO communications satellites) within the framework of Resolution No. 2325 of July 30, 1997, of the former Secretariat of Communications. In other words, the matters concerning the Registry for both GEO orbit services and for NGEO constellations are restructured, following some regulatory updates.

The provision of any satellite ICT service is subject to the general regime for the provision of ICT services established in this law (see Article 44).

As can be seen, the regulatory and control complexity is not entrusted to a single legislative entity (National Congress) but rather functions that can be assigned to different sectors of government management.

§ DNU[57] Decree No. 267/2015:[58] "Creates the National Communications Entity (ENACOM)," authority on communications. It grants the radio frequency licenses. It is an autonomous and decentralized entity in the area of the Ministry of Communications (currently within the scope of the Secretariat of Innovation, Science, and Technology of the Office of the Chief of Ministers by virtue of reorganizations of the structures of the National Public Administration). For its part, it acts as the Enforcement Authority of Laws Nos. 26.522 and 27.078 and their amending and regulatory norms, with full legal capacity to act in the areas of public and private law.

It is necessary to mention that only the most relevant ones have been pointed out here, since other regulations of a different hierarchy may be derived from the main

---

[56] *Resolution No. 12/2024*. By Secretariat of Innovation, Science and Technology. Available at https://servicios.infoleg.gob.ar/infolegInternet/anexos/395000-399999/399305/norma.htm.

[57] DNU Decreto de Necesidad y Urgencia (in spanish) / DNU Decree of Necessity and Urgency.

[58] DNU Decree No. 267/2015. Available on line at https://servicios.infoleg.gob.ar/infolegInternet/anexos/255000-259999/257461/norma.htm.

laws, through which their provisions are regulated, or requirements or functions are defined in a greater degree of implementation detail, specific to the activity in question.

2.10 Is There Any Effort Toward Capacity Building in the Space Sector, Both in Terms of Technologies and Regulatory Matters?

As presented in this chapter, the Argentine Republic is making efforts at the governmental level and also in the private sector for the development of space capabilities in terms of technology as well as institutions, education, and infrastructure.

The first steps were taken at the origins of the space age in the field of the Air Force, especially under the National Commission for Space Research (CNIE). But from 1991, with the creation of the National Space Agency (CONAE) with civil jurisdiction, the approval of the successive National Space Plans gave framework and impetus to the development of the space sector. Thus, space activity was established as a scientific State policy, which allowed important goals to be achieved over more than 30 years, such as providing the Argentine Republic with human capabilities, qualified knowledge, infrastructure, and its own satellites.

It is worth noting that the training of human resources is one of the pillars for achieving the proposed objectives, whether through CONAE's own institutions or through the entire educational system of the nation. Different undergraduate and graduate courses offered by universities throughout the country through public education as well as private education have allowed us to achieve a wealth of educational offerings that grow over time, allowing more young people to be introduced to STEM and other careers. Among the careers close to the space sector are undergraduate courses in aeronautical, aerospace, electronics, materials, and systems engineering. There is also a wide range of training for professionals in physics, chemistry, biology, medicine, geology, oceanography, mathematics, astrophysics, and astronomy and the entire range of needs that the multidisciplinary nature of space activity requires. Progress is also being made in the training of professionals specialized in space law, based on postgraduate courses.

The implementation of a wide range of graduate, doctoral, and postdoctoral courses based on the missions and functions established for CONAE in its founding law and successive National Plans has allowed both technical and professional human resources to stand out at national and international levels and has allowed Argentina to develop its own space technologies, including optical and radar Earth observation satellite missions and telecommunications. Among the specialized training and research institutions, the Balseiro Institute and the Mario Gulich Institute for Advanced Studies (the latter created by agreement between CONAE and the National University of Córdoba) stand out, offering specialized careers in space systems, geomatics, Earth remote sensing, and use of spatial data, among others, many of them with scholarship opportunities for both nationals and for students and researchers from abroad, mainly from Latin America and the Caribbean.

In turn, this allowed the development of a promising private sector, which strengthens Argentina's space economy, either from the emergence of new entrepreneurs or companies for the development of high technology, components, and/or services. Some of these entities that started with small projects, some of them with contributions from the national or provincial government for their first developments, are already making their way, even with a presence abroad.

Some of the relevant milestones of the nation in terms of technological capabilities are as follows:

- Four SAC series optical satellites launched.
- Two SAOCOM SAR satellites in Polarimetric L Band launched and operational.
- Two telecommunications satellites (ARSAT) operational.
- Two operational ground Telemetry, Tracking and Command (TT&C) stations: one at the Centro Espacial Teófilo Tabanera (CETT) in the province of Córdoba and one in Tolhuin, Province of Tierra del Fuego.
- A new station is being built at the General Belgrano Base in the Argentine Antarctic, the southernmost in the southern cone.
- Laboratories and testing facilities for satellites and space technologies (under the orbit of CONAE or INVAP in Bariloche).
- Capacity for the development and construction of solar panels for satellites, through areas of the national scientific and technological system.
- Development of a launcher for placing national satellites into orbit and providing services to third parties. Tests were carried out on preliminary versions. Development work continues.
- Research centers throughout the country.
- Private sector aerospace clusters.
- Small technology developments in university centers.
- Software development capabilities.
- Supplier development.
- Projects for the use of artificial intelligence applied to the space sector.

However, in terms of regulatory efforts, Argentina participates in the United Nations multilateral negotiation space processes, mainly in the Committee on the Peaceful Uses of Outer Space and PAROS. It also participates in other United Nations forums, as well as in those technical and specialized forums that allow for a rigorous international analysis of the progress made in this field and in its different areas of competence. It is common for Argentine experts to participate in international congresses and conferences, including as speakers.

Taking that into consideration, there have been some recent updates in the field of telecommunications. However, although Argentina has a certain degree of development of its legal framework for space activities, because of the growth of private sector players, it seems necessary to include some updates in order to harmonize the existing regulations that are being approved worldwide or to introduce the necessary modernizations. Given the relevance of projects that may be carried out in international cooperation or through domestic or foreign investments, this update and harmonization will not only further strengthen legal certainty for operators who want to develop within the space ecosystem but will also allow Argentina to maintain its status within the international segment.

2.11 How Does the Argentine Republic Engage in International Cooperation in the Space Sector, Both in Terms of Technologies and Representation in International Organizations? Are There Any Partnerships with Other Latin American Countries?

International cooperation is one of the fundamental pillars within the courses of action of the National Space Plan, in line with the country's foreign policy, as it is a founding principle of space activity in accordance with the provisions of the Outer Space Treaty. In this way, the Argentine Republic works actively to strengthen international collaboration relations in the field of the space sector, where for more than 30 years of civil space experience, starting with the creation of CONAE, it has signed government agreements with other States as well as the Space Agency CONAE, with other space agencies, academic institutions, universities, and research centers.

In space matters, the entity implementing government agreements is the National Commission for Space Activities (CONAE), with the counterpart being the space agency of the respective State or the competent authority regarding space activity. On the other hand, there are also institutional cooperation agreements which are signed by CONAE.

One of the first cooperation agreements was reached in 1991 between the USA and Argentina, which brought together the space agencies NASA and CONAE, respectively. This is a long-standing scientific and technical relationship that continues to this day and which also led to the signing of the Artemis Agreements in 2023.

It is worth remembering that there were already antecedents of conversations previously held by representatives of the space area of both countries that go back at least to 1986, but after the creation of CONAE as a civil agency, it was when those conversations took shape in a series of optical satellite developments (the SAC series). Thus, we find the SAC-B satellite launched by a launcher provided by the USA and also the SAC-A satellite launched into orbit aboard NASA's Space Shuttle Endeavour on December 4, 1998, departing from the Kennedy Space Center (KSC) in Cape Canaveral, Florida, USA. This mission was also a joint mission between NASA and CONAE. It was then followed by SAC-C, which also included international collaboration from NASA (USA), ASI (Italy), INPE (Brazil), CNES (France), and DSRI (Denmark).[59] Finally, within the framework of the National Space Plan, the progression of space missions led to the SAC-D/Aquarius satellite in

[59] Groetzner et al. (2021), p. 51.

scientific-technical collaboration between CONAE and NASA. The objective of this mission was to observe the ocean, measure ocean salinity, and make observations for climate and the environment. It was also fully developed and built in Argentina, on which the main instrument, NASA's Aquarius, was mounted. It was successfully launched on June 10, 2011, from the USA (Vandenberg) with a Delta II launcher, provided by the USA, having fulfilled its operational mission. Technologies from the space agencies of Italy (ASI), France (CNES), Canada (CSA), and Brazil (AEB/INPE) were also incorporated into the SAC-D/Aquarius platform.

In the area of satellite of Earth observation, the SAOCOM satellite mission[60] also stands out, a constellation of two satellites (SAOCOM 1A and SAOCOM 1B) Synthetic Aperture Radar (SAR) polarimetric in L Band, developed and built in Argentina, forming the Italian-Argentine System of Satellites for Emergency Management (SIASGE) between ASI and CONAE. Its main objectives are the measurement of soil humidity (e.g., with applications for agricultural production) and applications in emergencies (detection of hydrocarbon spills at sea, monitoring of water cover during floods). The SIASGE system is part of the government agreement signed between Argentina and Italy and is made up of the SAOCOM 1 constellation and the Italian COSMO-SkyMed satellite constellation. The SAOCOM satellites launched in 2018 and 2020 are operational, providing Earth information for both the country and users around the world who request it.[61]

The next satellite mission in cooperation is the SABIA-Mar mission, dedicated essentially to providing information and products for the study of the primary productivity of the sea, the marine ecosystems, the carbon cycle, the dynamics of coastal waters, the management of fishery resources, and the water quality in coasts and estuaries.[62] This is a project within the framework of the bilateral relationship between Argentina and Brazil, where each one develops its own satellite.

Among the nations with which ties of cooperation have been maintained over the years, either through government agreements or through agencies and institutions, are Germany, Australia, Brazil, Canada, China, Denmark, Spain, the USA, ESA, France, the Netherlands, Belgium, Italy, Japan, Norway, Poland, the Russian Federation, Sweden, and Ukraine.

As for specialized forums, multilateral organizations, and institutions, the following can be mentioned:[63]

- United Nations Committee on the Use of Outer Space (UN COPUOS)
- Group on Earth Observations (GEOSS)
- Committee on Earth Observations Satellites (CEOS)

---

[60] See SAOCOM Mission at CONAE's official web page. https://www.argentina.gob.ar/ciencia/conae/misiones-espaciales/saocom.

[61] For access to satellite images and products go to the following links: https://catalogos.conae.gov.ar/catalogo/catalogo.html / https://geoportal.conae.gov.ar/mapstore/#/viewer/openlayers/geoportal / https://www.argentina.gob.ar/ciencia/conae/aplicaciones-de-la-informacion-satelital.

[62] Source: www.conae.gov.ar.

[63] Source: https://www.argentina.gob.ar/ciencia/conae/institucional/organismos-multilaterales.

- The International Charter "Space and Major Catastrophes" (CHARTER)
- United Nations Platform for Space-Based Information for Disaster Management and Emergency Response (UNSPIDER)
- Committee on Space Research (COSPAR)

In terms of technology, agreements are also made with specialized institutions in order to carry out projects for the development of focused research. Here are some of them:[64]

- International Society for Photogrammetry and Remote Sensing (ISPRS)
- Latin American Society of Experts in Remote Sensing (SELPER)
- International Astronautical Federation (IAF)
- GEONETCast global satellite data distribution network

Finally, the following are highlighted as examples of international agreements:

- Ibero-American Network of Space Agencies, of which CONAE is a member.
- Latin American and Caribbean Space Agency. Although the constitutive agreement was signed by Argentina, as of the date of this work, it has not been ratified by the nation.
- Artemis Accords. On July 27 of 2023 Argentina became the 28th nation to sign the Artemis Accords (see previous Sect. 2.3 on this chapter).

In terms of deep space international cooperation, two stations have been deployed for deep space exploration missions. One of them is called Deep Space 3 (DS3) located in Malargüe, province of Mendoza. It was built based on an agreement reached by Argentina through CONAE and the European Space Agency (ESA). It was inaugurated in 2012. The other Deep Space Station CLTC-CONAE-NEUQUÉN is the product of interinstitutional agreements between China Satellite Launch and Tracking Control General (CLTC) and CONAE, the province of Neuquén, and the governments of Argentina and the People's Republic of China. It is located near the town of Bajada del Agrio, province of Neuquén, having entered into operation in 2018. Both agreements make 10% of the use of the antennas' operating time available to CONAE and its projects in cooperation with national and international partners. For more information, see https://www.argentina.gob.ar/anuncios-de-oportunidad-permanentes/red-de-estaciones-cltc-conae-neuquen-y-esa-ds3-malargue.

2.12 *How Does the Private Sector Conduct Its Activities in the Field of Space Exploration?*

Space activities in the Argentine Republic are carried out under the regulatory guidelines previously set out and within the framework of the execution of the National Space Plans, to which reference should be made to avoid duplication of

[64] Source: https://www.argentina.gob.ar/ciencia/conae/institucional/otros-ambitos-multilaterales.

exposition. In turn, as stated, they are open to both the governmental and nongovernmental sectors (private sector) in all their branches and areas of action. The implementation modality will depend on the case, based on the provisions of the applicable rules and regulations. This may include the establishment of legal entities (companies, enterprises) in the country, especially when they are foreign, authorizations, licensing, registrations, and even taking out insurance.

2.13 What Are the Plans for Space Activities in the Argentine Republic? Are Manned Flights and Spaceports Being Planned?

The deployment of public policies in space matters for the Argentine Republic is established at the national level through National Space Plans. This arises from Article 2 of Decree No. 995/91 ratified by Law 24.061,[65] which places under the responsibility of CONAE *"to propose the National Space Plan for the Use and Development of Space Science and Technology for peaceful purposes, as well as its financing mechanism, which must be approved by the NATIONAL EXECUTIVE BRANCH.*"

The National Space Plan (NSP) *"defines the framework and specifies the objectives that guide the investments and activities necessary for Argentina to take advantage of the benefits of accessing outer space with its own means and instruments, concentrating efforts to participate in the best positions together with the international community of countries with access to these technologies."*

These words mark the beginning of the **first National Space Plan "Argentina in Space 1995-2006," approved by Presidential Decree No. 2076/94** which declares the space activity as an area of scientific-technological activity and as a national priority and CONAE's strategic plan. Given its complexity and length, it is suggested to read the full text.[66] Thus, the objective of a National Space Plan is that "it be one of the national projects that allows concentrating means and resources, and in which different human groups come together to achieve it" (conf. Decree No. 2076/94).

The vision proposed for its creation was to understand it "as an important national project," where "the actions to achieve its objectives imply the direct or indirect participation of a number of human groups from the production area, the government, the academic sector and the national Science and Technology system." For which "it is to be expected that in the course of each action the different sectors mentioned will be explicitly incorporated, with specific commitments" (conf. Decree No. 2076/94).

---

[65] See supra n. 37 y 38.

[66] Presidential Decree No. 2076/94 and the 1st National Space Plan at the following link: http://servicios.infoleg.gob.ar/infolegInternet/anexos/10000-14999/14118/norma.htm.

The Space Plan aims to offer society a complete overview of spatial information, promoting its use and exploitation. To this end, it proposes developing its own space technologies for the protection of the environment, for the use of the productive scientific and educational sectors, for security, and for the society as a whole. Therefore, it is planned to develop satellites for remote sensing, scientific uses, and communications, capable of responding to specific national needs and requirements and to complement the international offer. This development of own technologies also includes launch vehicles, as well as all associated ground infrastructure for launching.

Through space-satellite capabilities and technologies, it is projected to achieve maximum benefit back to society, creating in turn new sources of employment in industries producing high value-added goods and services and developing competitive advantages for the local productive system as a whole. At the same time, it seeks to promote the inclusion of the national industry in the international market, expanding local productive sectors.

Furthermore, since the first Space Plan, one of the fundamental objectives pursued is to ensure that activities and investments for space activity are also carried out through international cooperation coordinated with different countries and with other space agencies.

It is often said that Argentina is a "space country" due to (a) its great geographical extension; (b) the fact that extensive primary exploitations are related to agricultural, fishing, forestry, mining, and hydrocarbon production; (c) the potential exposure to natural and anthropogenic catastrophes; (d) the distribution of the population throughout the territorial extension; and (e) the regional and international links and commitments assumed by Argentina that will allow its strategic insertion in the concert of nations for its technological space development.

Therefore, by making intensive use of the products of science and space technology, the Argentine Republic is sought to be inserted into the small group of countries that have the capabilities to develop its own space technology.

To this end, in order to manage and implement the spatial policies reflected in the different National Space Plans, different courses of action were articulated in them, among which are the following:

- **Use and Management of Spatial Information** from data and products obtained by satellites and the applications developed.
- **Terrestrial Infrastructure for Data Reception and Control of Satellites and Launchers**. This covers all the programs, technologies, and activities of planning, tracking, telemetry, and command (TT&C), and the reception, processing, and distribution of data from own and third-party satellite missions and launch tracking.
- **Satellite Systems.** This is one of the priority courses of action foreseen in the Space Plan, with the aim of satisfying that segment of spatial information necessary for the country while integrating own missions with those of other space agencies.
- **Integration, Testing, and Qualification**. This involves developing highly qualified infrastructures for the development of national space technologies and mis-

sions, the production of materials, and the integration with the industrial sector (including in the certification of parts and components with space quality) which allow ensuring extreme conditions in the space environment, as well as vibrations at the time of launch into space.
- **Exploration and Peaceful Use of Outer Space**, based on own missions and in participation through articulated cooperation with other nations and space agencies and with the privated sector.
- **Education and Capacity Building and Institutional Development.** This includes a close relationship with research groups, the deployment of specialized training and capacity building programs, and the consequent development of highly qualified human resources through the training of technicians and professionals in the disciplines and subjects related to space activity and the use of space information and knowledge of space law. To this end, educational programs are planned from childhood, undergraduate, graduate, doctoral, and postdoctoral levels within the scope of the National Space Agency, as well as with the national and provincial educational system, and the national scientific and technological system within the framework of Law No. 25.467.[67] Currently, some master's degrees are developed in cooperation with other space agencies (e.g., CONAE-ASI within the framework of the agreement by the Mario Gulich Institute of Advanced Space Studies and the National University of Córdoba). This segment also includes international cooperation, regional integration, institutional participation in specialized forums, and collaboration in the deployment of regulatory frameworks for the activity at the international and national level.
- **Access to Space.** This line of action includes the development of a launch vector for the placement of national satellites into orbit and the provision of launch services to third parties, as well as the construction of the respective launch platform, its auxiliary facilities, and the integration and testing facilities. Although it does not arise from the first Space Plan, it is not ruled out that in the future, based on the generation of capabilities in the private sector, as is currently the case, authorization may also be implemented for the establishment of launchers and launch bases through the granting of licenses, as occurs in other nations that contemplate this in their regulatory frameworks.

In turn, given the dynamism of space activity, whether due to technological progress, the fulfillment of goals and objectives, or new strategic visions, these plans are subject to review, giving rise to a new updated version when appropriate. In this regard, since the first plan, the following have been approved:

- **PEN Decree No. 1330/99 (Modifies PEN Decree No. 2076/94).** Establishes the National Space Plan for 1997–2008, as well as that the actions provided for in it have the character of Strategic Plan of the National Commission for Space

---

[67] The *Law No. 25.467* describes the National Science, Technology, and Innovation System, the objectives of the national scientific and technological policy, and the structure of the system, among other items. Available on line at https://servicios.infoleg.gob.ar/infolegInternet/anexos/65000-69999/69045/texact.htm.

Activities. See in full length in the following link: http://servicios.infoleg.gob.ar/infolegInternet/verNorma.do?id=61059.
- **PEN Decree No. 532/05** (Period 2004–2015). Declares the development of space activity as a State policy and a national priority. It establishes also that this plan and the actions planned for said period have the character of Strategic Plan of the National Commission for Space Activities (CONAE). See the Plan in the following link: http://servicios.infoleg.gob.ar/infolegInternet/anexos/105000-109999/106502/norma.htm.

A preliminary updated version of the "National Space Plan for the period 2016–2027"[68] was approved by the CONAE Board of Directors and submitted to the National Executive Branch years ago. Given the change of national government at the end of 2023 with the assumption of a new president in charge of approving and promoting the respective Decree, it is expected that a process of new analysis of the draft proposed Plan will be opened. Nevertheless, considering that it is the basis on which a national public policy is projected, with an impact on the socio-productive, scientific, technological, and educational sectors and international commitments, the systematic review and approval should be done at least at 5 years in a projection of 10 years, for each plan.

Finally, since the enactment of Law No. 25.467 on "Science, Technology and Innovation" (2001), the objectives pursued by the said law were taken into account for the definitions of public space policies to be contained in the National Space Plans (including the Geostationary Satellite Plan headed by ARSAT). Finally, it should be noted that, in line with the new private sector players that have emerged at the national level, the National Space Plan should include their participation in the different segments of expression, whether they carry out space activities directly or indirectly. It is therefore necessary to establish an updated framework that defines, at a minimum, what is meant by space activity at the national level.

2.14 What Are (and Should Be) the Perspectives of the Argentine Republic on Regulatory Matters Related to Space Debris, Militarization and Weaponization of Space, and Exploitation of Space Natural Resources?

In terms of regulations, as already noted, the Argentine Republic has ratified the Space Treaty, thus reaffirming the use and exploration of outer space for peaceful purposes, having incorporated it into current national legislation. Furthermore, as can be seen from Presidential Decree No. 991/95 (ratified by Law No. 24.061), which created CONAE as a civil space agency, its recitals state that the Argentine Republic "rejects all offensive military use of space activities, and recognizes its

[68] Source: https://www.argentina.gob.ar/ciencia/conae/plan-espacial.

willingness to work in this field with a high sense of peace, responsibility and transparency."

All of which is reaffirmed year after year, as can be read in the national declarations at the COPUOS sessions, as well as in its interventions in the treatment of the topics of the Prevention of an Arms Race in Outer Space before the First Committee of the UN and as could be seen in the sessions of the Open-ended Group approved by Resolution 76/231. Likewise, Argentina has assumed international commitments regarding the nonproliferation of nuclear weapons and the nonconducting of nuclear tests.

Regarding space debris issues, the Argentine Republic does not currently have a law that includes the Space Debris Mitigation Guidelines of the Committee on the Peaceful Uses of Outer Space (COPUOS) at the national level. However, as a COPUOS Member State, the Argentine Republic fully adheres to the Guidelines, as can be seen in the compendium supported by UNOOSA.[69] Furthermore, it supports IADC Space Debris Mitigation Guidelines.

Moreover, in a vision of sustainability of the space environment, the procedure established for the Registry of Objects Launched into Outer Space approved by Presidential Decree No. 125/95 provides for the obligation to provide information on the non-contamination measures that the registrant must adopt, even for the end of the useful life of the object.

In the preliminary inquiries that were able to be carried out, CONAE has already established some general directives and others of a more specific nature, among which are the Engineering and Safety Assurance Directive and the Product Assurance Directives that address requirements on collision prevention and prevention and mitigation of space debris that implement the COPUOS Guidelines, considering the recommendations of the IADC and ISO standards. Therefore, it is expected that these will be the basis of the standards applicable at the national level for space operators from both the governmental and nongovernmental sectors, given their status as space authority, coordinator of the space system, and under whose orbit is the Registry of Objects Launched into Outer Space.

Regarding the exploitation of space resources, a bill was presented in the Senate of the nation in 2019 with the aim of granting people residing in the country permits for the exploration and exploitation of minerals in space (including the moon and asteroid). However, it did not reach parliamentary status.

It is expected that in the not-too-distant future, both the UNCOPUOS Space Debris Guidelines and the Long-Term Sustainability Guidelines will be included in local regulatory provisions. The same applies to issues related to the exploration and exploitation of space resources, taking into account the space framework provided by the space treaties but, at the same time, any new regulations that may be reached from the Working Groups established under COPUOS or United Nations frameworks.

[69] See https://www.unoosa.org/oosa/en/ourwork/topics/space-debris/compendium.html.

3 Final Remarks

After what has been discussed in this chapter, by way of conclusion, it is worth making some final reflections.

In terms of the development of human capabilities, knowledge, technologies, and opportunities, the Argentine Republic has been able to achieve many of the objectives set out when creating its national space agency in just over 30 years and to project public policies for the development of space activity through successive National Space Plans. Clear proof of this are its highly qualified human resources that have allowed it to develop its own satellites; build, develop, and manage its own satellite missions, the respective infrastructures, and stations; and, at the same time, provide support, space data, and services to other nations and space agencies around the world. Astronomy and radio astronomy have also made significant progress, since the Argentine Republic has a territory with unique conditions of clear, dark, and quiet skies for the activity, which also allowed the location of projects in different regions of the country.

Another of its strengths is that it has a long tradition of bilateral and multilateral cooperation, which has allowed it not only to grow but also to position itself among the countries with its own quality space industry. In this sense, a national educational and scientific-technological system has been a key tool for the deployment of space science and technology, which has allowed this technological advance to be put at the service of the socio-productive sectors, national security, assistance in the event of catastrophes, and collaboration with other nations. However, it still needs to continue developing and growing.

This is why, given the generation of capabilities achieved, a new time is here, paving the way for new opportunities, as was pointed out at the beginning. If the global space economy is expected to be grow to $1.8 trillion by 2035, it is necessary to be prepared to participate in this segment of the economy. And to do so, an efficient, modern, and dynamic order is required in accordance with the guidelines of the space treaties. For this reason, it seems like a propitious time for a review of the national space regulatory frameworks, in order to bring them up to date and to provide clear and ordering tools both for the State as the authority of authorization and control (as the Space Treaty regulates and has been incorporated into national legislation) but fundamentally for the private sector space actors who want to carry out their projects in the nation.

At the same time, space activity is becoming more and more collaborative. Therefore, in the face of the possibility of internal projects that are opened through bilateral, regional, or multilateral cooperation agreements (as proposed in the Artemis Accords or others), it is imperative to have harmonized legal frameworks in accordance with international requirements that allow the productive sector to participate both nationally and internationally in the best way and at the same time to be able to receive investments for new projects at the local level. These projects must be carried out within frameworks of transparency, sustainability, and security of operations.

A better way to achieve this could be through a new National Space Law, which could systematize and include in a single orderly text the different scattered regulations, as well as advance on those points that still need updating and/or regulation for their operability.

References

Argentine Law No. 17.989 Outer Space Treaty & Rescue Agreement. http://servicios.infoleg.gob.ar/infolegInternet/anexos/205000-209999/208688/norma.htm

Argentine Law No. 19.865. Vienna Convention on the Law of Treaties. http://servicios.infoleg.gob.ar/infolegInternet/anexos/215000-219999/217116/norma.htm

Argentine Law No. 23.335 Convention on International Liability for Damage. http://servicios.infoleg.gob.ar/infolegInternet/anexos/20000-24999/23571/norma.htm

Argentine Law No. 24.158 Convention on Registration of Objects Launched into Outer Space. https://servicios.infoleg.gob.ar/infolegInternet/verNorma.do?id=556

Argentine Law No. 24.430 National Constitution (1994) Orders the publication of the official text of the National Constitution (sanctioned in 1853 with the reforms of 1860, 1866, 1898, 1957 and 1994). http://servicios.infoleg.gob.ar/infolegInternet/anexos/0-4999/804/norma.htm

Argentine Law No. 25.467 National Science, Technology and Innovation System. Objectives of the national scientific and technological policy. Structure of the System. https://servicios.infoleg.gob.ar/infolegInternet/anexos/65000-69999/69045/texact.htm

Argentine Law No. 26.092. Creates the Argentine Company of Satellite Solutions Sociedad Anónima AR-SAT. http://servicios.infoleg.gob.ar/infolegInternet/anexos/115000-119999/115886/texact.htm

Argentine Law No. 27.078 Information and Communications Technologies. Digital Argentina. https://servicios.infoleg.gob.ar/infolegInternet/verNorma.do?id=239771

Argentine Law No. 27.208 Declares the development of the satellite industry as a state policy and a national priority regarding geostationary telecommunications satellites, and approves the Argentine Geostationary Satellite Plan 2015-2035 to be executed by the company AR- SAT. https://servicios.infoleg.gob.ar/infolegInternet/anexos/250000-254999/254823/texact.htm

Azcárate Ortega A (2023) Not a Rose by Any Other Name: Dual-Use and Dual-Purpose Space Systems, Lawfare, Monday, (June 5, 2023, 8:15 AM). https://www.lawfaremedia.org/article/not-a-rose-by-any-other-name-dual-use-and-dual-purpose-space-systems

Azcárate Ortega A, Lagos Koller H (2023) The open-ended working group on reducing space threats through norms, rules and principles of responsible behaviours: the journey so far, and the road ahead. Air Space Law 48(Special Issue):19–40. © 2023 Kluwer Law International BV, The Netherlands (p 26)

Catani CE (2024) Reflexiones jurídico-técnicas desde la perspectiva de la ética para la sostenibilidad del espacio ultraterrestre. ISSN 3008-816X. https://cedaeonline.com.ar/2024/10/13/reflexiones-juridico-tecnicas-desde-la-perspectiva-de-la-etica-para-la-sostenibilidad-del-espacio-ultraterrestre/

CONAE Resolution n. 260/99 (1999) Official Gazette of the Nation No. 29.153 (1st Section, May 24, 1999). https://www.boletinoficial.gob.ar/detalleAviso/primera/7195327/19990524

CONAE Resolution No. 330/96 (1996). Official Gazette of 22-Aug-1996 Number: 28462 Page: 3. https://www.boletinoficial.gov.ar/detalleAviso/primera/7161462/19960822?busqueda=1

CONAE Resolution No. 463/97 (1997) Registry of Space Operators. Official Gazette of 11-Nov-1997 Number: 28771 Page: 4. https://servicios.infoleg.gob.ar/infolegInternet/anexos/45000-49999/47215/norma.htm

COPUOS, Space Debris Mitigation Guidelines of the Committee on the Peaceful Uses of Outer Space (2010), available online at https://www.unoosa.org/pdf/publications/st_space_49E.pdf
COPUOS, Guidelines for The Long-Term Sustainability of Outer Space Activities of the Committee on the Peaceful Uses of Outer Space, A/RES/74/82. https://www.unoosa.org/res/oosadoc/data/documents/2021/stspace/stspace79_0_html/st_space79S.pdf
DNU Decree No. 267/2015. Creates the National Communications Entity (ENACOM). https://servicios.infoleg.gob.ar/infolegInternet/anexos/255000-259999/257461/norma.htm
Groetzner L et al (2021) Mirar la Tierra desde el Espacio: 30 años de la Agencia Espacial Argentina. 1ª edición. Ciudad Autónoma de Buenos Aires. Comisión Nacional de Actividades Espaciales, 2021. Libro digital, PDF. Archivo Digital: ISBN 978-987-96864-2-3. https://www.argentina.gob.ar/sites/default/files/mirarlatierradesdeelespacio-conae-30aniversario.pdf
Osorio CM (2003) Aproximaciones a la Tecnología desde los Enfoques en CTS. Universidad del Valle, Colombia. Red CTS+I, OEI
Presidential Decree N° 603/92 (1992) Control Regime for sensitive and war material exports. https://servicios.infoleg.gob.ar/infolegInternet/verNorma.do?id=12381
Presidential Decree No. 125 (1995), Official Gazette No. 28,192 of July 25, 1995. https://www.boletinoficial.gov.ar/detalleAviso/primera/7152296/19950725?busqueda=1
Presidential Decree No. 1330/99. Modifies PEN Decree No 2076/94. New National Space Plan. http://servicios.infoleg.gob.ar/infolegInternet/verNorma.do?id=61059
Presidential Decree No. 2076/94 (1994) National Space Plan. http://servicios.infoleg.gob.ar/infolegInternet/anexos/10000-14999/14118/norma.htm
Presidential Decree No. 532/05. National Space Plan (Period 2004-2015) http://servicios.infoleg.gob.ar/infolegInternet/anexos/105000-109999/106502/norma.htm
Presidential Decree No. 995/1991 (1991) ratified by Law No. 24.061. https://servicios.infoleg.gob.ar/infolegInternet/anexos/5000-9999/6295/texact.htm
Resolution No. 12/2024 from Secretariat of Innovation, Science and Technology. https://servicios.infoleg.gob.ar/infolegInternet/anexos/395000-399999/399305/norma.htm
Secure World Foundation. (2023) Capacidades Globales de Contraespacio: Una evaluación de fuentes abiertas. Resumen Ejecutivo 04/2023
Stephan H, Schmidt-Tedd B, Schrogl K-U (2021) Cologne Commentary on Space Law. Outer Space Treaty, Dykinson. Ed, ISBN 8411220583, 9788411220583 Spanish translation by Rafael Moro Aguilar
United Nation General Assembly, Resolution 1962 (XVIII) (1963). Declaration of Legal Principles Governing the Activities of States in the Exploration and Use of Outer Space
United Nation General Assembly, Resolution 2222 (XXI) (1967), Treaty on Principles Governing the Activities of States in the Exploration and Use of Outer Space, including the Moon and Other Celestial Bodies. https://www.unoosa.org/oosa/en/ourwork/spacelaw/treaties/introouterspacetreaty.html
United Nation General Assembly, Resolution 2345 (XXII) (1968) Agreement on the Rescue of Astronauts, the Return of Astronauts and Return of Objects Launched into Outer Space. https://www.unoosa.org/oosa/en/ourwork/spacelaw/treaties/introrescueagreement.html
United Nation General Assembly, Resolution 2777 (XXVI), (1972) Convention on International Liability for Damage Caused by Space Objects. https://www.unoosa.org/oosa/en/ourwork/spacelaw/treaties/introliability-convention.html
United Nation General Assembly, Resolution 3235 (XXIX), (1975) Convention on Registration of Objects Launched into Outer Space. https://www.unoosa.org/oosa/en/ourwork/spacelaw/treaties/introregistration-convention.html
United Nation General Assembly, Resolution 34/68 Agreement Governing the Activities of States on the Moon and Other Celestial Bodies. (1979). https://www.unoosa.org/oosa/en/ourwork/spacelaw/treaties/intromoon-agreement.html
United Nation General Assembly, Resolution 76/231. https://undocs.org/Home/Mobile?FinalSymbol=a%2Fres%2F76%2F231&Language=E&DeviceType=Desktop&LangRequested=False

UNOOSA, A/RES/62/101 Recommendations on enhancing the practice of States and international intergovernmental organizations in registering space objects (2007). https://www.unoosa.org/oosa/oosadoc/data/resolutions/2007/general_assembly_62nd_session/ares62101.html
World Economy Forum, McKinsey Company (April, 2024) "Space: The $1.8 trillion opportunity for global economic growth". https://www.weforum.org/publications/space-the-1-8-trillion-opportunity-for-global-economic-growth/

Brazil

Ian Grosner

Contents

The contents of this chapter are written for academic purposes and personal capacity. It should not be interpreted as the position of AEB nor of the Republic of Brazil.

I. Grosner (✉)
Legal Department, Brazilian Space Agency, Brasilia, DF, Brazil

I. Grosner (ed.), *Space Regulation in Latin America*, Space Regulations Library 11, https://doi.org/10.1007/978-3-032-05828-7_4

Abstract Brazil has a rich history of involvement in space activities dating back to the 1960s. The Brazilian Space Agency (AEB) is the main regulatory body responsible for overseeing space activities in the country. The AEB has issued regulations governing space activities, such as the Brazilian Space Regulation (REB). Brazil's space program has achieved significant milestones, including the successful launch of satellites and the development of space technology. The country's space activities have a dual-use nature, serving both civil and defense purposes. Brazil is committed to space exploration, as evidenced by its participation in international collaborations and its efforts to promote the development of the space sector.

1 Introduction

Brazil's air and space program has a rich and extensive history that dates back to the establishment of the Brazilian Ministry of Aeronautics in 1941.[1] From its inception to the present day, Brazil has made significant strides in the development of its aerospace sector, with a multitude of noteworthy events and achievements contributing to its progress.

In 1946, the idea of creating a technical center emerged after a visit to the Massachusetts Institute of Technology (MIT). This center, which would later be called the Brazilian Aeronautics Technical Center (CTA), was proposed by Professor Richard H. Smith and then Colonel-Aviator of the Brazilian Air Force (FAB), Casimiro Montenegro Filho.[2] Their idea was to establish a higher school of aeronautics, leading to the creation of the Technological Institute of Aeronautics (ITA). The ITA was established by Presidential Decree No. 27,695 of 1950 and later defined by Law No. 2,165 of 1954. This marked the first unit to be established in the CTA.

In 1950, the Brazilian Society of Air Law was established, and it is now known as the Brazilian Association of Air and Space Law (SBDA).[3] It is interesting to note

[1] Decree-Law No 2,961 of 1941.
[2] Moraes and Chiaradia (2007), p. 125.
[3] SBDA.

that the creation of the SBDA precedes the development of esteemed institutes in the realm of air and space law, such as the Institute of Air and Space Law (IASL), associated with McGill University, in Canada, founded a year later, in 1951. Even the prestigious International Astronautical Federation (IAF) was established in 1951, while the International Institute of Space Law (IISL) and the International Academy of Astronautics (IAA) were founded in 1960.

The history of Brazilian space development dates back to the 1960s, when the country was spurred into action by the launch of the first artificial satellite, Sputnik 1, by the former Union of Soviet Socialist Republics (USSR) on October 4, 1957. Brazil, recognizing the significance of space exploration, emerged as a pioneer among developing nations in investing in and institutionalizing its space program. The country identified the vast potential of its national territory to contribute to advancements in this crucial sector, leading to active efforts in space research and development.

Also in 1960, the Brazilian Interplanetary Society (SIB) decided to propose the creation of a civil space research institution in the country during the Inter-American Meeting for Space Research. They sent a letter to the then Brazilian President of the Republic, Janio Quadros, suggesting this initiative.[4]

The development of the space sector in Brazil started in 1961 with the establishment of the Organizational Group of the National Commission for Space Activities (GOCNAE) by Decree No. 51,133 on August 3, 1961. GOCNAE was under the authority of the National Research Council (CNPq) and had the responsibility to recommend space policy, support scientific research and human resource development, and foster international collaboration. Therefore, it is evident that Presidential Decree No. 51,133, issued on August 3, 1961, stands as the pioneering piece of legislation governing space law and policy in Brazil. From an administrative standpoint, it is clear that Brazil has been actively engaged in space programs for over 60 years, showcasing its long-standing commitment to space exploration and research.[5]

On the global stage, Brazil joined 17 other nations in establishing the United Nations Committee on the Peaceful Uses of Outer Space (COPUOS) *ad hoc*, on December 13, 1958, through UNGA Resolution No. 1348 (XIII). Notable members of this committee included the USA and the USSR. Both countries were pivotal players in the space race at the time.

In the six decades since then, numerous space missions have been successfully completed, with more tasks yet to be accomplished. It is essential to inquire about the current state of space law and policy in Brazil and how they are affecting its space program.

The objective of this chapter is to conduct a comprehensive analysis of the primary legal documents and regulations pertaining to the Brazilian space program.

---

[4] Grosner and Silva (2023), p. 15.

[5] Grosner and Silva (2023), p. 16.

2 Topics

This work aims to provide a comprehensive overview of the regulations governing the space industry in Latin America and the Caribbean.

The focus of this chapter will be on the regulatory framework in Brazil.

2.1 Which International Space Treaties Has Brazil Signed as a Party?

The International Geophysical Year, sponsored by UNESCO and with the participation of other sectors of the UN complex, including the Scientific Committee on Oceanic Research (SCOR), took place between July 1, 1957, and December 31, 1958. It mobilizes teams of scientists from many countries to study the physical properties of the Earth and the interaction between the Sun and our planet. It is the first major global effort by the best scientific expertise available, with a clearly peaceful spirit. It was a large-scale scientific program, with the participation of several countries, including Brazil, Argentina, Chile, the USSR, the UK, and the USA.

After a few years, the United Nations General Assembly unanimously adopted Resolution 1962 (XVIII) on December 13, 1963. This resolution, entitled "Declaration of Legal Principles Regulating Activities in the Exploration and Use of Outer Space," marked a significant milestone.

The UNGA Resolution 1962 (XVIII) serves as a principled doctrinal framework. It provides a soft law legal guideline to be used in the creation or translation of specific norms of law for inclusion in international acts. These acts are intended to be incorporated into the domestic law of countries in the manner specified by each country.

During the years from 1967 to 1979, a golden age of space treaties emerged, marked by significant involvement from Brazil.

Brazil has signed four of the five main treaties in the space area, namely:

- Treaty on Principles Governing the Activities of States in the Exploration and Use of Outer Space, including the Moon and Other Celestial Bodies, approved by the UN General Assembly on December 19, 1966, opened for signature on January 27, 1967, in force since October 10, 1967. Depositary countries: the USSR, the UK, and the USA. Introduced in Brazil by Presidential Decree No. 64,362, of April 17, 1969
- Agreement on the Rescue of Astronauts, the Return of Astronauts and the Return of Objects Launched into Outer Space, approved by the UN General Assembly on December 19, 1967, opened for signature on April 22, 1968, in force since December 3, 1968. Depositary countries: the USSR, the UK, and the USA. Introduced in Brazil by Presidential Decree No. 71,989, of March 26, 1973
- Convention on International Liability for Damage Caused by Space Objects, adopted by the UN General Assembly on November 29, 1971, opened for signature on March 29 1972, in force since September 1, 1972. Depositary countries:

the USSR, the UK, and the USA. Introduced in Brazil by Presidential Decree No. 71,981, of March 22, 1973
- Convention on Registration of Objects Launched into Outer Space, adopted by the UN General Assembly on November 12, 1974, opened for signature on January 14, 1975, in force since September 15, 1976. Depositary: UN Secretariat-General. Introduced in Brazil by Presidential Decree No. 5,806, of June 19, 2006

2.2 *Is Brazil a Member of COPUOS?*

Brazil played a significant role in the establishment of the Committee on the Peaceful Uses of Outer Space (COPUOS) as one of the 18 member countries. In 1958, the United Nations General Assembly, through resolution 1348 (XIII), formed an *ad hoc* COPUOS. The 18 states that were part of this committee included major powers such as the USA and the former USSR, both at the forefront of the space race.

On November 27, 1961, the COPUOS, which at that time had 24 members and had gained permanent status, convened for its inaugural session. Ambassador Geraldo de Carvalho Silos, serving as the representative of Brazil, held the role of rapporteur during this significant committee meeting.

Since then, Brazil has played a crucial role in all meetings and deliberations in COPUOS. Brazil has a permanent delegation in Vienna. In a scenario characterized by the multiplication of governmental and private space actors and the centrality of space activities in modern societies, COPUOS has played a leading role in regulating space activities and fostering cooperation between countries.

The permanent delegation of Brazil works to defend the strengthening of the Committee as the multilateral forum of the United Nations with a mandate to deal with the exploration and peaceful uses of outer space, particularly with a view to ensuring Brazil's interests in the space area. This includes the negotiation of norms that facilitate cooperation with other countries and access to space technologies.

The country's active participation in the Committee seeks to ensure that Brazil is recognized as a relevant actor in the space area, whose economic and strategic value is growing. Recently, there have been efforts to strengthen the relationship between the United Nations Office for Outer Space Affairs (UNOOSA) and the Brazilian space organizations, such as the Ministry of Science, Technology and Innovation, the Brazilian Space Agency (AEB), the National Institute for Space Research (INPE), and others. This has been achieved through virtual and in-person meetings.

In the recent past, Brazil took on the leadership position of COPUOS and also chaired the Working Group on the Definition and Delimitation of Outer Space of the Legal Subcommittee.[6] Brazil actively engaged in discussions regarding space resources, long-term sustainability guidelines, and the development of the Space Agenda 2030.

---

[6] UN A/AC.105/1285 (2023). Paragraph 76, p. 13.

2.3 Has Brazil Signed the Artemis Accords?

Brazil was indeed the first country in Latin America to sign the Artemis Accords on June 15, 2021. By joining the agreement, Brazil committed to participating in peaceful and responsible space exploration, including the goal of returning humans to the Moon. This significant step solidified Brazil's position as a major player in international space cooperation.

Artemis has been included in the recent edition of the Brazilian National Space Activities Program (PNAE) for the 2022–2031 decade. It will contribute to the following PNAE strategic objectives:

- Foster the development of scientific and technological innovation for the space sector
- Actively consolidate, in all sectors of Brazilian society, the understanding of the direct and indirect, existing, and potential benefits of the space sector for Brazil

2.4 Can Space Activities Be Classified as Dual Use, or Are They Only for Defense or Civil Purposes?

Brazil's space activities have had a dual-use nature since the 1960s, serving both defense and civil purposes.

This was further reinforced by the recent federal Law N. 14,946 of 2024, which explicitly defines space activities as dual use in articles 2, IV and 5, §1.

2.5 Is There a Registry of Space Objects Maintained by the United Nations?

In compliance with AEB Ordinance No. 96 of November 30, 2011, the duties of the Brazilian Space Agency (AEB) include overseeing the establishment and management of the National Registry of Space Objects. This comprehensive registry is routinely updated whenever Brazil fulfills its role as a "launching State" according to the terms outlined in the Convention on the Registration of Objects Launched into Outer Space, also known as the "Registration Convention," enacted on January 14, 1975 (General Assembly Resolution 3235 (XXIX).

Article 6 of the AEB Ordinance No. 96 establishes that "Brazilian space objects" to be registered are (a) space objects developed in Brazil by a Brazilian government entity or the private sector by a foreign entity duly authorized to operate in the sector or through a bilateral initiative, whose launch takes place in Brazilian territory or in the territory of another country; (b) space objects developed by a Brazilian entity abroad, with or without the participation of a foreign entity, which are launched from Brazilian territory or another country; (c) space objects developed abroad by a foreign entity, as a result of an order from a Brazilian entity, whose launch takes place from Brazilian territory or another country; and (d) space objects developed abroad by a foreign entity, without the participation of a Brazilian entity and without having been ordered by a Brazilian entity, whose launch takes place from Brazilian territory.

Additionally, a registry of Brazilian and foreign satellites in commercial operation in Brazil is made available by Brazilian National Telecommunications Agency (ANATEL). For ANATEL, Brazilian space objects are considered to be satellites that use orbital and radio spectrum resources notified by Brazil, or distributed or assigned to it, and whose control and monitoring station is installed in the national territory.

Finally, in 2024, the federal Law N. 14.946 created the Brazilian National Space Registry (RESBRA) in Articles 25 and 26.

Article 25 mandates that the Brazilian Space Agency (AEB) will create and manage the Brazilian Space Registry (RESBRA). This registry will serve as a comprehensive system for gathering, analyzing, and retaining data and information related to Brazil's space endeavors, in accordance with the country's international commitments concerning the formalization of its registration status.

RESBRA's records may encompass a wide range of data and information related to national civil space operations, activities, artifacts, as well as licenses and authorizations associated with civil space activities. This may also include information about the granting of rights and any relevant transactions. The AEB will implement a regulation to outline how RESBRA will operate.

2.6 Does Brazil Have a National Specific Space Act or Regulations?

As seen before, in Brazil, the space sector's institutionalization started in 1961 with the establishment of GOCNAE. This was set up through Presidential Decree No. 51,133 on August 3, 1961.

GOCNAE was granted the authority to not only propose space policy but also to play a crucial role in promoting scientific research and the training of human resources. Moreover, it actively encourages international cooperation in the field of space exploration.

FAB also took on the responsibility of consolidating the defense space program, further solidifying the dual nature of the Brazilian space program.

Since 1967, the Brazilian Federal Constitution has included space law as an autonomous branch of law. It may be the only constitution in the world that explicitly mentions space law.

In the current 1988 Brazilian Federal Constitution, Article 22, I, states that:

> Article 22. The Union has the exclusive power to legislate on: I – civil, commercial, criminal, procedural, electoral, agrarian, maritime, aeronautical, *space* and labor *law*;

Many years later, after facing numerous logistical and budgetary challenges, Brazil finally established its Brazilian Space Agency (AEB) through Law No. 8,854 of 1994.

2.6.1 Law No. 8,854 of 1994

The Brazilian Space Agency (AEB) was created on February 10, 1994, by Law No. 8,854/1994, as a federal agency linked to the presidency of the republic, replacing the Brazilian Commission for Space Activities (COBAE).

The first regulatory structure of the AEB was established in Presidential Decree No. 1,329, of December 6, 1994.

The powers of the AEB are specifically outlined in Article 3 of Law No. 8,854/1994:

- To implement and enforce the Brazilian National Policy for the Development of Space Activities (PNDAE), as well as to propose guidelines and implement actions arising from it
- To propose the updating of the PNDAE and the guidelines for its implementation
- To prepare and update the Brazilian National Program for Space Activities (PNAE) and their respective budget proposals
- To promote relationships with similar institutions in Brazil and abroad
- To analyze proposals, sign international agreements in coordination with the Brazilian Ministry of Foreign Affairs (MRE) and the Brazilian Ministry of Science, Technology and Innovation (MCTI), for cooperation in space activities, and oversee their implementation
- To provide opinions on space-related issues for analysis and discussion in international forums, as COPUOS, and to represent them, in coordination with the Brazilian Ministry of Foreign Affairs (MRE) and the Brazilian Ministry of Science, Technology and Innovation (MCTI)
- To encourage the participation of universities, educational institutions, and research and development organizations in space-related activities
- To stimulate the participation of the private sector in space activities
- To promote scientific research and technological development in space-related activities
- To enhance national entities' access to knowledge acquired through space activities, with the aim of advancing their technological capabilities
- To coordinate the joint use of space technical facilities, aiming at the integration of available means and the rationalization of resources
- To identify commercial opportunities for the use of space technologies and applications, with the aim of encouraging business ventures in service provision and goods production
- To establish standards, issue licenses, and grant authorizations related to space activities
- To apply quality and productivity standards in space activities

The AEB has the authority to engage in its operations either directly or indirectly through the use of contracts, agreements, and arrangements, both within Brazil and internationally.

The AEB is led by a president and four directors as stipulated in Decree No. 11,192 of 2022. The president of the republic appoints these officials and must be Brazilian citizens with impeccable moral character and recognized competence.

2.6.2 Law No. 14,946 of 2024: A New Era for Brazilian Space Activities

Law No. 14,946 of 2024, also known as the Brazilian General Law of Space Activities, marks a significant achievement for the Brazilian space sector. This law consolidates and updates the legal framework governing space activities in the country. It introduces several new features and brings Brazil in line with international best practices.

Law No. 14,946 of 2024 establishes the general rules for Brazilian space activities, ranging from research and development to the exploration and use of outer space. The law covers topics such as:

- Definition and classification of space activities: The law defines space activities and classifies them into different categories, including launching space vehicles, operating satellites, and exploiting space resources.
- Agencies and entities involved: The new law sets up the institutional framework for managing space activities, defining the responsibilities of the Brazilian Space Agency (AEB), Brazilian Air Force (FAB), and other involved agencies.
- Licensing and authorization: The law establishes a new licensing and authorization system for space activities to ensure safety and environmental protection.
- International cooperation: As per Law No. 8,854 of 1994, Law No. 14,946 of 2024 promotes global collaboration in space endeavors, acknowledging inter-country partnerships as crucial for sector development.

Law 14.946/2024 brings in a range of updates and additions compared to the previous legislation. Notable changes include:

- Recognition of the dual nature of space activities: The law explicitly recognizes the dual nature of space activities, that is, their importance for both civil and defense purposes.
- Encouragement of private sector participation: The objective of the law is to encourage the involvement of private companies in the space industry by employing methods such as forming partnerships between the public and private sectors and granting service concessions.
- Protection of the space environment: The law establishes measures to protect the space environment, such as preventing space pollution and mitigating the environmental impacts of space activities.
- Space resources: This legislation officially acknowledges and regulates the utilization of space resources within the country. By enacting this law, Brazil joins a select group of nations, becoming the fifth country in the world to have a domes-

tic legal framework that approves the use of space resources. This significant development paves the way for future space exploration and potential economic opportunities related to space resource utilization within Brazil's borders.
- Modernization of the regulatory framework: The new law introduces updated regulations for space activities, taking into account the latest advancements in technology and aligning with the best practices followed internationally.

In short, Law No. 14,946/2024 signifies a major step forward for the Brazilian space industry. It establishes a modern and comprehensive legal framework that is in line with the demands and opportunities of the twenty-first century. This new law solidifies Brazil's position as a significant contributor to the global space landscape and sets the stage for the growth of a more dynamic and innovative space sector.

2.7 *Does Brazil Have a Space Agency?*

Since 1994, Brazil has had its own space agency called the AEB.

The AEB was officially established on February 10, 1994, with the primary goal of formulating, coordinating, executing, and controlling Brazil's space policy. The AEB has been instrumental in developing Brazil's space program and has achieved significant milestones in space research, technology development, and satellite launches. Its efforts have contributed to both domestic and international space exploration, positioning Brazil as a key player in the global space community.

2.8 *What Is the Primary Regulatory Body Responsible for Overseeing Space Activities?*

The Presidential Decree 1,953 of 1996 is a significant milestone in structuring and organizing the Brazilian space program. It established the National System for the Development of Space Activities (SINDAE), demonstrating the Brazilian government's commitment to space exploration and utilizing space technologies for the country's development.

The AEB is the main coordinating body for SINDAE and is responsible for developing and implementing national space policies and programs. The agency is tasked with proposing updates to the National Policy for the Development of Space Activities (PNDAE) and the National Program for Space Activities (PNAE), as well as coordinating and overseeing the execution of PNAE initiatives. To support these responsibilities, the AEB has a higher council, which is a decision-making body comprised of representatives from various government ministries and agencies involved in space activities, as well as members of the scientific and industrial communities.[7]

---

[7] AEB. Sistema Nacional de Desenvolvimento das Atividades Espaciais (SINDAE).

The main sectoral bodies responsible for carrying out strategic projects and activities under the PNAE are the National Institute for Space Research (INPE) and the Department of Aerospace Science and Technology (DCTA), under the authority of the Air Force Command (COMAER) of the Ministry of Defense (MD).

The National Institute for Space Research (INPE) is dedicated to advancing science and technology in the fields of space and the terrestrial environment. INPE aims to provide unique products and services that benefit Brazil. Over the past 50 years, the institute has conducted extensive research, development, and applications in the space sector. Its activities range from the annual monitoring of deforestation and land cover dynamics in the Amazon to the development of research and instrumentation for space sciences. INPE is a national leader in remote sensing, space sciences, atmospheric sciences, Earth system research, and space engineering and technology. In addition to providing operational services for weather and climate forecasting and monitoring deforestation in the Amazon, INPE conducts satellite tracking and control, fire and lightning monitoring, air pollution measurements, as well as high-quality industrial testing and trials.

The DCTA is responsible for planning, managing, conducting, and overseeing activities related to science, technology, and innovation within the Air Force Command. The DCTA has departments located in different areas, including Brasília, Alcântara, Natal, and São José dos Campos. It brings together a significant number of high-level personnel, totaling around 5,500 military personnel and civil servants. This includes engineers, researchers, and technicians from various specialties who work on cutting-edge projects of great strategic value to the country.

SINDAE, as participating executors, also maintains an industrial base. Although still small, this industrial base has achieved high technical levels with engineers trained in the production of optical cameras, solar panels, propulsion systems, energy supply, mechanical structures, thermal control, and telecommunications. Additionally, the business sector has a space systems project integrator.

In the academic sector, the country is home to eight aerospace engineering courses, with a total of 200–300 students demonstrating increasing involvement in space activities and projects.

In summary, Decree 1.953/1996 and the creation of SINDAE represent a historic milestone for the Brazilian space program. The AEB, as the central body, has the mission of coordinating and driving the development of the space sector, contributing to the scientific, technological, and socioeconomic progress of the country.

2.9 *What Are the Primary Regulations Governing Space Activities, and How Are Private Companies Performing Space Activities Authorized, Monitored, and Supervised?*

As explained before in item 2.6., since the enactment of Law No. 8,854 of 1994, the AEB has been granted the authority to effectively regulate space activities within the country. This authority includes the power to authorize, monitor, and supervise private companies involved in space exploration and utilization.

Furthermore, the enactment of Law 14,946 of 2024 has contributed to further strengthening the AEB's role by establishing specific conditions for licensing, authorization, and supervision of the private sector in the context of space resources. This law outlines detailed requirements and procedures in Articles 12–24 that private entities must adhere to in order to obtain the necessary permits and oversight from the AEB. It is through these regulations and procedures that the responsible use of space resources is promoted, ensuring that space activities are conducted in compliance with Brazilian laws and regulations. Ultimately, this contributes to the promotion of safety and sustainability in space exploration and utilization.

2.9.1 The Brazilian Regulations from AEB: REBs

Since 1994, in accordance with Article 3, XIII, of Law No. 8,854, the presidency of the AEB has been granted the authority to set forth regulations and grant licenses and permits for activities related to space.

The AEB Ordinance No. 698, of August 31, 2021, establishes the Brazilian Space Regulation (REB), which sets out the standards for the Operator's License for Space Activities (REB 1) and the Launch Authorization in Brazilian Territory (REB 2).[8]

In a short period after, the AEB Ordinance No. 1,019, of December 23, 2022, published the third part of the Brazilian Space Regulation (REB 3), which establishes the Insurance Requirements for Space Launch.

In recent times, the space industry has undergone significant changes, primarily attributed to the increasing engagement of private entities. This has resulted in the emergence of numerous companies in the space launch sector and the establishment of private launch facilities. The impact of these developments became apparent with the successful inaugural commercial launch of the Alcantara Space Launch Center (CLA), by South Korean company Innospace, during Operation Astrolabe, on March 19, 2023. In November 2025, a new operation is planned with the same South Korean company, the Spaceward operation.

Legal certainty is essential for the smooth operation of commercial activities. It is crucial to have clear regulations in place to ensure the safety and effectiveness of these activities.

2.9.1.1 REB 1

Part 1 of the REB, Launch Operator License, is composed of the following items:[9]

- General information about the license
- Requirements for obtaining the license

[8] Grosner et al. (2022), p. 5.

[9] AEB (3).

- Required documentation
- Issuance procedures
- Monitoring of the licensee
- Administrative sanctions
- Administrative appeals

The Launch Operator License is an administrative approval granted to a legal entity, associate, or consortium with headquarters or representation in Brazil. This license allows the holder to conduct space launch activities from Brazilian territory, in compliance with the conditions specified in this Regulation.

The license will be valid for 5 years and may be renewed for equal and successive periods.

In Brazil, private legal entities conducting space activities such as launching orbital or suborbital payloads and conducting flight tests of space devices are required to follow the REB procedure, with the exception of model rocket and meteorological balloon activities, which have their own regulations. It is important to note that these rules do not apply to activities involving public actors, such as the National Institute for Space Research (INPE) and/or the FAB.

The licensing terms may include restrictions or conditions that take into account Brazil's national security interests, foreign policy, and international obligations. For instance, the license may consider countries under UN sanctions or those deemed dangerous by Brazil. The Brazilian Space Agency (AEB) may consult with relevant government bodies and entities to assess any potential conflicts with national security and foreign policy interests related to proposed space launch operations. These bodies may include the Ministry of Foreign Affairs (MRE), the Brazilian Intelligence Agency (ABIN), the presidency of the republic, the Federal Police Department (DPF), and the Armed Forces.

A Special Licensing Commission will be established, consisting of a minimum of three members appointed by the president of the AEB. At least one member must be a civil servant from the AEB or another entity of the Federal Public Administration. Their primary responsibility will be to review and handle the necessary documentation. The AEB's Directorate of Strategic Intelligence and New Business (AEB/DIEN) will serve as the technical secretariat for the Commission.

2.9.1.2 REB 2

Part 2 of the REB, Launch Authorization, is composed of the following items:[10]

- General information about the authorization and its process
- Transfer of the authorization
- Authorization requirements (redirection to the annexes)
- Monitoring of the authorization

[10] AEB (3).

- Administrative penalties (equivalent to administrative sanctions)
- Administrative appeals

Launch Authorization is the administrative act intended to grant the release of space launch activities or a set of space launches in Brazilian territory, according to the conditions established in this Regulation and the legislation in force.

REB 2 is intended for:

- Private launch operations conducted by Brazilian companies or those with representation in Brazil, from Brazilian territory
- Private launch operations carried out by Brazilian companies in another country

Space launch activities of a military nature (Navy, Army, and Air Force) under the responsibility of FAB are exempt from this Regulation.

The Launch Operator License (REB 1) is required to formalize the application and grant the Launch Authorization (REB 2).

The Launch Authorization process will require the party authorized to conduct the space launch to obtain comprehensive insurance coverage. This insurance should cover any potential damages caused to third parties or to the infrastructure of the public launch center as a result of the space launch. The specific amounts of coverage required will be determined by the AEB (the relevant authority). For further details, please refer to the REB 3 document (please remember the following text: Sect. 2.9.1.3 below).

Item 6.1.5 of REB 2 states that liability for damages resulting from space launches will be governed by the international treaties and conventions that regulate space activities, of which Brazil is a signatory. It will also be governed by other applicable standards. The liability will be the sole responsibility of the authorized party and will not be reduced or transferred to the public administration due to private contracts, including insurance contracts, that may exist between the authorized party and third parties that stipulate the division of the financial obligations for which they are responsible.

The regulations in this document are based on the standards set by the Federal Aviation Administration (FAA), linked to the United States Department of Transportation (DOT), related to part 450[11]—streamlining of launch and reentry licensing requirements—and part 420,[12] license to operate launch sites. These standards are divided into Annexes A, B, C, D, and E and have been adapted to Brazilian legislation. Compliance with part 450 of the FAA means meeting the requirements of this Regulation, except for any reserved items that do not apply or have already been referenced in the AEB regulations.

The space launch, whether civilian or military, will be meticulously overseen by the Brazilian Space Agency (AEB) through the Special Licensing Commission. The

[11] FAA 14 CFR Part 450 (namely, the Launch and Reentry Licensing Requirements).

[12] FAA 14 CFR Part 420 (namely, the License to Operate a Launch Site).

AEB will be responsible for controlling, monitoring, and supervising civilian space launches, ensuring that all operations and payloads are duly registered and that there are no conflicts with commercial operations. In the case of military launches, FAB will take charge, but they are required to inform the AEB about the operation and payload to ensure coordination and avoid potential conflicts.

2.9.1.3 REB 3

The AEB, through Ordinance No. 1,019, of December 23, 2022, published the third part of the Brazilian Space Regulation (REB 3), which establishes the Insurance Requirements for Space Launches.

The purpose of REB 3 is to protect society and the Brazilian state in the event of an accident during a space launch operation carried out by private companies within the national territory. It states that for a launch to occur, the company must obtain an Operator's License (REB 1) and a Launch Authorization (REB 2).

The company will only receive permission to launch if it provides all the required information for assessing the safety of the operation and calculating the insurance value. This assessment will be done according to the methodology developed by the AEB and presented in the third part of the REB.

In order to obtain a Launch Authorization, the applicant must provide the information required by the methodology issued by the AEB for conducting a maximum probable loss analysis for the applicable authorized operation, as stated in Annex B of the REB, Part 2, item 450.31 (a) (6).

The document outlines the various obligations that companies must meet in the event of accidents, property damage, personal injuries, environmental harm, and other direct or indirect losses. These obligations are necessary for obtaining the insurance required for space launches. The specific insurance amount to be secured by a private entity planning a space launch from Brazilian territory will be determined by the Licensing Commission. This determination will involve comparing the particular launch scenario with the reference values provided in Annex A of the regulation (see Table 1).

Table 1 Reference values for taking out insurance

Maximum payload	Insurance values (in US$)
Up to 300 kg	10–40 million
301–1000 kg	40–100 million
1001–10,000 kg	100–150 million
10,001–25,000 kg	150–360 million
Over 25,000 kg	360–500 million
Airdropped (up to 500 kg)	10–60 million

2.10 Is There Any Effort Toward Capacity Building in the Space Sector, Both in Terms of Technologies and Regulatory Matters?

The National Space Activities Plan (PNAE) serves as a pivotal instrument for the Brazilian state, outlining the strategic framework for space activities. Over the years, the Brazilian Space Agency (AEB) has meticulously crafted five editions of the PNAE, in 1996, 1998, 2005, 2012, and the latest in 2022. These iterations have been instrumental in delineating space activities, guiding principles, and significant projects aimed at addressing the economic, industrial, strategic, and political imperatives, along with other applications deemed advantageous for the nation. The current PNAE, in its fifth edition, spans the period from 2022 to 2031, encompassing a comprehensive array of facets encompassing missions, space access mechanisms, applications, and scientific, technological, and educational programs. For more comprehensive insights, please refer to Sect. 2.13.

The current PNAE, for the period of 2022–2031, emphasizes the importance of capacity building within Brazil's space sector. This entails a strategic investment in human resources and technological development to bolster and advance the technical, technological, and industrial capabilities of the country's space industry. The aim is to foster a skilled workforce and enhance the technological infrastructure to position Brazil as a prominent player in the global space arena.

Over the past three decades, Brazil has made significant regulatory advancements in its space sector. A key milestone in this progress was the establishment of the AEB, which has played a pivotal role in shaping and strengthening the regulatory framework governing the country's space activities. The establishment of the AEB has not only contributed to regulatory advancements but has also facilitated strategic planning, research, and development initiatives in Brazil's space industry. The agency's involvement has been instrumental in fostering international collaborations and positioning Brazil as a key player in the global space arena.

It is worth noting the recent establishment of the Brazilian Space Program Development Committee (CDPEB) through Presidential Decree No. 9,839 of 2019. This committee, which operates under the auspices of the President's Office of Brazil, is tasked with overseeing and driving the development of Brazil's space program. Additionally, the creation of the Brazilian National Space Council (CNE) via Presidential Decree No. 11,224 of 2022 is a significant milestone. The CNE, also under the Brazilian President's Office, is responsible for providing strategic governance and direction for Brazil's space program. These institutions are pivotal in shaping the future trajectory of Brazil's endeavors in space exploration and development.

2.11 How Does Brazil Engage in International Cooperation in the Space Sector, Both in Terms of Technologies and Representation in International Organizations? Are There Any Partnerships with Other Latin American Countries?

Brazil has actively engaged in international partnerships within the space sector, joining forces with diverse countries and organizations to propel its space exploration and technology advancement efforts.

Brazil has engaged in partnerships with countries like China, France, and Argentina to work on the creation of satellites. These satellites serve various purposes including telecommunications, Earth observation, and scientific research.

Therefore, Brazil has taken part in international initiatives to share satellite data and conduct joint research projects.

As mentioned earlier, since the 1960s, Brazil has been actively represented in international forums. The country has been a member of the United Nations Committee on Peaceful Uses of Outer Space (COPUOS) since 1958. Additionally, AEB is also a member of the International Astronautical Federation (IAF), a global organization that brings together space professionals from diverse countries.

Brazil has established enduring and robust partnerships with Latin American countries in the realm of space exploration. An exemplary illustration of this is the SABIAMAR Project, a collaborative initiative between Brazil and Argentina aimed at developing a satellite constellation tailored for maritime surveillance and environmental monitoring. Brazil has been a significant contributor to international space cooperation, leveraging its expertise and resources for diverse projects. The nation has actively pursued the enhancement of its partnerships with neighboring countries in Latin America, with the aim of fostering regional development and fostering collaboration within the space sector.

While Brazil is not currently a member of the Latin American and Caribbean Space Agency (ALCE), it actively participates in other regional and international space initiatives. The country's engagement in international cooperation has helped to enhance its reputation as a spacefaring nation and contribute to global efforts in space exploration and technology development.

2.12 How Does the Private Sector Conduct Its Activities in the Field of Space Exploration?

In Brazil, the private sector's involvement in space exploration has seen significant growth, attributed to advancements in technology, government backing, and expanding commercial prospects. Noteworthy entities and endeavors have surfaced, contributing to the advancement of the Brazilian space industry.

Brazil has several hubs of innovation in the space sector. The oldest and main hub is located in Sao Jose dos Campos, in the state of Sao Paulo. It has become a center for space-related research, development, and innovation, hosting numerous research institutes, universities, and companies involved in the space sector.

- Research Institutes: The National Institute for Space Research (INPE) and the Brazilian Aerospace Institute (IAE) are prominent research institutions located in Sao Jose dos Campos. They conduct research on various space-related topics, including satellite technology, rocket propulsion, and space science.
- Academia Partnerships: The city has strong university partnerships with institutions such as the Institute of Technology of Aeronautics (ITA), the University of Campinas (UNICAMP), and the Federal University of Sao Carlos (UFSCar). These partnerships provide various programs and research opportunities in aerospace engineering and related fields.
- The São José dos Campos Technological Innovation Park (PIT): The PIT is recognized as a top hub for the advancement of aerospace technologies in Latin America. Boasting a dynamic ecosystem, PIT serves as a nexus that fosters collaboration among corporations, academic institutions, research centers, and emerging companies, all working together to pioneer groundbreaking solutions within the space industry.

In recent years, an increasing number of emerging companies have ventured into the Brazilian space industry, introducing new and inventive methods for space exploration. These start-ups specialize in various niches including the manufacturing of satellites, providing launch services, developing space applications, and conducting space data analytics.

It is worth mentioning that the Brazilian Startups Alliance serves as a valuable platform that facilitates collaboration, networking, and support for emerging start-ups. Through this alliance, start-ups are connected with investors, mentors, and industry experts, providing them with the essential resources and guidance needed to thrive and make strides toward success.

The Association of Air and Space Industries in Brazil (AIAB) represents companies involved in the aerospace industry in Brazil. It serves as a platform for industry dialogue, advocacy, and cooperation. The AIAB works with government agencies to shape policies that support the growth and development of the Brazilian aerospace sector. It also promotes collaboration between industry players and fosters international partnerships.

The private sector engages in a variety of key activities, including:

- Satellite Development and Manufacturing: Brazilian companies are actively involved in the development and manufacturing of satellites for various purposes, including telecommunications, Earth observation, and scientific research. It is possible to mention Visiona, a joint venture between Embraer and Telebras, which is a prominent Brazilian company specializing in the design, development, manufacturing, and operation of satellites.

- Launch Services: Several private companies are currently investigating the potential of offering launch services for satellites. However, this field poses significant challenges and has high entry barriers.
- Space Applications: The private sector is developing and commercializing various space applications, such as satellite imagery analysis, remote sensing, and space-based communication services.
- Space Data Analytics: Companies are leveraging space data to extract valuable insights and information for various industries, including agriculture, environmental monitoring, and urban planning.

In conclusion, the private sector in Brazil is significantly expanding its involvement in the nation's space exploration endeavors. This increased participation is fostering innovation, promoting entrepreneurial initiatives, and fueling the expansion of the Brazilian space industry.

2.13 What Are the Plans for Space Activities in Brazil? Are Manned Flights and Spaceports Being Planned?

Brazil has been actively involved in space exploration for several decades.

The Brazilian Space Programme (PEB) must meet society's needs, with the highest possible levels of effectiveness and efficiency. It is with this objective that PNAE 2022–2031 is established as an instrument of the Brazilian state.[13]

The PNAE 2022–2031 delineates Brazil's strategic objectives for space exploration during the 10-year period spanning 2022–2031. This structured framework emphasizes several pivotal domains, encompassing satellite development, advanced space technology, scientific research in space, fostering international partnerships, and the bolstering of aerospace infrastructure within the nation. It focuses on several key areas:

- Satellite development and launch: Brazil aims to develop and launch various satellites for telecommunications, Earth observation, scientific research, and other purposes.
- Space research: The plan includes initiatives to conduct scientific research in space, such as astronomy, astrophysics, and space medicine.
- International cooperation: Brazil seeks to collaborate with other countries and space agencies on various space projects.

The PNAE does not specifically reference manned flights as a defined objective, but it does explore the potential for involvement in international human space exploration initiatives.

The CEA Alcantara Space Launch is a major initiative focused on the development of a spaceport in Alcantara, Brazil. This strategic spaceport is intended to

[13] Grosner et al. (2022, 2023), p. 507.

serve as a crucial launch site for a wide range of rockets and satellites, aiming to support a diverse array of space missions. Despite encountering significant challenges and experiencing some delays, the project continues to be of paramount importance to Brazil's ambitious space exploration endeavors.

2.14 What Are (and Should Be) the Perspectives of Brazil on Regulatory Matters Related to Space Debris, Militarization and Weaponization of Space, and Exploitation of Space Natural Resources?

Brazil's stance on regulatory issues pertaining to space debris, militarization and weaponization of space, as well as the exploitation of space natural resources is intricate and continually developing. As a party to international agreements like the Outer Space Treaty, Brazil is dedicated to the peaceful exploration and utilization of space. Nonetheless, the nation acknowledges the increasing significance of space endeavors and the necessity of harmonizing global collaboration with its own domestic interests.

Law 14,946 of 2024, also known as the Brazilian General Law of Space Activities, provides a framework for Brazilian space activities and reaffirms the AEB as the responsible authority for the civil sector. The law addresses various aspects of space exploration, including the protection of space objects, the licensing of space activities, and the regulation of space debris. Please refer to Sect. 2.6.2 for more information.

Brazil has expressed significant concern about the increasing threat of collisions and other potential dangers resulting from space debris in orbit. In response, a new law has been enacted (Law 14,946 of 2024), requiring the AEB to establish comprehensive regulations aimed at reducing the generation of space debris and to implement systems for tracking and monitoring existing debris. Furthermore, Brazil is actively collaborating with international organizations, including COPUOS, UNOOSA, and the Inter-Agency Space Debris Coordination Committee (IADC), among others, to address the global challenge of space debris.

Brazil has consistently maintained a principled stance against the militarization and weaponization of outer space. The country firmly believes that such actions not only jeopardize international peace and security but also hinder the exploration and utilization of space for peaceful purposes. Brazil advocates for the implementation of robust, legally binding measures aimed at preventing the weaponization of space. As a member of the Group of 77 (G77), a coalition of developing nations, Brazil actively collaborates with other member states to advance initiatives that promote disarmament and nonproliferation in outer space. The country's commitment to this cause underscores its dedication to upholding international peace and security while fostering the responsible use of space for the betterment of humankind.

In regard to the utilization of natural resources in space, Brazil acknowledges the potential advantages and difficulties linked to such endeavors. Law 14,946 of

2024 in its Art. 2, XII, grants the AEB the authority to regulate and encourage the exploration and utilization of space resources, within the framework of international law and national interests. Brazil is also engaged in discussions within COPUOS concerning the establishment of international standards and principles governing the exploitation of space resources.

In summary, Brazil's approach to regulatory issues concerning space debris, militarization and weaponization of space, and the use of space natural resources is based on its dedication to peaceful space exploration, international collaboration, and its own national interests. Law 14,946 of 2024 sets out the legal framework for Brazilian space activities and designates the AEB as the responsible authority. Brazil is actively engaging in international initiatives to tackle these issues and advocate for the sustainable and responsible utilization of outer space.

2.15 Other Relevant Topics

Brazil's current lack of extensive academic programs in space law and policy highlights the necessity for broader educational options to cater to the country's increasing participation in space endeavors.

A new educational program needs to be developed to cover the theoretical and practical components of space law and space policy. Providing enhanced access to space law education for Brazil's legal professionals, government officials, and industry stakeholders can yield substantial benefits. For example, establishing a robust space law and policy framework could lead to significant economic and diplomatic opportunities for the entire continent.

Potential sources to increase space law in the country can be established through academic journals such as the *Journal of Space Law*, *Space Policy*, *International Journal of Air and Space Law*, and Brazilian law journals.

Finally, it is important to note that the Higher School of Lawyers in Brasilia (ESA-DF) has been offering the sole foundational course dedicated to space law since 2020. Additionally, in 2024, the AEB School (AEB Escola) offered an introduction course to space law for the first time, which is completely free of charge and available online.

3 Final Remarks

Brazil has a long history of involvement in space activities, dating back to the 1960s. The country has made significant strides in the development of its space program, both domestically and internationally. Brazil is a member of various international space organizations, including COPUOS, and has signed several key space treaties.

The AEB is the primary regulatory body responsible for overseeing space activities in Brazil. It establishes and manages the National Registry of Space Objects and regulates private companies involved in space exploration. The AEB has also issued regulations governing space activities, such as the Brazilian Space Regulation .

Brazil's space program has achieved significant milestones, including the successful launch of satellites and the development of space technology. The country's space activities have dual-use nature, serving both civil and defense purposes. Brazil's commitment to space exploration is evident through its participation in international collaborations and its efforts to promote the development of the space sector.

Despite the progress made, the Brazilian space program still faces challenges such as the need for continued investment in research and development, the qualification of human resources, and the consolidation of partnerships with the private sector.

However, the outlook for the future is promising. With the growing demand for space services and products, the Brazilian space sector has great potential for growth. The AEB, as the central body of SINDAE, will play a fundamental role in this process, seeking to consolidate Brazil as a space power and seize the opportunities offered by the new era of space exploration.

References

AEB (1). https://www.gov.br/aeb/pt-br/assuntos/programa-espacial-brasileiro/objetos-espaciais-brasileiros

AEB (2). https://www.gov.br/aeb/pt-br/programa-espacial-brasileiro/politica-organizacoes-programa-e-projetos/sistema-nacional-de-desenvolvimento-das-atividades-espaciais-sindae

AEB (3). https://www.gov.br/aeb/pt-br/servicos/licenciamento/normas-para-atividades-espaciais

Grosner I, Silva BC, Grosner I (org) (2023) Série Direito e Política Espacial: volume 1: Direito Espacial Internacional: contextualizado e comentado. Dialética. São Paulo

Grosner I et al (2022) What is Brazil doing to develop its commercial space program? In: Froehlich A (ed) Space Fostering Latin American Societies. Springer, Chan, pp 1–26

Grosner I et al (2023) The New Brazilian National Programme of Space Activities – PNAE (2022-2031): what to expect. In: Blount PJ et al (eds) Proceedings of the International Institute of Space Law 2022. Eleven, The Hague, pp 507–519

Moraes RV, Chiaradia APM (2007) Instituições e agências brasileiras. In: Winter OC, Prado AFBA (orgs) A conquista do espaço: do Sputnik à Missão Centenário, São Paulo, Livraria do Físico, pp 123–149

SBDA. https://sbda.org.br/historico/

UN A/AC.105/1285 (2023) Report of the Legal Subcommittee on its sixty-second session, held in Vienna from 20 to 31 March 2023. United Nations

US Embassy. Brazil is the first Country in Latin America to sign the Artemis Accords (2021). https://br.usembassy.gov/brazil-is-the-first-country-in-latin-america-to-sign-the-artemis-accords/#:~:text=

Chile

Victoria Valdivia

Contents

V. Valdivia (✉)
Universidad de Santiago de Chile , Santiago, Chile

Global Fellow, European Space Policy Institute, Vienna, Austria
e-mail: victoria.valdivia@espi.global

I. Grosner (ed.), *Space Regulation in Latin America*, Space Regulations Library 11, https://doi.org/10.1007/978-3-032-05828-7_5

Abstract Chile's space history began in 1958 and has evolved into a complex dynamic over the years. Early engagement in space activities laid the foundation for the development of robust capabilities, particularly in space diplomacy. However, the country has faced significant challenges in establishing a cohesive national space structure that supports the development of sustainable, long-term space programs. These challenges have directly impacted the decision-making process, including the regulation of national space activities. Despite early achievements, the lack of a consolidated national framework has hindered the ability to advance and sustain comprehensive space initiatives. This paper explores the evolution of Chile's space capabilities, the difficulties encountered in creating a unified space infrastructure, and the implications for national policy and regulation. By examining these factors, this chapter aims to provide insights into how Chile can overcome current obstacles and enhance its space program's effectiveness and sustainability

1 Introduction

Chile's involvement in space activities can be traced back to 1958, with the establishment of a collaboration agreement with the United States as part of the "Minitrack Network" project. This initiative saw the deployment of a tracking station in the Metropolitan Region, just a few kilometers from Santiago, the country's capital. While the Chilean government played a key role in formalizing this agreement, it appears that Chile was selected for the station's location due, in part, to the strong ties between the Chilean Instituto Geográfico Militar (Military Geographic Institute) and the United States. These ties were characterized by extensive collaboration in the field of cartography, including the introduction of aerophotogrammetry and the production of Chile's first satellite maps in 1978, with a particular focus on the Austral-Antarctic region.[1]

Following the initiation of the Minitrack Network project, Chile's defense sector, especially the Army, began developing space-related capabilities to support routine operations. Given that these developments occurred during the early stages of the global space race—amid the Cold War—it is logical to consider how traditional concepts of hard power, geopolitics, and national security were inherently

[1] Pinto and Meza (2023).

connected to these activities.[2] The strategic implications of outer space, particularly for national defense, became increasingly evident, leading to the creation of the Advisory Committee on Outer Space Affairs under the Ministry of Defense in 1975. This committee reflected Chile's early recognition of the geostrategic importance of outer space, contextualized within the structural transformation of the international system and a period of national development driven by the pressures of international sanctions. In this sense, being exposed to the benefits of space technologies and the regional strategic competition for their development—closely linked to bilateral tensions and crises over territorial issues—it became evident that Chile needed to develop its own indigenous space capabilities.[3]

Therefore, since 1975 and throughout the 1980s, several Advisory Committees on Outer Space Affairs were created under the Ministry of Defense. These committees functioned as a pre–space agency, bringing together the intersectoral efforts that the State had been developing since 1958 in the field of outer space activities. Evidently, given the geopolitical context of the time—marked by international crises and a growing sense of uncertainty regarding national security, with two potential conflicts involving the borders with Peru and Argentina—the main concern was closely tied to defense activities. In particular, the aim was to establish mechanisms of control to prevent any violation of national sovereignty by states possessing space capabilities. To this end, the Committee was established as a Joint and Interagency Body, involving the Army, Navy, and Air Force, as well as academia, the industrial sector, and the Ministry of Foreign Affairs, with the mandate to: (1) propose a national space policy; (2) define the structure and organization of a National Space Committee; and (3) advise the President of the Republic, General Augusto Pinochet, on all scientific, diplomatic, industrial, and technological applications of outer space activities.The formation of those committees was likely influenced by several factors, including Chile's exposure to the strategic applications of space technology during the 1978 Beagle Channel crisis with Argentina. During this conflict, remote sensing played a crucial role in providing intelligence and situational awareness.[4] Additionally, Chile's long-standing engagement in space diplomacy, beginning with its participation in the 1967 Outer Space Treaty,[5] underscores the nation's commitment to the peaceful and strategic use of space.

Thereby, the diplomatic involvement of Chile begun on the preliminary talks that conducted to the creation of the Commission for Peaceful Uses of Outer Space (COPUOS) and in the formulation of the Space Treaty of 1967, probably as a consequence of the country's active involvement during the International Geophysics Year celebrated during 1957–1958 and its extensive experience within the Antarctic

---

[2] Valdivia (2020a).

[3] Valdivia (2016b).

[4] González (2023).

[5] Treaty on Principles Governing the Activities of States in the Exploration and Use of Outer Space, including the Moon and Other Celestial Bodies, 1967, G.A. Resolution 2222 (XXI), https://www.unoosa.org/oosa/en/ourwork/spacelaw/treaties/outerspacetreaty.html.

Treaty System, a model that has inspired the formulation of the Outer Space Treaty and some aspects on its multilateral governance.[6]

With 66 years of tradition in space law and diplomacy, Chile has consolidated an accurate space political behavior turning itself into a trustable space player and—despite the few space projects developed—into a relevant space player in the South American region.

After the end of the Cold War, during the "Pax Americana" period, space technologies have been massified, as part of the globalization processes, decreasing access barriers to services, data, and platforms. Following the global tendency, the decrease of uncertainty and conflictive perception in the international arena quickly produces the transference of knowledge and technologies from defense sector to civilians (Valdivia 2020b), incentivizing the participation of civilian programs and, slowly, the creation of private space activities. Currently, following the end of the Pax Americana, the international liberal order faces multiple challenges, including a crisis of multilateralism and the emergence of strategic competition among international actors—extending even to outer space activities. This phenomenon has generated a unique moment in which civilian and state activities in space increasingly overlap and mutually influence one another in the pursuit of strategic objectives. For civilian actors, space has become a domain linked to economic and educational opportunities, while for states, it remains a key arena for defining international order and, consequently, global power structures. This evolving context has also renewed the interest of both established and emerging space powers, blending elements of soft power, smart power, and, at times, hard power, and thereby contributing to a more complex and volatile space environment.[7]

During this same process, Chile launched its first satellite "FASAT- Alpha," being the beginning of the national satellite project under the umbrella of Minister of Defense in Chile and as a joint initiative that would complete its third platform in 2011 (FASAT-C component of the "Sistema Satelital de Observación de la Tierra" or SSOT); in addition, the defense institutions—such as the Army and the Navy—have developed their own specialized services in critical segments of outer space activities. An example of this is the Army's Satellite Space Operations Center, which contributes to a permanent and evolving infrastructure of national space capabilities. Likewise, several civilian institutions and public services have begun to develop space-related capacities linked to their operational needs. These include, for instance, the use of satellite imagery for homeland security by the Chilean police forces (Carabineros de Chile and the Investigative Police, PDI), applications within the agricultural sector, and environmental monitoring conducted by entities such as CIREN (the Natural Resources Information Center of the Ministry of Agriculture), among others. In parallel, the academic sector begun with the creation of academic offer in several areas, such as remote sensing, aerospace engineering, and scientific

[6] Valdivia (2024a).

[7] Valdivia (2024b).

disciplines derived from the geosciences area: contributing to creating a working force mostly in the area of enginery.

Nowadays, Chile faces a significant imbalance between the limited job opportunities in the national space sector and the growing pool of qualified professionals, primarily in engineering. Despite this growing talent base, Chile still lacks a national space agency or a formal organizational structure to coordinate and lead its space activities. This absence generates significant challenges and risks for national security, further widening the gap between the country's existing capabilities and global advancements in space situational awareness. Moreover, the emergence of unregulated actors within the national space arena—engaging in international activities on behalf of the State without a clear mandate or institutional linkage—reflects an "emptiness of power" resulting from the lack of regulatory frameworks and the absence of a coherent and functional state body for outer space affairs. This, combined with the still-evolving nature of the national space policy, adds an additional layer of complexity to the overall governance landscape.

Chile is thus positioned at a critical juncture, marked by the deregulation of space activities, the rise of third-party actors, and the pressures of the rapidly growing "new space" industry. This is all unfolding amid increasing international uncertainty and an urgent need to reinforce global principles governing outer space activities. Given Chile's long-standing tradition of space diplomacy, strengthening these principles aligns closely with the nation's interests.

2 Topics

Chile presents a dual image regarding space activities. On the one hand, the country demonstrates strong capabilities in space diplomacy, actively participating in multilateral and international forums and leading various initiatives. On the other hand, it faces significant challenges in designing, consolidating, and implementing a long-term, sustainable space program. This duality creates cognitive dissonance, affecting the decision-making process and the potential engagement of national stakeholders. Consequently, space remains a highly specialized field dominated by space engineering, with limited space for interdisciplinary contributions. This isolation of the "space community" has led to centrifugal processes, resulting in significant inconsistencies in developing functional ecosystems, despite the presence of necessary actors.

This paradox in the Chilean context stems from the historical framework of national space activities. Influenced by external drivers such as the Cold War, international sanctions over the country, bilateral crisis and the uncertainty characteristic of transitional times at international Order. Chile's early approach to outer space was predominantly shaped by a securitized perspective, emphasizing activities perceived as potential threats to national sovereignty—such as the exploitation of space capabilities by adversarial states—rather than by a developmental or problem-solving rationale. This security-centered orientation, rooted in geopolitical tensions and

A/AC.105/C.2/2025/CRP.9

State, area or organization	United Nations treaties (1) 1967 OST	(2) 1968 ARRA	(3) 1972 LIAB	(4) 1975 REG	(5) 1979 MOON	Other agreements (6) 1963 NTB	(7) 1974 BRS	(8) 1971 ITSO	(9) 1971 INTR	(10) 1975 ESA	(11) 1976 ARB	(12) 1976 INTC	(13) 1976 IMSO	(14) 1982 EUTL	(15) 1983 EUM	(16) 1992 ITU
Cameroon	S	R				S		R					R			R
Canada	R	R	R	R		R		R		b			R			R
Cape Verde						R		R								R
Central African Republic	S		S			R		R								R
Chad						R		R								R
Chile	R	R	R	R	R	R	R	R					R			R
China	R	R	R	R		R		R					R			R
Colombia	R	S	R	R		R	R	R					R			R
Comoros								R					R			R
Congo								R								R

Fig. 1 Status of international agreements relating to activities in outer space (UNOOSA 2004)

the legacy of territorial disputes, constrained the formulation of a broader vision of space as a tool for national development and public policy innovation. Consequently, the establishment of comprehensive national strategies, planning frameworks, and long-term programs in space affairs was delayed, reinforcing institutional fragmentation and limiting the country's strategic autonomy in this domain. This misalignment is evident in the low priority given to space issues in political statements and decisions. For example, the creation of a national authority to govern space activities has remained an incomplete task for 44 years. This absence has also led to a diminished perception of the social profitability of national space activities and raised questions about political decisions, particularly concerning state investment in projects perceived by society as nonessential for their well-being and daily life.[8]

2.1 *Which International Space Treaties Has Chile Signed as a Party?*

With a strong tradition in space law, Chile has ratified the entire *corpus iuris spatialis*, which is composed of 16 binding international instruments, as indicated in the UNOOSA report, *Status of International Agreements Relating to Activities in Outer Space* (as of January 1, 2024; see Fig. 1).

[8]As demonstrated by the very low societal participation in public consultation processes (https://minciencia.gob.cl/noticias/informe-ejecutivo-conoce-los-resultados-del-proceso-de-consulta-ciudadana-para-la-actualizacion-de-la-politica-nacional-espacial/), such as the one conducted in 2022 regarding the proposal for a new space policy formulation, there is a significant issue. In this process, fewer than 30 individuals responded to the survey out of a population of 18 million. Of those respondents, nearly 90% were affiliated with ACHIDE, a private organization hired to conduct certain tasks related to the process. This situation makes it impossible to validate the sample and highlights the almost negligible interest of the general public in space activities.

It is also important to highlight the active role of Ambassador Raimundo González-Aninat, a key figure in the development of space law in Chile. Ambassador González played a pivotal role during the codification of several international instruments, such as the Moon Agreement in 1979.

2.2 *Is Chile a Member of COPUOS?*

In line with its long-standing tradition of space diplomacy and early involvement in the movements that led to the creation of COPUOS, Chile became a member of the committee on December 18, 1973, following the adoption of United Nations General Assembly Resolution A/RES/3182 (1973).

Since joining, Chile has played a pivotal role within COPUOS, under the leadership of Ministery of Foreign Affairs, holding positions such as chair and vice chair while also leading numerous international and regional initiatives. These include efforts within COPUOS itself, as well as collaborations with other UN bodies. Notable initiatives include Chile's recent contributions to protecting dark and quiet skies, under the dram of COPUOS agenda item; its participation in the Open-Ended Working Group on Reducing Space Threats through Norms, Rules, and Principles of Responsible Behaviours (OEWG PAROS), and the Space Conference of the Americas. Additionally, Chile has actively supported various nonbinding initiatives and working groups, all aimed at strengthening the principles of international space activities, enhancing space governance, and promoting the peaceful and resilient use of outer space. In this sense, the work carried out by Chile's space diplomacy sector has been consistently aligned with the country's foreign policy objectives, reflecting a coherent and long-standing commitment to international cooperation. Chilean ambassadors, like Ambassador Lagos and Ambassador Cousiño, and diplomats have played an essential role in this regard, demonstrating notable leadership and professionalism in multilateral forums. Their sustained engagement has not only ensured Chile's active participation in the formulation of global space governance but has also strengthened the country's image as a reliable, principled, and constructive actor within the international community—one firmly grounded in respect for international law and in the fulfillment of its commitments.

2.3 *Has Chile Signed the Artemis Accords?*

Regarding the long space law and policy background of Chile, the Artemis Accords have been a long-term debate at the level of national stakeholders. Due to its nature, the Artemis Accords (AA) demanded a complete review of the aspect of the space political behaviors[9] of the state, to reduce the possibilities of creating cognitive

[9] Valdivia (2023).

dissonance and potential contractions with the international commitments adopted by Chile along the space law history.

The discussion, which has taken over 2 years to reach a final decision, has received a positive endorsement from the "Consejo de Ministros en Materia Espacial" (Space Ministries Council), an advisory body that includes all ministries and state secretariats involved in space affairs.[10] Despite the outcome of the national debate regarding potential interactions with the Moon Agreement, Chile remains committed to endorsing the peaceful use of outer space and seeks to achieve international consensus on future regulatory norms for celestial mining and the establishment of colonies on celestial bodies, including the Moon.

Particularly on the foresight for space/celestial mining, it is in the Chilean interest to be an active part of the coming debates about future regulations on this activity, even more considering that the main economic activity of the country is settled at the mining activity of copper, being the major component of the national GDP.[11] In this sense, the future of space/celestial mining would impact over the future of the Chilean economy and through it, the development factors and possibilities of future generations of Chileans, a very sensitive aspect to consider under the considerations of the principles contended into the Outer Space Treaty 1967.

Finally, on October 25, 2024, Chile has signed the Artemis Accords with NASA, with the presence of the current national Ministry of Science, endorsing the principle of pacific uses of outer space and the protection of space heritage, particularly on space sustainability emerging concerns and the preservation of celestial bodies' environment.

2.4 *Can Space Activities be Classified as Dual Use, or Are They Only for Defense or Civil Purposes?*

Regarding the historical development of space capabilities in the national context, Chile's space program can be primarily classified as dual use, encompassing both civilian and military capabilities. However, the situation is more complex than the straightforward international distinctions typically made.

As a developing country, Chile faces several challenges in advancing its space capabilities. These challenges arise from a combination of public concerns, which demand state investment in addressing basic needs such as access to essential services and the need for technological investment to address the geographic challenges posed by the country's extensive length and its tri-continental presence, including the Chilean Antarctic Territory. Additionally, Chile's national

[10] Jerez (2024).

[11] The mining sector in Chile accounted for approximately 13.6% of the country's gross domestic product (GDP) in 2022 (Garside 2024).

geomorphology creates isolated areas and extreme environments, complicating efforts to maintain accurate levels of national connectivity and access to public services.

Moreover, frequent natural disasters exacerbate the tension between public concerns—such as the need for immediate shelter and rebuilding after major events like earthquakes, floods, and fires—and long-term planning processes. These disasters drive rapid responses from stakeholders and decision-makers, often leading to a focus on short-term solutions due to the urgency of emerging public needs.

In the context of Chile's space capabilities development, the introduction of space technologies initially appeared to offer a broad solution to several public concerns that were prominent on the national agenda. These technologies promised more effective solutions through innovation and capability building. However, during the early decades of human space activities, the high costs of access to space limited the available options for benefiting from these advancements (Valdivia 2016a). Consequently, the initial engagement with space technologies came primarily from the military sector. Beyond the historical context of the Cold War and global polarization, the Chilean military has played a versatile role, responding to various situations beyond its traditional functions, particularly in emergency and disaster response.

Following the engagement with the Minitrack Network, and likely driven by geopolitical and strategic awareness of the potential of space, the development of space capabilities remained within the defense sector. This sector adopted a comprehensive approach, involving the Navy and Air Force in the vision for national space capabilities. Programs such as FASAT have aimed to create knowledge and technological development, focusing on dual-use services like remote sensing. These capabilities have been extensively utilized in situations related to the "estados de excepción constitucional" (constitutional exception status /CES), where national security, civil population, or infrastructure is critically jeopardized by disasters, conflicts, or crises, requiring immediate state action.

In the area of education and training for space activities, the "Academia Nacional de Estudios Políticos y Estratégicos" (ANEPE) has played a central role in promoting the principles of outer space activities among future operators and users. Under the leadership of Navy Colonel Karel Blaha, ANEPE has modernized postgraduate diplomas and introduced a diploma program in "aerospace studies," covering space policies, law, technology analysis, space systems, and counterspace analysis. This initiative has extended to the training of foreign students from Brazil, Paraguay, and Nigeria, contributing to the development of space education at national, regional, and international levels.

Simultaneously, during the 1980s, civilian society also began to play a role in shaping a national ecosystem for space capability development. Encouraged by a vision of generating skilled workers and scientists for indigenous space platforms, the state supported early engagement with academia, notably the Universidad de Chile at the Peldehue facility where the Minitrack Network operated. This collaboration led to significant knowledge transfer, particularly through cooperation with NASA.

Following the success of Universidad de Chile, other universities joined in establishing space studies programs, predominantly in engineering and technology, reflecting the early focus on space activities within universities.

Space law and diplomacy have traditionally been managed by the Ministry of Foreign Affairs, which has been central in regulating national space activities and maintaining connections with the emerging space sector. The Ministry's role has been crucial in fulfilling international commitments under the corpus iuris spatialis, including the registration convention. This responsibility extends to raising awareness among new operators, such as universities involved in satellite activities in low Earth orbit (LEO). The Ministry has also facilitated various national-level collaborations, including AMERIGEOS and the GEOS group.

From 2010 to 2020—and continuing to the present—new actors, including the Ministry of Science, Technology, and Innovation, regional governments, private sector entities, and universities such as DUOC UC, have become increasingly involved in space-related activities, particularly in the fields of outreach and science communication. Between 2014 and 2023, Chile's active participation in World Space Week—an annual global celebration held from October 4 to October 10, established by United Nations General Assembly Resolution No. 54/68, adopted on December 6, 1999—has been made possible through the voluntary leadership of its National Coordinators, Mg. Victoria Valdivia (2014–2017; 2017–2023) and Mg. Franco Orellana Walden (2017–2020). Together with a national coordination team composed of volunteers from diverse institutions, they ensured Chile's sustained engagement with the World Space Week Association and the organization of major national events each year. This continued commitment enabled a series of landmark initiatives, including the first 21st-century space-related transmission broadcast live from the Chilean Army's Antarctic Base "General B. O'Higgins R.", which reached over 1,200 students across continental Chile, demonstrating the value of space-based communications in supporting Antarctic science and peace. Another notable example was the first event held from Easter Island, connecting local students with international space professionals through coordination with the Rapa Nui Planetarium, a private institution. Over the years, an expanding network of organizations and civil actors has joined these initiatives, reinforcing Chile's growing culture of public participation in space. In this context, individual actors—including space professionals and astronomy experts—have played a decisive role in promoting societal engagement with outer space. Among these, the ShakthiSAT mission stands out as a pioneering initiative, providing girls with free, certified training in space engineering through a collaboration between an individual space professional and the non-governmental organization SpaceKidz India. This initiative has contributed to strengthening STEM education and inspiring a new generation of young women to pursue careers in the space sector.

In 2025, the Chilean Army inaugurated the "Satellite Operations Center of the Army" (Centro de Operaciones del Ejército), a collaborative initiative that supports emergency organizations during situations that threaten human security, such as major disasters. Building on its long-standing tradition in communications, this center is pioneering the ability to maintain satellite communication (SATCOM) capabilities across the Army's area of responsibility. This is a crucial support for scientific development in regions like Antarctica and contributes to military operations other than war (MOOTW) aimed at national development. Therefore, although the capability falls under the defense sector, its operational benefits are designed to support national development goals.

Thus, the development of space capabilities in Chile involves a three-pronged approach: technical capabilities for national emergencies managed by the Ministry of Defense; space law, diplomacy, and policy led by the Ministry of Foreign Affairs; and civilian capabilities represented by educational NGO, natural person leaded initiatives and academic initiatives. Under this framework, all space activities conducted in Chile are characterized by dual-use capabilities.

2.5 *Is There a Registry of Space Objects Maintained by the United Nations?*

Regarding the Convention on Registration of Objects Launched into Outer Space (Registration Convention), which Chile adopted in 1975, all space objects launched on behalf of Chile must be registered with the United Nations. Currently, the national register includes three satellites from the FASat program (Alpha, Bravo, and Charlie) and four satellites from the Universidad de Chile's project (Suchai I, II, III, and PlantSat).[12] According to the Registration Convention, only registered platforms recognized by the Chilean State are considered national space platforms, and the state holds recognized liability for them. Consequently, the FASat-D satellite, which is not registered by Chile, is considered to belong to a third state (which has registered it), according to publicly available information on the UNOOSA online register index.

2.6 *Does Chile Have a National Specific Space Act or Regulations?*

Despite its long tradition in outer space activities, Chile does not have a specific space law to comprehensively regulate national space activities. Although Chile has adhered to various norms at specific historical periods, such as Ministerial Orders governing the operation of FASat-Charlie and coordinating space activities within the Ministry of Defense, there is no overarching legislation.

Despite the incorporation of international treaties, such as the corpus iuris spatialis, into Chilean law, there remains a significant gap between the development of space-related projects and the ability to codify national laws to regulate this emerging economic, scientific, technological, and societal sector.

---

[12] UNOOSA (s/f).

In terms of specific regulations, Chile has seen more advanced regulation in the area of geodata, particularly with the "Ley IDE" (Proposed Law for Geospatial Data Infrastructure), led by the Servicio Nacional de Información Territorial (SNIT). However, despite notable advances in intersectoral use and production of geoinformation, standardization of data and metadata, and the creation of GIS systems, there is still no specific law to regulate the integration and standardization of geoinformation produced by national entities.

Regarding space policies, although mandated since 1980, the first formal space policy was only developed in 2014. This policy has been a valuable instrument due to the previous lack of public concern and the absence of a national strategy for space activities. From a sectoral perspective, space has been included in defense sector policies through the Defense White Papers since 1997. However, only the 2017 Defense White Paper addressed space from a meta-territorial perspective, recognizing its broader strategic importance beyond remote sensing for defense purposes. This perspective was further refined in the 2020 National Defense Policy, which regarded space as a critical dimension for all national defense institutions, moving beyond the traditional focus on satellite operators (Valdivia 2019).

In 2022, the Ministry of Science and Technology made another attempt to formalize a national space policy. However, this new document reiterates the methodological issues identified by specialists in 2014. Additionally, the public consultation process has been criticized for low engagement and involvement from the same individuals who proposed the text. The document was published in July 2025 and, as expected, highlights a lack of attention on the public issue agenda and an understanding of the outer space arena. This deficiency is linked to inadequate methodologies in space policy, led by operators without the participation of civil society, creating a false representation of interest in this activity. Additionally, the complex political environment, especially toward the end of Boric's administration with only 6 months remaining until the presidential election, suggests that this document is unlikely to effect any significant change or address unresolved social issues.

Most regulations in Chile have taken the form of decrees or presidential orders that establish advisory committees. However, these committees have not functioned effectively over the past 60 years. As a result, there is a lack of regulation in this area, indicating limited capacity to integrate space activities as a normalized aspect of state action and administration. Moreover, it is important to note that outer space is not considered a public issue or an independent topic on the national agenda. Instead, it is viewed as part of broader state activities, similar to other issues that the government addresses, but it is not regarded as a strategic or key area of focus.

2.7 *Does Chile Have a Space Agency?*

The creation of a national space agency has been on Chile's public agenda since 1975, with severals advisory councils repeatedly tasked with exploring this possibility. However, to this day, Chile does not have a dedicated space agency or a national authority with similar rank or functions. Instead, Chile has adopted an intersectoral coordination model as a transitional approach, with several ministries holding specific responsibilities related to outer space. For instance, the Ministry of Foreign Affairs is responsible for Chile's international representation in multilateral space forums; the Ministry of Defense has historically overseen the operation of certain space platforms and the utilization of space assets for defense purposes; and the Ministry of Science, Knowledge, and Technology shares responsibility for supervising national space activities in coordination with the Ministries of Foreign Affairs, Defense, and Transport and Telecommunications.

As a result of this fragmented approach, multiple entities in Chile have emerged, sometimes leading actions in determined areas of the space sector. This lack of a cohesive vision for space benefits has contributed to a "vacancy phenomenon" in space activities. Over the past 67 years, various individuals and civil organizations have attempted to position themselves as the national space authority or even self-designated as a "space agency," despite the absence of such an institution. One notable example is the Advisory Commission on Space Activities, which was established in 2012 to provide input on Chile's future space activities, including defining a national space policy and proposing a national space agency. This "committee" adopted the title "space agency," which was more symbolic than substantive. It was dissolved in 2014 and replaced by a new advisory commission, now known as the "Council of Ministries for Space and Digital Development," tasked with defining national space policy and proposing the structure and functions of a potential national space agency.

The lack of a formalized space authority has impacted Chile's ability to integrate and coordinate both national and international cooperation, delaying the country's potential to capitalize on emerging opportunities in the new space economy.

Currently, Chile has an advisory board led by the Ministry of Foreign Affairs, but it is not a space agency. Similarly, the "executive secretariat" of the Ministry of Defense is not the national authority on space activities; it functions as a coordination body for outer space activities related to the Ministry of Defense, including managing Chilean space platforms during constitutional exception status (CES) or emergencies.

Therefore, the absence of a national authority—whether a space agency or a similar organization—has created challenges, including the risk of third-party organizations, such as nongovernmental organizations (NGOs) or other civil society groups, taking advantage of or usurping functions traditionally associated with a national space agency. This lack of control over such representations, particularly overseas, underscores the need for a formal national space authority.

2.8 *What Is the Primary Regulatory Body Responsible for Overseeing Space Activities?*

According to Decree No. 24/2022, the main regulatory body overseeing space activities in Chile is the Consejo de Ministros en Materias Espaciales (Council of Ministries on Space Affairs). This council is made up of six state secretariats:

Interior and Public Security, Foreign Affairs, National Defense, Transport and Telecommunications, National Assets, and Science, Technology, Knowledge, and Innovation.

The council oversees sectoral advisory boards, such as the Comité Ejecutivo Espacial (Space Executive Committee) within the Ministry of Defense. However, this committee is not a permanent fixture. It serves as a consultative body rather than a decision-making authority. The council provides advice but does not have the power to make decisions regarding funding, project execution, program approval, or the establishment of laws and policies.

2.9 *What Are the Primary Regulations Governing Space Activities, and How Are Private Companies Performing Space Activities Authorized, Monitored, and Supervised?*

The primary regulations governing space activities in Chile are derived from international space treaties that have been incorporated into national law. According to the principles outlined in the corpus iuris spatialis, all space activities conducted on behalf of Chile, as well as those occurring within its territory, must adhere to these principles, such as the peaceful use of outer space.

Due to the absence of dedicated national space regulations, there are currently no specific rules governing private space activities. Consequently, private entities involved in space activities are regulated in the same manner as other businesses in Chile, primarily with respect to tax regulations and general legal aspects of their operations.

2.10 *Is There Any Effort Toward Capacity Building in the Space Sector, Both in Terms of Technologies and Regulatory Matters?*

Actually, in Chile, there are several initiatives driven by individuals who are working to build capabilities and raise awareness about the country's need for space development. One of the most impactful is the ShakthiSAT mission—an international endeavor aiming to train 12,000 girls from 108 countries in STEM and the fundamentals of space activities, culminating in the collaborative construction of a CubeSat to be launched into lunar orbit in 2026.

The ambassador for Chile is Victoria Valdivia, and the initiative currently includes 17 Chilean girls who are actively involved. A key factor in enabling this participation has been the support of the Regional Secretariat of Science and Technology (SEREMI) for the Austral Macrozone, especially since Chile contributes with the southernmost group of students taking part in this global effort that brings together astronauts, stakeholders, and space professionals from around the world.

Also, there are several initiatives regarding the development of future space security specialists. Particularly in space law and policies, the Universidad Católica del Maule is collaborating with the United Nations Institute for Disarmament Research (UNIDIR) on a research project led by Victoria Valdivia. This project aims to establish a network of specialists in space security and safety.

Moreover, the Academia Nacional de Estudios Políticos y Estratégicos (ANEPE) offers annual courses on space policy, space law, space systems, and counterspace analysis through its postgraduate programs. These courses are enriched by specialist lectures on various aspects of space activities, exposing students, both civilian and military, to major international trends in outer space dynamics.

Finally, at the school level, there is a national NGO, MARTEENS, which for the past 10 years has been providing extracurricular activities for children in low-income areas, teaching STEM through role-playing as aspiring "astronauts." This NGO has participated in several national initiatives and, over the years, has developed educational programs and research that validates its educational model.

2.11 How Does Chile Engage in International Cooperation in the Space Sector, Both in Terms of Technologies and Representation in International Organizations? Are There Any Partnerships with Other Latin American Countries?

Chile engages internationally through the Ministry of Foreign Affairs and its dedicated offices, such as the "Dirección de Seguridad Internacional y Humana" (DISIN) and the "División de Ciencias, Energía, Educación, Innovación y Astronomía" (DECITY). As with all international cooperation involving the state, agreements impacting national actions must be managed through these ministries.

In international organizations, Chile's official national delegation is led by the official representative of Chile in that organization, who is a member of the Chilean diplomatic corps. Depending on the subject, specialists with proven expertise may also be included in the delegation.

Chile currently holds several partnerships for space activities with regional countries, including a bilateral agreement with Brazil. Additionally, Chile is a member of various regional and multilateral organizations, such as the International Astronautical Federation (Latin America and Caribbean subcommittee), COPUOS (group of Latin America and the Caribbean), AMERIGEOS, and GEOS, among others.

2.12 How Does the Private Sector Conduct Its Activities in the Field of Space Exploration?

There is no evidence of such activities in Chile. The closest related activity might be the training of analog astronauts, conducted abroad by individuals. However, these activities do not create or consolidate capabilities at either the national or international level. They are typically individual pursuits akin to extreme outdoor or tourism activities, rather than being part of a scientific or training program within the framework of a space program. The most notable emerging development that could signify a shift in this regard is the case of Matilde Gate, a Chilean student currently participating in a NASA training program, aspiring to become the first Chilean woman astronaut.

2.13 What Are the Plans for Space Activities in Chile? Are Manned Flights and Spaceports Being Planned?

There is no evidence of such activities in Chile.

2.14 What Are (and Should Be) the Perspectives of Chile on Regulatory Matters Related to Space Debris, Militarization and Weaponization of Space, and Exploitation of Space Natural Resources?

As the space domain becomes increasingly competitive and congested, the proliferation of space debris is leading to a rise in both controlled and uncontrolled reentries. This escalation poses significant risks to natural ecosystems, critical infrastructure, and civil society, heightening hazards and challenges for both international and human security. For Chile, given its extensive territorial reach and high latitudes, this issue is of particular concern. The entire national territory frequently falls within reentry windows. Additionally, Chile's natural connection to the Antarctic environment heightens its vulnerability. Space debris, accumulating at locations like Point Nemo, has the potential to impact the Antarctic Circumpolar Current and various coastal ecosystems, posing threats to human security, among other concerns.[13] Moreover, the use of counterspace capabilities has led to substantial amounts of space debris. If these activities are not classified as operations

[13] Valdivia (2024c).

involving new types of weapons, they still impact the conduct of space operations and the functionality of space platform.[14]

The growing militarization of outer space necessitates regulatory measures to govern the use of force and engagement rules in space activities to prevent harm to civilian populations. Chile's reliance on space-based data and information underscores the need for robust regulations governing the presence and military use of outer space. It is crucial to adopt binding norms to prevent the weaponization of space and the deployment of weapon systems that could affect space platforms from Earth. This is vital for international security and safety and to mitigate the creation of additional space debris, which directly impacts the oceanic environment.

Consequently, emerging trends in space security and sustainability demand proactive engagement from states, especially those directly affected. Chile should focus on advancing national legislation to regulate outer space activities, establishing a functional framework to address national security challenges arising from space activities and international interactions. This includes adopting emergency protocols and gathering scientific evidence to support decision-making and policy formulation based on data.

2.15 *Other Relevant Topics*

Space activities in Chile remain an unfinished task. Over the years, rapid technological advancements and technology-based solutions have widened the gap between regulations and emerging trends, necessitating significant flexibility from the state to address these challenges and reduce uncertainty. To achieve this, it is crucial to establish a national authority capable of overseeing, supervising, and regulating space activities. Such an authority would align its commitments with national interests and political objectives, thereby enhancing Chile's international image.

Given the pressing need for a national space law, the development of a sustainable, long-term, and efficient space program must be grounded in Chile's public concerns regarding space. Without this foundational context, space projects risk being ineffectual and failing to address public issues, thus limiting their social impact.

As space becomes increasingly complex, congested, and competitive, emerging threats and hazards, such as counterspace capabilities, pose risks to international security. These developments can lead to new phenomena, such as diminished civilian connectivity due to conflicts in other regions on Earth, potentially affecting critical services vital to human life. The cross-domain nature of outer space amplifies its strategic importance, necessitating a proactive approach to mitigate negative effects on populations. While no single country can solve these issues alone, effective

[14] Óp. Cit Valdivia (2024a).

collaboration begins with a comprehensive understanding of current activities and their national consequences.

In this context, the development of space capabilities should adopt a holistic approach, incorporating technical, legal, policy, diplomatic, educational, communication, and outreach aspects. Given Chile's limited number of highly skilled space professionals, it is essential to attract and retain talent to transfer experience and knowledge to new generations, inspiring them to contribute to the national space sector. A functional space ecosystem could foster innovative solutions and attract international expertise, particularly in critical areas such as disaster response. However, the sustainability of this ecosystem over time is crucial for adding value to ongoing activities.

Chile's unique natural laboratories, such as its dark and quiet skies, Antarctic territory, and the Atacama Desert, enhance its relevance to international space actors. As demand grows for locations to test space technologies—particularly those related to human presence on celestial bodies—Chile's Austral territories become increasingly attractive. Dark and quiet skies are essential for both astronomical research and ground control of space missions, including satellite tracking and deep space exploration. The high latitudes of Chile, especially the Austral-Antarctic region, are well suited to enhance the resilience of polar orbit space operations. Moreover, the potential for reduced cloud cover due to climate change is drawing interest to Chile's southern territories, which may see increased involvement from space and astronomical programs.

This underscores the need for strong protection of Antarctica's dark skies, both through national legislation and by advocating for an addendum to the Antarctic Treaty's environmental protocol. Such measures would aim to mitigate the impacts of major facilities in protected areas and prevent international disputes or competitive tensions.

In this vein, during the 67th session of the United Nations Committee on the Peaceful Uses of Outer Space, held in Vienna, the Chilean Mission to international organizations based in the city organized a presentation titled "Preserving Dark and Quiet Skies: Responsible Practices for Science and Development within the Framework of APEP-Space." This discussion aimed to promote the protection of dark and quiet skies.[15]

3 Final Remarks

Outer space has long been a source of inspiration and evolution for humankind, driving innovation and transforming our understanding of the universe. The stars and the mysteries of space have fueled a continuous quest for knowledge and technological advancement.

---

[15] Minrel (2024).

From the outset, human space activities have been characterized by their cross-sectoral benefits, influencing various dimensions of state power. The development of outer space activities has consistently been intertwined with policies, regulations, and societal impacts—reflecting the broader ways in which power is manifested. Moreover, as societies engage with space technologies, these activities often become intertwined with public concerns. Therefore, the creation of space capabilities encompasses more than just engineering or technical skills; it involves a broader scope that integrates multiple facets of society.

To fully grasp the evolution of space activities within a country and assess the scope of its space sector, it is crucial to understand its historical development and contextualize it accordingly. There is no uniform trajectory for space activities, even among countries within the same regional area or those sharing cultural similarities such as language. This is evident in Latin America, where diverse incentives and approaches to space development reflect a rich tapestry of regional heterogeneity.

In the specific case of Chile, its early involvement in space activities appears logical as it stems from a mix of international interest—due to its geographical conditions and particularities—and close collaboration with the United States during the Cold War. As a Latin American country historically influenced by the United States, Chile's geographical advantages for space activities helped initiate its involvement in the field, making it one of the few countries in the region engaged in interdisciplinary space activities for decades. However, this same driver, which integrated outer space activities into state functions, has not been driven by societal demands or evolving needs. As a result, it has not reached its full potential, leading to several challenges and incomplete processes, such as the development of a national regulatory framework.

The slow development of national space regulations can be majorly explained by the major difficulties in adopting a national space authority, potentially due to the incidence of difficulties during the 1970s–1990s, including the impact of bilateral tensions, natural disasters, internal crises, etc. Despite those variables impacting over the decision-making process, there have been some advances in the technical area of space activities, particularly in the formulation of projects and adoption of space capabilities, like the three national satellites belonging to the FASat project and the inclusion of universities with their own research projects.

The early exploitation of the benefits of space, like remote sensing, has reinforced the use of space for national situations, like major disasters or issues linked with national security, as has been demonstrated in 1978 during the collaboration received in the context of the crisis with Argentina.

However, with the end of the Cold War and the Pax Americana decade, space activities shifted from almost exclusive state participation to include other actors such as NGOs, universities, and private entities. This shift consolidated several changes within the space industry and ecosystem. These changes occurred while Chile was attempting to establish its initial framework and mindset on space activities. Since then, the rapid evolution of space activities, including the emergence of the new space sector, has widened the gap between Chile's awareness of the need for a more structured and stable space ecosystem and the evolving international landscape.

The reiteration of dynamics at the national level reflects the consequences of inadequate regulation and organization of space activities. This also leads to duplication of efforts and contributes to making the exploitation of indigenous capabilities less effective and profitable. Additionally, due to a cognitive bias in understanding space activities, the predominance of specialized engineers has narrowed the visibility of the need to include a cross-disciplinary perspective to accelerate societal evolution toward the consolidation of space public concern. Consequently, certain processes, such as the formulation of space policy, reproduce the same shortcomings, notably the failure to identify this public concern, which is key to stimulating public action and ensuring long-term and sustainable state involvement.

Chile has a clear need for space-based data and products due to various factors, such as the country's longitudinal extent and its geographic and topographic composition. The generation of accurate geographic knowledge is critical for conducting efficient disaster response, particularly given the country's high latitude, which presents ongoing and significant hazards. Space capabilities are essential for enhancing societal resilience and for future strategic planning. However, major challenges in the regulatory framework and shortcomings at the decision-making level have delayed the application of these benefits in emergency situations.

From the perspective of innovations and international security, emerging trends at the international level are presenting new challenges in international relations. The rise of counterspace capabilities, dual-use technologies, and their intersection with international and interstate conflicts underscores the need for measures in outer space activities to prevent the emergence of space conflicts that could undermine the principles enshrined in the corpus juris spatialis. In this context, Chile's unique natural laboratory environment is likely to attract interest for testing space technologies or establishing facilities for satellite tracking and command and control operations for deep space missions. Chile must remain vigilant about these trends and make significant efforts to regulate space activities at the national level, safeguarding its interests, values, and strategic vision in this domain.

Addressing this issue is crucial for maintaining consistent, coherent, and credible political behavior. Such stability is preferable for the integrity of the international space system compared to forming partnerships or making compromises that might create uncertainty and misperceptions about the state in the short and medium term. Therefore, Chile must remain vigilant, proactive, and strategic. Any collaboration, partnerships, or private initiatives conducted within national borders are significant. They not only are observed by other states but, in a high-uncertainty environment, can influence the country's ability to gain or lose partners and engage in collaborative processes. This is particularly important for Chile, given its status as a developing country and the critical role these processes play in its advancement.

Beyond the well-known successes of specific space initiatives, the state must adopt a comprehensive framework to expedite the political decision-making process, leveraging the country's strongest space capabilities, which appear to be more aligned with space diplomacy and policy rather than the technical aspects of space operations. It may be more effective for Chile to utilize its existing capabilities rather than investing heavily in acquiring a satellite platform, which could place a significant financial strain on the state. If Chile aims to participate in space activities as a state—beyond the preferences of individual figures—it must clearly define its objectives: why, when, how, and with whom. Answering these fundamental questions will provide an initial framework to identify the types of space activities that will best serve national needs while aligning with its cultural heritage and unique characteristics.

Moreover, it is crucial for Chile to recognize that space activities extend beyond low Earth orbit (LEO) and encompass a range of domains, including cyberspace and astronomy. A complex and holistic vision for the future of space activities will offer the state a strategic compass to address current and future concerns impacting daily life and provide an opportunity to contribute to international security by reinforcing the principles governing outer space activities.

References

Garside M (2024, mayo 24) Chile: mining sector's share of GDP. Statista. https://www.statista.com/statistics/1056760/chile-mining-sector-contribution-gdp/

González JM (2023, diciembre 21) 45 años del Conflicto del Beagle: Diciembre de 1978, una Navidad al borde de la guerra entre Chile y Argentina. Nuevatribuna.es. https://www.nuevatribuna.es/articulo/global/historia-diciembre-1978-borde-guerra-chile-argentina/20231221091036221089.html

Jerez S (2024, agosto 7) Histórico: Chile firmará los Acuerdos de Artemis por el inminente regreso de los humanos a la Luna. BioBioChile. https://www.biobiochile.cl/noticias/ciencia-y-tecnologia/adelantos/2024/08/07/historico-chile-firmara-los-acuerdos-de-artemis-por-el-inminente-regreso-del-los-humanos-a-la-luna.shtml

Minrel (2024, junio 20) Chile organiza panel de discusión para promover la protección de los cielos oscuros y silenciosos. Minrel. https://www.minrel.gob.cl/noticias-anteriores/chile-organiza-panel-de-discusion-para-promover-la-proteccion-de-los

Pinto A, Meza M (2023) Historic evolution of the Military Geography Institute of Chile. Revista geográfica de Chile Terra Australis 2(2). https://doi.org/10.23854/07199562.202258esp.pinto3

Treaty on Principles Governing the Activities of States in the Exploration and Use of Outer Space, including the Moon and Other Celestial Bodies, 1967, G.A.Resolution 2222 (XXI). https://www.unoosa.org/oosa/en/ourwork/spacelaw/treaties/outerspacetreaty.html

UNOOSA (s/f) Online Index of Objects Launched into Outer Space. Unoosa.org. Recuperado el 7 de noviembre de 2024, de https://www.unoosa.org/oosa/osoindex/search-ng.jspx?lf_id=

Valdivia V (2016a) Desarrollo espacial en América del Sur Una historia de fracasos y llegadas tarde. Boletín IEEE. https://dialnet.unirioja.es/servlet/articulo?codigo=5998268

Valdivia V (2016b) El espacio ultraterrestre como factor para el desarrollo y su presencia en la Política Internacional. La situación de Chile y América del Sur. Hacia la profundización de una política espacial con perspectiva estratégica para nuestro país. Universidad de Santiago

Valdivia V (2019) Política Espacial Nacional. Cuadernos de Trabajo ANEPE. https://anepe.cl/wp-content/uploads/2020/11/Cuaderno-de-Trabajo-N%C2%B016-2019.pdf

Valdivia V (2020a) Hipótesis de conflicto en el espacio ultraterrestre. De la geopolítica a la inteligencia espacial. Cuaderno de trabajo 3:1–22. https://www.publicacionesanepe.cl/index.php/cdt/article/view/864

Valdivia V (2020b, junio 30) Cuando la tecnología conoció a la geopolítica. AthenaLAB. https://www.athenalab.org/when-geopolitics-meets-technologies-space-development-and-changes-on-traditional-powers-balance/

Valdivia V (2023) The creation of space capabilities on developing countries, the role of space policies formulation at the beginning of LATINAMERICAS Space era. In: International Astronautical Congress (ed) 36th IAA symposium on space policy, regulations and economics (E3) Interactive Presentations - 36th IAA symposium on space policy, regulations and economics

Valdivia V (2024a) Remove before launch: collisions between space activities regulated under the Outer Space Treaty and the Antarctic Treaty System. In: International Astronautical Conference (ed) IISL Colloquium on the law of outer space

Valdivia V (2024b) Armas contraespaciales en Antártica. Ciclos de conocimiento e innovación, implicancias y rinocerontes grises. Cuaderno de trabajo 3:1–18. https://www.publicacionesanepe.cl/index.php/cdt/article/view/1075

Valdivia V (2024c) Counterspace capabilities within the Antarctic Treaty System: uncovering the emerging hazard from space technologies for the principle of peaceful uses of Antarctic territory and its governance. XI Scientific Committee on Antarctic Research (SCAR) Open Science Conference

Mexico

Fermín Romero

Contents

F. Romero (✉)
Fundacion Acercandote al Universo (FAU)/Approaching the Universe Foundation, Mexico City, Mexico
e-mail: presidencia@fau.org.mx

I. Grosner (ed.), *Space Regulation in Latin America*, Space Regulations Library 11, https://doi.org/10.1007/978-3-032-05828-7_6

Abstract This chapter provides a comprehensive view of current Mexico's space regime based on the Law creating the Mexican Space Agency (LAEM), its participation in the international space community, and its national space activities. Likewise, it addresses the various aspects of space activities in the country, through government institutions, industry, academia, and organized civil society in the space field, including Mexico's adherence to international space treaties and membership in organizations and relevant forums, national regulations, and future plans, based on the constitutional reform in space matters that seeks to generate a National Space Development Law with a long-term vision that articulates the "quadruple helix" and that turns Mexico into a relevant actor in the global space community with the capacity to promote the peaceful, safe, responsible, and sustainable use of outer space. It is important to note that this chapter covers the period from the establishment of the AEM in 2010 to its restructuring under the Sheinbaum administration in 2025, overseen by the Agency for Digital Transformation and Telecommunications (ATDT).

1 Introduction

As the exploration and use of space increase and become more frequent, the importance of having the broadest and strongest possible legal framework becomes even more urgent. Outer space law is fundamental for a variety of purposes, ranging from those most relevant to national space agendas to those of general interest to humanity, such as ensuring the peaceful, responsible, sustainable, and equitable use of outer space, as set forth in the United Nations Outer Space Treaties and Principles.

The current global context of space development is defined by the New Space Race and New Space, which is permeated by a geopolitical reconfiguration on a global scale, in which space powers are in open competition for leadership and space dominance of Earth's orbits (Low Earth Orbit (LEO), Medium Earth Orbit (MEO) and Geosynchronous earth Orbit (GEO)), the cislunar region, the resources of the Moon, Mars, and other celestial bodies and seek to impose their hegemony in the areas of security, politics, defense, economics, commerce, and space exploration, with the support of large multinational technology corporations whose influence on the shaping of regulations, policies, and global decisions is highly significant.

From this perspective, Mexico, in its current status of space development, requires, in order not to be marginalized from these processes, the design of an up-to-date, dynamic, flexible, innovative, and visionary legal architecture that integrates the regulation of all national space activities, promotes their development, and is complemented with the provisions established in the five space treaties, principles, resolutions, and other norms codified within the United Nations for the peaceful use of outer space.

Therefore, it is important to review the background and the current regulatory framework; analyze the fundamental aspects for the formulation of a National Space Development Law and the opportunities and challenges of such law tending to the formulation of a solid Mexican space program; outline considerations that drive, promote, and regulate space activity and national, and foreign investments; as well as foresee its impact on national development and future prospects. This is particularly true in light of the Mexican space sector's current scenario, as outlined by the government of Claudia Sheinbaum. The laws and regulations in force provide a comprehensive framework for the regulation and development of space activities in Mexico, which seeks to balance technological progress with security and compliance with international obligations.

2 Topics

This section will provide a comprehensive overview of Mexico's involvement in the international space community and its domestic space activities. We will now review various aspects of Mexico's space activities, including its adherence to international treaties and membership in relevant organizations, domestic regulations, and future plans. By examining these aspects, let us gain a deeper understanding of Mexico's position in the global space community and future space aspirations, according to the Sheinbaum administration's proposed restructuring of the space sector.

2.1 Which International Space Treaties Has Mexico Signed as a Party?

Prior to the creation of the current Mexican Space Agency (AEM), the Ministry of Foreign Affairs (MoFA/SRE) was responsible for leading the space agenda in specialized international forums.

> Mexico's foreign policy has been characterized by a clear commitment to the peaceful use of space. The general lines of action of Mexico's foreign policy in space matters in COPUOS have been oriented towards promoting the ratification and accession of Member States to the United Nations Outer Space Treaties, strengthening the active presence of our country in the promotion of international cooperation in favor of the peaceful use of outer space, and perfecting the international legal regime of outer space to regulate the aspects related to its use (Romero Vázquez 2010, p. 64).

Some examples of how Mexico's foreign policy reflects its commitment to the peaceful use of space are ratifying all five of the major UN treaties governing outer space activities, demonstrating its adherence to international norms and principles; regularly participating in the Committee on the Peaceful Uses of Outer Space (COPUOS) meetings and contributing to the development of international space law and policy; fostering international cooperation in space activities and working with other countries and international organizations to promote joint projects and initiatives; supporting efforts to mitigate the problem of space debris, which poses a threat to both human spaceflight and satellite operations; and promoting transparency and accountability in space activities, supporting measures to ensure that space technologies are used responsibly and ethically. These general examples highlight Mexico's commitment to the peaceful use of space and its role in shaping the international legal and policy framework for space activities.

Mexico is a state party to the five multilateral treaties (signed and ratified) codified within the United Nations that make up the current space law (United Nations Office for Outer Space Affairs-UNOOSA 2017; see Table 1).

2.2 *Is Mexico a Member of COPUOS?*

Mexico is a country with a strong commitment to multilateralism, international cooperation, and the United Nations since 1945 when it was one of the 51 founding countries of the UN. Mexico is a founding state of the Committee on the Peaceful Uses of Outer Space (COPUOS) of the United Nations (UN) and its role in shaping international space policy since December 12, 1959.

As part of Mexico's active participation in space affairs, coordinated by the United Nations Office for Outer Space Affairs (UNOOSA), COPUOS Secretariat,

Table 1 Multilateral treaties signed and ratified by Mexico

1	Treaty on Principles Governing the Activities of States in the Exploration and Use of Outer Space, including the Moon and Other Celestial Bodies. Adopted by the General Assembly in its resolution 2222 (XXI), opened for signature on January 27, 1967, entered into force on October 10, 1967
2	Agreement on the Rescue of Astronauts, the Return of Astronauts and the Return of Objects Launched into Outer Space. Adopted by the General Assembly in its resolution 2345 (XXII), opened for signature on April 22, 1968, entered into force on December 3, 1968
3	Convention on International Liability for Damage Caused by Space Objects. Adopted by the General Assembly in its resolution 2777 (XXVI), opened for signature on March 29, 1972, entered into force on September 1, 1972
4	Convention on Registration of Objects Launched into Outer Space Adopted by the General Assembly in its resolution 3235 (XXIX), opened for signature on January 14, 1975, entered into force on September 15, 1976
5	Agreement Governing the Activities of States on the Moon and Other Celestial Bodies. Adopted by the General Assembly in its resolution 34/68, opened for signature on December 18, 1979, entered into force on July 11, 1984

the contribution of Dr. Sergio Camacho-Lara stands out. Dr. Sergio Camacho-Lara served as director of UNOOSA from 2002 to 2007. Previously, Dr. Camacho "was Chief, Space Applications Section of UNOOSA focusing on capacity building in space science, technology, and space policy. Before that, he was Chief, Committee Services and Research Section also at UNOOSA and worked on the organization of the Third United Nations Conference on the Exploration and Peaceful Uses of Outer Space (UNISPACE III). Working with Member States of the Committee on the Peaceful Uses of Outer Space (COPUOS), he contributed to implementing the recommendations of UNISPACE III. Highlights of that implementation have been, the establishment of the Space Generation Advisory Council, the establishment of the International Committee on GNSS, and the establishment of the United Nations Platform for Space-based Information for Disaster Management and Emergency Response (UN-SPIDER)" (The Hague Institute for Global Justice 2023).

He also contributed to the establishment of the Regional Centres for Space Science and Technology Education, affiliated to the United Nations, particularly he supported the Regional Centre for Space Science and Technology Education for Latin America and the Caribbean (CRECTEALC). Dr. Camacho was also the first secretary general of CRECTEALC.

> As staff of the United Nations Secretariat and later as a member of the delegation of Mexico to COPUOS, he was involved in many issues dealt with by the Committee and its Scientific and Technical Subcommittee and Legal Subcommittee. As a delegate of Mexico to COPUOS, he was Chair of its Action Team on Near-Earth Objects (NEOs) and Chairman of the Working Group of the Scientific and Technical Subcommittee on NEOs which led to the establishment in 2014 of the International Asteroid Warning Network (IAWN) and the Space Mission Planning Advisory Group (SMPAG). These are among the issues that benefit from the long-term sustainability of activities in outer space … (The Hague Institute for Global Justice 2023).

In 2018, Mexico chaired COPUOS and the "UNISPACE+50" Summit. The Latin American and Caribbean Group to the United Nations (GRULAC) and 123 UN member countries elected Mexico to chair COPUOS (Gobierno de Mexico 2018). From that position, Mexico promoted (and continues to promote) the peaceful, safe, equitable, responsible, and sustainable use of outer space.

2.3 *Has Mexico Signed the Artemis Accords?*

Mexico signed the NASA Artemis Accords on December 9, 2021. Artemis, a framework for cooperation in lunar exploration, is the American international space program that seeks to bring mankind back to the Moon 50 years after the first human landing on the Moon during the American Apollo mission.

According to NASA the Artemis Accords are a multilateral commitment to promote "Principles for Cooperation in Civil Exploration and Peaceful Uses of the Moon, Mars, Comets and Asteroids" that propose rules for those seeking to take advantage of the possibilities offered by the Moon. These Accords establish that governments and private companies that want to initiate operations on the Moon must do so for peaceful purposes and with transparency and seek to create standards for working collaboratively, providing mutual assistance in case of emergency, publishing scientific data and findings, protecting the heritage and historical sites on the Moon, and good management of space debris (NASA 2024). The Artemis Accords also provide for the extraction of resources from lunar soil, called in situ resource utilization (ISRU).

Mexico's adherence to the Artemis Agreements will boost the Mexican space sector, as it will promote scientific and technological space development through the exchange of information, the development of joint projects with NASA and space companies, and, eventually, the creation of Mexican space companies. The Ministry of Economy estimates that by 2025 the aerospace industry could become the tenth most important in the world, with more than 400 companies in the country, generating 110,000 jobs and 12 billion dollars in exports.

Mexico's participation in the NASA Artemis Program will generate great interest among the public, which will boost awareness of the importance of space, and will foster the creation of new technologies developed in Mexico, which is important to take advantage of this opportunity to work together with NASA and the Artemis partners to promote Mexico's space development (SRE, 2021).

2.4 *Can Space Activities Be Classified as Dual Use, or Are They Only for Defense or Civil Purposes?*

Mexico's space activities must be for peaceful use, regardless of their civilian or military use. In Mexico, the Ministry of Economy regulates the export of technologies, software, and dual-use goods (civil, military, or nuclear use, including software and technology susceptible to deviation for the manufacture and proliferation of conventional weapons and weapons of mass destruction). In order to obtain a prior export permit for dual-use goods, software, conventional weapons, their parts, and components, it is necessary to have a "Manifestation of use and end-user and its modifications to obtain a prior export permit for conventional weapons, their parts and components, dual-use goods, software and related technologies," which allows to state the information related to the use and end user of the goods. Mexico is the third largest exporter of some advanced technologies (parts and structures) related to the aeronautics, medical equipment and devices, smartphones, microprocessors, computers, and information technology sector and the second largest destination for software investment in Latin America (Gobierno de Mexico, Secretaria de Economia, 2019).

Mexico, like many other countries, is involved in various international forums and mechanisms that seek to regulate and control the proliferation of dual-use technologies. These mechanisms help to prevent sensitive technologies from falling into the hands of non-state actors or states that could use them to develop weapons of mass destruction or for destabilizing purposes; they help to reinforce the international regimes established to control proliferation and facilitate cooperation between countries to share information and best practices and develop common export control policies (Romero Vázquez 2025a).

Mexico plays an important role in international efforts to control the proliferation of dual-use technologies. Its participation in various fora and mechanisms demonstrates its commitment to international security and nonproliferation through its support for initiatives such as the Prevention of an Arms Race in Outer Space (PAROS) Treaty, which prevents weapons in orbit, the placement of weapons on celestial bodies, and the threat of the use of force against objects in outer space. Mexico is an active member of several international forums and mechanisms related to dual-use technologies. Some of the most prominent export control regimes are the Missile Technology Control Regime (MTCR) (Romero Vázquez, 2025a), Nuclear Suppliers Group (NSG), the Australia Group, and the Organization for the Prohibition of Chemical Weapons.

2.5 *Is There a Registry of Space Objects Maintained by the United Nations?*

Mexico's involvement in the United Nations's Registry of space objects and its compliance with reporting requirements is part of its commitment as a founding State Party to COPUOS. In accordance with Article II of the Convention on Registration of Objects Launched into Outer Space, resolution 3235 XXIX of the United Nations General Assembly, the Mexican Space Agency (AEM) established the national registry of objects launched into Earth orbit or beyond since March 1, 2013. And its maintenance is responsibility of the General Coordination Office for Space-related Security and International Affairs of the Mexican Space Agency. Mexico has 17 objects launched into outer space registered with UNOOSA (Gobierno de Mexico 2021).

The Mexican government is obligated to keep the registry of objects launched into space up to date with the UNOOSA, a requirement that the restructured AEM must fulfill in due time.

2.6 *Does Mexico Have a National Specific Space Act or Regulations?*

Currently, in the domain of space regulation Mexico counts with the Law creating the Mexican Space Agency (LAEM[1]), the General Lines for Mexico's Space Policy (LGPEM[2]), which require updating, and the National Space Activities Program

[1] Ley de creación de la Agencia Espacial Mexicana (LAEM).

[2] Lineas Generales de Política Espacial de México (LGPEM).

(PNAE[3] 2020–2024). The AEM Governing Board established the necessary periodic review and updating of the General Guidelines for Mexico's Space Policy, which were published in the *Official Journal of the Federation* (DOF) on July 13, 2011 (Diario Oficial de la Federación, 2011). The first review was to take place in the fourth 2-month period of 2012, and they were to be updated at least every 4 years, which has not yet occurred.

However, Mexico is immersed in the constitutional reform on space matters, focused on the modification of Articles 28 and 73 with the purpose of establishing "space activities as priority areas for national development, as well as being a guideline to enrich the legislation in the space sector" (Gobierno de Mexico, AEM 2023), which will allow as a next step to formulate and approve in the Congress the secondary law: a National Space Development Law. The current legislative process of the reform is being approved in the Senate and subsequently requires the approval of the local Congresses to be published in the *Official Journal of the Federation*.

> "The main objective of the reform is to foster national scientific and technological research and development in the space field, as well as to promote international cooperation in this field, with the purpose of turning Mexico into a relevant space actor at a regional and global level, in the following decades. To achieve these objectives, the reform will establish clear provisions on the regulation, supervision and promotion of space activities in Mexican territory." "The constitutional reform on space matters in Mexico represents a significant step for the development and regulation of space activities in the country. The enactment of this reform will have—without a doubt—a far-reaching positive impact that will allow the establishment of an adequate legal framework (National Space Development Law and its regulations), to promote exploration, development, as well as the strengthening of the Mexican Space Agency (AEM)…"

The electoral process and the change of administration in 2024 temporarily interrupted the legislative process for the approval of the constitutional reform on space matters; however, once the LXVI Legislature of the Mexican Congress of the Union is installed, on September 1, 2024, both chambers will resume their agenda and review the matters that were left pending in the previous legislature, to proceed with their attention, complete the legislative process in progress, and reach the decree of the reform to be published in the DOF (Altamirano 2024). In addition to restructuring the space sector, the government of President Sheinbaum must take up the reform and work with the Senate to resume the legislative process and promote its approval as soon as possible. This will enable the introduction of the National Space Development Law initiative. As can be seen, space regulation in Mexico is currently undergoing a process of development and consolidation in which the restructured AEM must play a relevant role, despite the lack of sufficient financial resources to enable the development of the national space sector. Although the country has taken significant steps in recent years to establish a solid legal framework for its space activities, including the constitutional reform on space matters promoted by various sectors concerned, there are still numerous challenges and opportunities from the design and introduction to the legislative process of the National Space Development

[3] Programa Nacional de Actividades Espaciales (PNAE).

Law. A great challenge, especially in the new administration of President Claudia Sheinbaum, in which the restructured AEM was move from the Ministry of Infrastructure Communications and Transport to the new Agency for Digital Transformation and Telecommunications (ATDT[4]), under a capability-reduced scheme focused on the Mexican space program presented in FAMEX 2025, which reflects ATDT's priorities for the space sector.

We have already emphasized that among the advances in space regulation in Mexico are the Law creating the Mexican Space Agency (LAEM) in 2010, the LGPE (2011), and the PNAE (2015 and 2020–2024). From this perspective, we can say that the current regulatory framework in Mexico is incomplete, although evolving, considering that space regulation is a dynamic field that requires constant updating to adapt to rapid technological advances, new needs, regulatory challenges such as funding for space activity, inter-institutional coordination for adequate legislative harmonization, research and development of national capacities, as well as opportunities in the sector to attract foreign direct investment. This looks for the development of a national space industry with applications of technology in various sectors (agriculture, fisheries, cadastre, urban planning, navigation, communications, etc.), participation in international space missions, the launching of space vehicles; investment in research, technological development and space infrastructure. To achieve these objectives of the Mexican Space Program; the country needs to training specialized human capital in the space sector, both at the technical and scientific level; the use of space technologies to solve national problems, such as natural resource management, disaster prevention; the improvement of connectivity; inter-institutional coordination in space activities (AEM, AFAC5[5], Ministry of National Defense, universities or other institutions); space traffic management; cooperation with other countries and international organizations to access advanced technologies and knowledge, as well as to participate in projects of international scope, among others.

Beyond the LAEM, it is still necessary to develop more detailed and specific legislation to regulate the various space activities described above, i.e., a regulation designed to favor space development in Mexico. This is the great challenge for the new ATDT in charge of the restructured AEM. This represents a window of immense opportunities to boost economic growth, innovation, and social development in the country. Each of the space areas and activities included in the secondary legislation, the National Space Development Law, will generate new regulations, codes, official standards, and other normative provisions applicable to the sector with the consequent impulse and promotion of productive activities.

[4] Agencia de Transformación Digital y Telecomunicaciones (ATDT).

[5] Agencia Federal de Aviación Civil (AFAC).

2.7 Does Mexico Have a Space Agency?

In the 1990s, the Mexican Space Society (SEM[6]) unsuccessfully proposed the creation of a space agency. This was after a prior effort that generated the developments that laid the groundwork for the creation of the National Commission for Outer Space (CONEE[7]) on August 31, 1962, whose objective was to promote the peaceful exploration of outer space and which was abolished by presidential decree on March 11, 1977, transferring its functions to the Secretariat of Communications and Transport (SCT[8]).

Faced with this reality, which dominated the national space agenda, the SRE[9] took the first step by inviting the agencies involved in space matters to an inter-secretariat meeting on 27 June 2003, which recognized the need for an effective and agile exchange of information on space matters in order to unify Mexico's position in international forums, among other things that had prevented the formulation of a national policy in this area. In response to this need, and with the support of INEGI[10], the Ministry of Foreign Affairs developed the electronic portal in July 2003: Information Exchange Mechanism on Space Matters, as an exclusive communication tool for the federal executive agencies with competence in space matters. (Romero Vázquez 2010, p. 79)

As a next step, during 2004 the SRE formulated a preliminary draft of Mexico's Space Policy—which consisted of a conceptual policy document, the first draft of the Law for the Creation of the Mexican Space Agency and a first draft of the National Space Activities Program (Pronae) —to promote inter-institutional coordination of the national space agenda. The document represented an attempt to fill the existing gaps in the space issue, with the long-term objective of contributing to the transformation of Mexico into a highly competitive country, with a global vision, where space science and technologies were integrated into the national agenda (Romero Vázquez 2010, pp. 79–80).

The initiative had its justification in the role traditionally exercised by the Ministry of Foreign Affairs as focal point for the national coordination of the space agenda with the competent governmental, academic and scientific institutions, as well as in the active trajectory in the international agenda of space affairs. The preliminary draft sought to articulate the multiple efforts deployed in Mexico in this strategic sector, in response to the urgent need to promote a comprehensive policy in this sector. (Romero Vázquez 2010, p. 80)

Thus, on December 1st, 2004, the Ministry of Foreign Affairs—through the General Directorate for the United Nations System—convened an inter-institutional meeting to present the preliminary drafts of Mexico's Space Policy; Law for the Creation of the Mexican Space Agency, and Pronae, to discuss them and define the critical path in order to promote the creation of the Inter-Institutional Commission on Space Affairs, whose purpose would be the establishment of the Mexican Space Agency. The proposal was well received by the participants who represented agencies of the Federal Executive, decentralized organizations and academic and research institutions linked to space activities. (Romero Vázquez 2010, p. 80)

[6] Sociedad Espacial de México (SEM).

[7] Comisión Nacional del Espacio Exterior (CONEE).

[8] Secretaría de Comunicaciones y Transportes (SCT).

[9] Secretaría de Relaciones Exteriores (SRE).

[10] Instituto Nacional de Estadística y Geografía (INEGI).

At the meeting, the advisability of establishing the Agency as a coordinating body at the federal level for national space policy and activities, as well as for Mexico's position at the international level, was raised. The Agency proposed by the Ministry of Foreign Affairs is of a civilian nature and its priorities coincide with those promoted by Mexico in international forums: the peaceful use of outer space; the prevention of natural disasters; distance education and telemedicine, among other issues related to national scientific development. As part of the strategy, the initiative was presented to the competent authorities of the Executive and Legislative branches. From this moment on, the draft Law for the Creation of the Mexican Space Agency—originated in the SRE—was promoted by different promoters of the initiative for its review and opinion in the House of Representatives. (Romero Vázquez 2010, p. 81)

Thus, the proposal for the creation of the Mexican Space Agency (AEM), presented by the SRE to all concerned institutions in government, academia, and industry, was joined by several support groups that promoted its entry into the House of Representatives on November 25, 2005. The House of Representatives approved the initiative on April 20, 2010. The Law creating the Mexican Space Agency (LAEM) was enacted on July 13, 2010, concluding its legislative process with its publication in the *Official Journal of the Federation* (DOF) on July 30, 2010.

In accordance with the Second Transitory Article of the LAEM, on September 7, the AEM's Governing Board was installed, which was devoted to organize four consultation forums with the active participation of specialists in the field, from which the AEM adopted the current operational structure (four of the five general coordination are homonyms of the titles of the forums); the results of the forums were a relevant input for the formulation of the General Lines of Mexico's Space Policy. (Diario Oficial de la Federación-DOF, 2011)

For 15 years, AEM has been responsible for coordinating space activity in Mexico. Following the 2024 elections and change in administration, the AEM restructuring, coordinated by the ATDT, began in early 2025. The integration of AEM's functions within the ATDT in the form of a simple "Dirección General Satelital" (DGS), established on January 29, 2025 (Diario Oficial de la Federación-DOF, 2025), and assuming space functions, is a restructuring presented as a "strengthening" that affects the entire national space sector. This restructuring slows down the outlined medium- and long-term space development. Although the current government proposes to leverage AEM's expertise, concerns persist in the academic community, organized civil society, and industry about whether this new structure and its resources will suffice to maintain the autonomy and scope of space projects. There are also concerns about the disarticulation of the sector and the loss of the original strategic vision.

Despite speculation about the "disappearance" of the AEM, the restructured AEM will remain in force as long as the Congress of the Union does not approve the repeal of the Law creating of the AEM (2010). Its facilities continue to operate with reduced capacity and new personnel. The restructured AEM also participates in forums such as the 4th Meeting of Space Agencies of the Member Countries of the Italo-Latin American Institute (IILA), which took place on June 3 in Rome, Italy (Gobierno de Mexico 2025). Currently, the "renewed" AEM is simpler and has fewer capacities, but there is still confidence that the authorities recognize the importance of this strategic sector and the need to strengthen it. Additionally, once approved, the ongoing constitutional reform will allow an initiative to be introduced to promote the National Space Development Law in Congress.

This analysis illustrates the transition from initial uncertainty to reaffirming the commitment to the Mexican space program under a new structure. This new approach seeks to integrate space with the country's digital transformation and telecommunications agenda. The success of the new projects and the real "strengthening" of the AEM will depend on continuity of investments, allocation of qualified human resources, and sufficient financial and material resources, as well as the effective execution of the announced plans.

President Sheinbaum's statement, "The AEM is not disappearing; it is being strengthened," regarding the controversy generated by the AEM director's resignation in January 2025, created more uncertainty than clarity under the current government.

Despite the government's lack of interest in and political will for the strategic space sector, universities and some national and international companies are fully committed, along with organized civil society and nongovernmental organizations (NGOs), such as Fundacion Acercandote al Universo (FAU), to boosting space activities in academia, industry, and society. This commitment aims to continue building national space capacities and promote a robust national space sector and ecosystem that will allow the country to take its place in the regional and global space community.

2.8 What Is the Primary Regulatory Body Responsible for Overseeing Space Activities?

The Mexican Space Agency (AEM), originally was a decentralized public agency with its own legal personality and assets, has technical and managerial autonomy to fulfill its attributions, objectives, and goals. The agency was part of the sector coordinated by the Ministry of Infrastructure, Communications, and Transport of Mexico. The AEM executes Mexico's space policy, through the development and application of the National Space Activities Plan (PNAE), the Mexican space program.

The AEM "is a decentralized public agency of the Federal Government and sectorized in the Ministry of Infrastructure, Communications and Transport" and has served to coordinate space activities in Mexico. This initial institutional architecture will change under President Sheinbaum's administration with the transfer of the AEM to the ATDT, where it is expected that the AEM and the Mexican space program will receive a greater boost.

The AEM is responsible for formulating and executing national space policy, promoting research and technological development, as well as promoting international collaboration (bilateral and multilateral), in addition to adherence to international treaties. Mexico is a party to international treaties such as the Treaty on Principles Governing the Activities of States in the Exploration and Use of Outer Space (OST), which demonstrates its commitment to international cooperation in the space field. The AEM has implemented various space programs, such as the development of Earth observation (EO), communications and navigation satellites, as well as participation in international missions and has also promoted research and development programs in the space sector, with the aim of strengthening national capacities and encouraging the participation of academic institutions and companies.

The LAEM, the current national regulatory framework for space, initiated a new stage for Mexico's space development and produced two important regulatory instruments, which to date guide the actions of the AEM, allowing it to fulfill its functions and achieve its institutional objectives. The first one is the agreement that announces the General Guidelines for Mexico's Space Policy (LGPEM), published in the *Official Journal of the Federation* (DOF) on July 13, 2011, which are in urgent need of updating, and the second one is the agreement that issues the National Program for Space Activities (PNAE), published in the DOF on April 14, 2015, a sort of first Mexican space program.

Despite being a brief law, which establishes the object, instruments of Mexico's space policy, functions, attributions, administrative and governing bodies (organization and operation), budget, and assets, the LAEM is transcendental because it establishes the governing body for space development in Mexico, the Mexican Space Agency (AEM). Therefore, in terms of space regulation, it is important to highlight some of its articles:

> Article 1. The Mexican Space Agency is hereby created as a decentralized public agency, with legal personality and its own assets and with technical and managerial autonomy for the fulfillment of its attributions, objectives and purposes.

> Article 2. The purpose of the Mexican Space Agency shall be to: I. To formulate and propose to the head of the Ministry of Communications and Transport the general lines of the Mexican Space Policy, as well as the National Program of Space Activities; II. To execute the Mexican Space Policy, through the elaboration and application of the National Program of Space Activities; III. To promote the effective development of space activities to expand the country's capabilities in the educational, industrial, scientific and technological branches in space matters; IV. To develop the scientific-technological capacity of the country through the articulation of the sectors involved in all the fields of space activity that make possible its performance within a framework of national autonomy in the matter; V. Promote the development of space systems and the means, technology and infrastructure necessary for the consolidation and autonomy of this sector in Mexico; VI. To facilitate the incorporation of the sectors related to this policy and particularly the participation of the productive sector, so that it acquires competitiveness in the markets of space goods and services; VII. Promote an active international cooperation through agreements that benefit space activities and that allow the active integration of Mexico to the International Space Community; VIII. Serve as an instrument of the State's leadership in this sector, to strengthen sovereignty; IX. To watch over the national interest and security, by means of a strategy that integrates scientific and technological knowledge, efficiency, experience and coordination capacity among the public entities of the Federal Public Administration; X. To guarantee and preserve the public interest and the protection of the population, as the basis for development, security, peace and prevention of

national security problems in Mexico; and XI. Receive from public, private and social entities, proposals and observations in the spatial area for their study and consideration.

In terms of space regulation, it is important to highlight both Articles (1 and 2), since they provide the instruments for Mexico's space policy, the functions, powers, and authorities of the AEM, which currently give legal support to space activities in Mexico in conjunction with the LGPEM and the PNAE.

Currently, through the integration of capacities, the creation of the General Satellite Directorate (DGS), interinstitutional coordination, and the participation of the private sector, the ATDT has assumed the functions of the restructured AEM, including the responsibility to carry out the Mexican space program. This includes merging the mission and objectives of the AEM with those of the MEXSAT satellite program. These efforts seek to give continuity to ongoing space projects and programs and to continue promoting the development of the space sector in Mexico. The AEM will exist as a government entity until the law that created it is repealed, the decree of its extinction is published, or the corresponding reforms are carried out. However, the ATDT is integrating its functions and resources to continue the sector's objectives from the DGS. Given the inertia of the sector and its broad, crosscutting activity in multiple agencies of the Federal Public Administration, the DGS will surely grow in importance, resources, and projects. Specifically, it is impossible for a single general directorate to encompass all the AEM's objectives, powers, attributions, functions, and activities.

2.9 What Are the Primary Regulations Governing Space Activities, and How Are Private Companies Performing Space Activities Authorized, Monitored, and Supervised?

Currently, the main legislation regulating space activities in Mexico is the Law creating the Mexican Space Agency (LAEM), supported in the agreement that announces the General Guidelines for Mexico's Space Policy (LGPEM), published in the *Official Journal of the Federation* (DOF) on July 13, 2011, and the agreement that issues the National Program for Space Activities (PNAE), published in the DOF on April 14, 2015. These also include The Orbit Plan: Roadmap for the Mexican Space Industry 2013, a document coordinated by the AEM and ProMexico, published on August 5, 2012, and The Orbit Plan 2.0: Roadmap for the Space Sector, published on June 9, 2017; both plans represent the joint work and the collaboration of experts from the "quadruple helix": government, industry, academia, and organized civil society in the space field (Gobierno de Mexico 2011, 2012, 2018).

The AEM is the public agency in charge of the space sector in Mexico and has contact with companies in the aerospace sector. The authorization for the creation of companies in the space sector is carried out between the SRE and the Ministry of

Economy (SE[11]), with the support of legal firms and notaries that manage the official procedures to generate the company's constitutive act of incorporation and registration in the Public Registry of Commerce. Together, both secretariats authorize, control, and supervise private companies that carry out space activities.

The AEM collaborates with the General Directorate of Standards (DGN[12]) of the Ministry of Economy (SE), redoubling joint efforts to develop Mexican standards to promote the industrial satellite component of the national aerospace sector. In 2015, the Technical Committee for National Space Standardization (COTENNE[13]) was created, composed of members of the AEM, academia, companies, government, and individuals and companies linked to space activity. The potential benefits of these standards, which contribute to the participation of small- and medium-sized companies in the value chain of industrial activity, are multiple as they enable Mexico to improve its competitiveness, allowing the national aerospace industry to compete and project itself into new markets (Gobierno de Mexico 2018).

The National Chamber of the Transformation Industry (CANACINTRA[14]) and the Mexican Federation of the Aerospace Industry (FEMIA[15]) affiliate and register companies in the aerospace sector (aeronautics and space).

The restructured AEM must define the government's new relationship with private and productive sectors involved in space activities, as well as with academic and organized civil society groups in the field of space.

2.10 Is There Any Effort Toward Capacity Building in the Space Sector, Both in Terms of Technologies and Regulatory Matters?

The main efforts toward capacity building in space sector can be visualized through a constitutional reform on space matters which is currently being promoted in the Mexican Congress through amendments to Articles 28 and 73 of the Constitution of the United Mexican States. The reform seeks to create the legislative framework that will allow the development of space activities related to industry, energy, telecommunications, health, agriculture, environment, urban development, climate change, natural disasters, and more. With this reform the space activity will be considered a priority area for national development at the constitutional level, and space technology will allow finding solutions to social problems, hand in hand with the current technological development. This reform lays the foundations for a new chapter in the generation of knowledge and innovation in the country and will

[11] Secretaria de Economía (SE).

[12] Direccion General de Normas.

[13] Comite Técnico de Normalizacion Nacional del Espacio (COTENNE), created in 2015.

[14] Camara Nacional de la Industria de la transformación (CANACINTRA).

[15] Federacion Mexicana de la Industria Aeroespacial (FEMIA).

encourage public and private investment in space research and exploration. It will also enable the development of space sector capacity building, both in technology and regulatory issues. It is crucial for President Sheinbaum's administration to take a stance on the constitutional reform regarding space and determine if it is included in their plans for the space sector.

Once the constitutional reform on space is approved, it will be essential to create a secondary law, the National Space Development Law, so that Mexico can take full advantage of the potential of the space sector, which will allow the country to regulate space activities and promote national and foreign investment to increase national space capabilities, reflected in more satellites, rocket launches, and ground stations. By providing a solid and comprehensive legal framework, this law must include at least certain fundamental elements such as the definition, in a clear and comprehensive manner, of space activities; use of the radio electric spectrum, through the allocation of frequencies for space communications; regulation of private space companies involved in the commercialization of space activities; the creation of an autonomous regulatory agency (independent from the AEM), which designates an authority in charge of regulating and supervising space activities such as launching, in-orbit operations, reentry, and the use of space resources; the establishment of a system of licenses, registration procedures, and permits for the performance of the different types of space activities; the protection of intellectual property, through the necessary mechanisms to protect intellectual property generated in the space sector; rules on civil liability and insurance, to cover possible damages caused to third parties by space activities or objects; protection of space objects, through measures (such as the UNOOSA operational guidelines) to avoid collisions and ensure the sustainability of outer space; and the promotion of scientific dissemination and education in space matters, as well as provisions to foster international collaboration and exchange of best practices in space matters, successfully implemented by third countries, among many other aspects that will promote Mexico's space development.

A regulatory, technological, and industrial development would create a robust national space industry through the development of satellites, rockets, and other space components, generating highly qualified jobs and promoting technology transfer; through innovation in various sectors, space technologies can be applied in sectors such as agriculture, communications, transportation, energy, and environment, among others, generating innovative products and services. The creation of a robust local supply chain for the space industry will generate new business opportunities for small- and medium-sized companies linked to the supply chain.

As part of the benefits associated with the development of national space capabilities, such as Earth observation (EO), satellites can provide high-resolution images to monitor climate change, deforestation, pollution, and other natural phenomena, allowing more informed decisions to be made for natural resource management and environmental protection; satellite communication systems can improve connectivity in remote and rural areas, facilitating access to basic services such as education, health, financial services, and entertainment; satellite navigation systems can improve logistics and transportation efficiency, reducing costs and delivery times. Another benefit of space regulation in Mexico is the STEM formation of highly qualified human capital. The space sector demands professionals in areas such as engineering, physics, mathematics, and computer science, which can contribute to improving the quality of education in the country; the promotion of space research motivates curiosity, ingenuity, and creativity, generating new knowledge and solutions to complex problems.

Space regulation will also allow to take advantage for greater use of natural resources. Mexico has a great diversity of natural resources that can be monitored and managed more efficiently using space technology; with development of applications for agriculture and fishing, the Mexican agricultural sector, among other industries, can benefit from geospace technologies such as remote sensing and global positioning to improve productivity and sustainability; collaboration with neighboring countries on space projects can generate mutual benefits and strengthen regional integration.

2.11 How Does Mexico Engage in International Cooperation in the Space Sector, Both in Terms of Technologies and Representation in International Organizations? Are There Any Partnerships with Other Latin American Countries?

Mexico has a wide international cooperation in space matters in terms of technology and the scope of multilateral organizations specialized in space matters such as UN COPUOS, ITU, the Space Conference of the Americas (CEA), CRECTEALC, G20, and space agencies, among others. Mexico also cooperates bilaterally in space matters with countries such as Argentina, Brazil, Chile, Colombia, Ecuador, Paraguay, Peru, and Venezuela, among others. At the regional level, in CELAC Mexico promoted the creation of the Latin American and Caribbean Space Agency (ALCE), whose headquarters are in Mexico.

In addition to collaboration with countries such as the United States, some European countries, India, South Korea, and Russia, Mexico gives high priority to regional space cooperation through the ALCE. Mexico expects the ALCE to help the region to strengthen technological sovereignty in space, to absorb Latin American talent to promote regional space development, and to position Latin America in a relevant place in the global space community.

> The objective of these instruments is to promote bilateral cooperation in various areas of peaceful exploration of outer space, as well as the development of space science and technology for the mutual benefit of the parties (Gobierno de Mexico 2022).

Beyond the national regulatory framework referred to (LAEM, LGPEM and PNAE), besides the international cooperation in space sector, a fundamental part of Mexico's space activity is carried out within the framework of the norms established by specialized international organizations such as the COPUOS and its Secretariat, the

United Nations Office for Outer Space Affairs (UN OOSA), headquartered in Vienna, Austria; the International Telecommunication Union (ITU), based in Geneva, Switzerland; and the Inter-American Telecommunication Commission (CITEL) of the Organization of American States (OAS), based in Washington, D.C., USA, among other intergovernmental organizations with competence in matters of telecommunications regulation, satellite radiofrequency spectrum, etc., which issue their own regulatory frameworks, regulations, and agreements that complement space regulation in Mexico.

The restructured AEM will have to establish the role it gives to international cooperation in the space field as one of its priorities.

2.12 How Does the Private Sector Conduct Its Activities in the Field of Space Exploration?

Currently, the few private sector companies in Mexico with activities in the space field are focused on providing satellite images for various purposes; some others are starting in the field of rocketry and launch platforms. Most of the developments of space missions (nanosatellites and Moon missions) have been carried out by public and private universities under the framework of NASA Artemis Program.

On November 13, 2020, a collaboration agreement was signed between the Mexican Space Agency (AEM) and the Mexican Federation of the Aerospace Industry (FEMIA), for the launching of the Mexican space industry, through which both entities seek to develop companies in the aerospace sector, boost job creation, and position Mexico on the world stage and to scale the capabilities of Mexican companies in the aeronautical sector toward the space sector, where just the satellite construction segment represents a market of 12.5 billion dollars (Navarrete 2020).

The signing of the AEM-FEMIA agreement marks the beginning of a new stage in the development of the space industry in Mexico. This collaboration is important for the sustainable development of the national space sector, promoting innovation and public and private investment, generating jobs, and increasing the country's competitiveness in this sector. This collaboration will allow the promotion of specific projects related to Earth observation, telecommunications, and space science and technology, among others, for the benefit of the Mexican population.

On September 20, 2023, the Ministry of Infrastructure, Communications, and Transport (SICT), through the Mexican Space Agency (AEM), reported that the "SME4SPACE," a European organization of companies working directly with the European Space Agency (ESA), conducted a working tour in Mexico, in order to articulate an agenda of industrial cooperation with Mexican companies (Gobierno de Mexico 2023a).

With this articulation, SME4SPACE will be able to support Mexican organizations and companies in the space sector to facilitate access to ESA and the programs offered by the European Union, as well as to take advantage of the current boom in "nearshoring" to install companies—in this case European companies—in Mexico. The articulation will promote the development of an ecosystem of cooperation and business exchange between small- and medium-sized Mexican and European companies in the sector, to contribute to the development of the growing Mexican space industry.

Current collaborations with NASA for scientific purposes are focused on the study of climate change, in order to deepen the understanding of global warming (EMIDSS-6), conducted by the Center for Aerospace Development of the National Polytechnic Institute (CDA-IPN), Universidad Nacional Autonoma de Mexico (UNAM), and AEM (Gobierno de Mexico 2024).

The Colmena Mission 1 was developed by the Space Instrumentation Laboratory of the Institute of Nuclear Sciences of the UNAM (LINX ICN UNAM) in collaboration with the AEM and NASA, a pioneer in testing the concept of using autonomous micro-robots in space exploration and mining tasks, which was designed for the Moon but also has interest in Mars exploration (LINX 2023). Colmena Mission 2, scheduled for 2027, although it failed to land on the Moon, boosted technological development and the formation of talent in Mexico. The main objective is the scientific study of the lunar regolith, which could not be carried out in the first mission. Colmena 2 is in progress awaiting the support of the new AEM.

The satellite project "Constellation AztechSat," focused on the monitoring of marine fauna, is a collaboration of five Mexican universities: Universidad Nacional Autonoma de Mexico (UNAM), Universidad Aeronautica en Querétaro (UNAQ), Universidad Panamericana (UP), Universidad Popular Autonoma del Estado de Puebla (UPAEP), and Universidad Politecnica de Queretaro (UPQ), coordinated by the AEM with NASA and completed on April 28, 2023, with its first phase called "Mission Concept Review" (MCR) (Gobierno de Mexico 2023b).

During the International Astronautical Congress (IAC) 2024 in Milan, Italy, the AEM participated in the meeting of members (companies and students) of the Latin American Space Industry Cluster, a project in which Mexico's leadership is relevant. The Mexican government's participation in the IAC 2025 in Sydney, Australia, through the restructured AEM, is not yet known.

Mexico's Ministry of Defense (SEDENA) and its contractors, particularly through FAMEX, have expressed new interest in security projects related to national space activities and the missions of SEDENA and SEMAR. In FAMEX 2025 la ATDT presentó el Programa Espacial Mexicano. Aviación 21 (2025), (Romero Vázquez, 2023b)

Similarly, Fundación Acercandote al Universo (FAU)'s space ecosystem, which unites affiliated companies and organizations, promotes technological project development and space entrepreneurship. This is achieved through different programs and projects such as the International Competition of Youth Entrepreneurship in the Space Sector, which is essentially Latin American and is currently in its 4th year.

2.13 What Are the Plans for Space Activities in Mexico? Are Manned Flights and Spaceports Being Planned?

Derived from the constitutional reform in space matters, the formulation of a National Space Development Law is expected that seeks to generate national space capacities in various areas, promote national and foreign investment in this sector, as well as provide legal certainty to investors. This legal framework will foster an attractive investment environment in segments such as spaceports, rockets, space tourism, potentially space mining, and of course Mexico's participation in manned flights in conjunction with other space agencies.

At the project level, there are potential collaborations with other countries for the development of spaceports and companies interested in investing in launching platforms and the development of space vehicles, which will be materializing in the coming years.

The evolution of space regulation in Mexico, despite its shortcomings, is experiencing significant progress in recent years, positioning the country as an increasingly relevant player in the international space scenario. The current regulatory framework, centered on the AEM, seeks to promote technological development, innovation, and the generation of added value in various sectors of the national economy.

Based on the limited information available about the Mexican space program under Claudia Sheinbaum's administration, it is difficult to ascertain the restructured AEM's stance on Mexico's plans for human spaceflight. However, given the budget cuts to the space sector, it is foreseeable that this topic will not be part of the space program.

2.14 What Are (and Should Be) the Perspectives of Mexico on Regulatory Matters Related to Space Debris, Militarization and Weaponization of Space, and Exploitation of Space Natural Resources?

The National Space Development Law in Mexico should include regulatory issues related to space debris, space militarization and weaponization, and exploitation of space natural resources (ISRU), which are issues of concern to Mexico's space community and its governmental institutions. The National Space Development Law will contain Mexico's firm positions on these issues that have to do with the peaceful, safe, responsible, and sustainable use of space activity.

Mexico's position on space debris is characterized by a proactive and collaborative approach. Mexico has expressed concern about the growing problem of space debris. Although Mexico is not a major source of this problem, it recognizes the importance of participating in the search for global solutions to mitigate its effects.

Mexico's government recognizes the seriousness of the problem and is committed to working with the international community in COPUOS to find sustainable and effective solutions. Mexico has emphasized the need for close international cooperation to address this challenge and believes that the only way to effectively address the space debris problem is through multilateral agreements and the implementation of common standards that emphasize prevention as the best strategy for dealing with space debris; the importance of having effective monitoring and tracking systems to identify and track operational and nonoperational space objects; and the exploration of technologies and possible space cleanup missions as a complementary measure to prevention and mitigation (Gobierno de Mexico 2024).

Militarization and weaponization of space are an issue where the official position (Mexico's Statement at 63rd Session of the Legal Subcommittee 2024 of UN COPUOS, 15-26 April 2024, Item 4. General Exchange of Views) is: "Mexico maintains its clear and firm position against the militarization of outer space and calls for transparency and international cooperation for its peaceful use."

Article II of the Outer Space Treaty (OST, 1967), which prohibits national appropriation of the Moon or other celestial bodies, is invoked to address the issue of space mining. The interpretation of this treaty with respect to the ownership of extracted resources is still the subject of much debate. In the analysis of the legal doctrine, the issue is complex if one considers exclusively the legality of the activity of extracting resources from celestial bodies. In practice, given the laxity of space law, some nations (the United States, Luxembourg, the United Arab Emirates, and Japan) and space companies with interests in these resources have already generated their own rules.

For Mexico, the need for a global regulatory framework for space mining is becoming increasingly evident, considering that this activity will have a significant environmental impact on celestial bodies. Mining and space tourism are emerging industries that represent a new frontier for humanity. They have the potential to transform the global economy and our way of life.

2.15 Other Relevant Topics

In addition to the regular activity of the AEM, in the past years, there is focus on three priority axes: satellite telecommunications and navigation, Earth observation and space exploration, and research and development carried out by some public and private universities to promote space missions such as Colmena (LINX ICN UNAM, 2023), (Romero Vázquez, 2024a) and AEM; EMIDSS6: CDA IPN, UNAM, and AEM; and Constellation AztechSat: UNAM, UNAQ, UP, UPAEP, UPQ, and AEM, or important astronomical projects. Some companies with the intention of investing or migrating to the space sector maintain the approval of the "constitutional reform in space matters" (Romero Vázquez 2023a) to venture into the nascent space ecosystem that will promote the various industries linked to the space sector that will be regulated by the National Space Development Law, in which the "quadruple helix" will actively participate.

Despite the progress made in recent decades, Mexico's space regulation still faces important lags and challenges that, although we have already described in broad terms, I summarize below in order of importance:

Lack of resources: Public and private investment in the space sector is very limited compared to that of other countries, including those with the same or lower levels of development than ours, which shows the importance that should be given to the development of this strategic sector.

Interinstitutional coordination: It is necessary to strengthen coordination among the different institutions involved in space activities. The effective articulation of the "quadruple helix" is fundamental to promote not only space development in Mexico but also effective regulation.

Development of a local supply chain: The creation of a robust local supply chain for the space industry is fundamental to guarantee the sustainable development of the sector.

Training of personnel: Greater public investment is required in the training of specialized professionals in the different areas of the space sector.

In parallel, these challenges also offer some opportunities for the growth, development, and consolidation of the Mexican space sector. Some of the most promising ones detected so far are the development of a commercial space industry, where the promotion of national space development will generate a local ecosystem that articulates the commercial space industry, generating new jobs and business opportunities, and the development of space applications to solve national problems, where space technologies can be used to address problems such as connectivity, food security, water management, and environmental protection, among many other pressing issues. An active participation in international space exploration projects will generate scientific and economic benefits for Mexico, in addition to increasing the involvement of Mexican astronauts in international space missions. However, the new administration in the restructured AEM and ATDT must endorse all of this.

3 Final Remarks

Although so far the LAEM, the LGPEM, and the PNAE have allowed—in past years—the AEM and the space sector to operate in Mexico, its current scope is limited, so it is necessary to have a national law that promotes the development of national capacities in space, encourages scientific research and the formation of specialized human capital, and promotes national and foreign investment while providing legal certainty to investors in the sector and promoting the generation of a space ecosystem and the corresponding local supply chain in industries such as satellite, ground stations, space ports and launch vehicles (rockets), space tourism, and analog stations, among other industries related to space activities, which are essential for the sustainable development of the sector.

Given the significant number of space-related issues in Mexico that the AEM was addressing, as outlined below, it is crucial for the reorganized AEM and the ATDT to establish a clear stance on the numerous issues beyond its Mexican space program that demand immediate and substantial attention. This will enable the country to continue developing national space capacities, promote Mexico's space development, and foster the growth of other industries and sectors.

A National Space Development Law in Mexico is a legal instrument of vital importance to articulate and consolidate the country's space sector and take full advantage of its potential, in the global context of the New Space Race and New Space. This law will establish a solid and coherent legal framework for space activities, providing legal certainty to all actors involved, including non-state actors such as companies, promoting investment and innovation in the nascent national space ecosystem, generating jobs, and contributing to the scientific-technological, economic, and social development of the country.

The National Space Development Law is crucial for the development of the space sector in Mexico, for several reasons related to the following issues, the relevance of which is unquestionable:

- Legal certainty, defining the rights and obligations of public and private actors involved in space activities, avoiding conflicts, and ensuring a stable investment environment
- Investment promotion, which will attract domestic and foreign investment to the space sector by providing a clear and transparent regulatory framework to boost the national space ecosystem
- Technological development, which will support research, development, and innovation (R&D&I) in space technologies, software, and applications and generate national space knowledge and capabilities
- The creation of new highly skilled and remunerated jobs in the space sector, contributing to the economic development, value added productivity, and competitiveness of the country
- The development of practical space applications to solve various national problems, such as the management of natural resources, early warning systems to prevent disasters caused by natural phenomena, and the improvement of many public services
- Contributing to the strengthening of national security and sovereignty, by developing our own space capabilities and reducing dependence on foreign technologies
- Facilitate international cooperation in space, allowing Mexico to participate in projects of bilateral, regional, and global importance, such as NASA's Artemis program, and to access advanced technologies in collaboration with other countries and space agencies

This is in addition to ensuring the participation of the "quadruple helix" (government, industry, academia, and organized civil society) in the formulation of Mexico's space policy, in order to make the entire population aware of the importance of a law of this dimension and scope.

Based on the analysis of the information presented here, it is recommended that space regulation in Mexico, through the National Space Development Law, continue to evolve in the coming years, with emphasis on the following aspects:

An Expansion of the Regulatory Framework
Following the constitutional reform on space matters, the creation of a secondary law, the National Space Development Law, Mexico must work on the development of new laws, rules, regulations, and legislative harmonization to meet the needs of the space sector, which is constantly evolving. This will allow to articulate the national space sector in a cross-cutting approach.

Development of Indigenous Capabilities
The experience gained during the AEM's existence will compel it to seek autonomy in management, budget, and decision-making in order to promote strategic projects with a long-term vision. The AEM should focus on the development of national capabilities, the promotion of research and technological development, and international cooperation.

Strengthening the Space Industry
Throughout this review, we have considered the urgent need and importance of regulating space activities while encouraging and promoting the development of a national space industry/ecosystem, with the participation of private companies and the support of government, industry, academia, and organized civil society in the space agenda: the "quadruple helix."

Greater Investment in the Space Sector
The global trend, and it is expected that Mexico will not be excluded from this trend, is that public and private investment in the space sector will increase in the coming years, allowing the development of new technologies and applications with broad scientific and economic benefits.

The Development of Space Capabilities
Building national capacity in the space sector will enable the country to take advantage of space technologies to solve national problems such as natural resource management, disaster prevention, and improvement of communication services in remote areas.

Space Infrastructure
It is necessary to promote the development of space infrastructure, such as launch centers and ground stations, to support Mexico's space activities. The development of small, low-cost nanosatellites for Earth observation is another area in which Mexico should continue to invest. These satellites will be used for various applications such as communications, education, and scientific research.

Commercial Applications
Research, development, and innovation carried out in universities tend to be funded and linked with public and private entities to explore commercial applications of space technologies, such as telecommunications services, Earth observation and

satellite navigation, tourism, and space mining, among other sectors of the space, cislunar, and lunar economy. Universities and research centers in Mexico, such as UNAM and IPN, carry out important research in the space field, contributing to the development of national technology.

The Development of Specialized Human Talent

It is necessary to implement programs to train professionals in the space sector, through scholarships, specialization courses, academic exchanges with other countries, and the creation of research centers to stop the "brain drain" and repatriate national talent abroad.

Regional Cooperation

A country with greater space capabilities and solid regulation will strengthen cooperation with other countries in the region on space matters through the Latin American and Caribbean Space Agency (ALCE), the Space Conference of the Americas (CEA), the Community of Latin American and Caribbean States (CELAC), and the UN-affiliated Regional Centre for Space Science and Technology Education for Latin America and the Caribbean (CRECTEALC).

At the international level, Mexico will continue to strengthen its collaboration with other space agencies (NASA, ESA, JAXA, and ISRO, among others) and countries, as well as through conferences, networks, and forums, such as the OEI's Ibero-American Network of Space Agencies and the meeting of the space agencies of the member countries of the International Italo-Latin American Organization (IILA), which will allow access to new technologies and the exchange of knowledge, information, best practices, and expertise.

The global trend in space regulation outlines prospects for greater commercialization of space based on innovation and technological development but also promotes the protection of space resources and, consequently, space governance. In this context, space regulation in Mexico is adapting to both national and global challenges, combining national legislation, fulfilling its obligations, and strengthening international cooperation, with the aim of ensuring that space activities are carried out in a safe, responsible, peaceful, and sustainable manner.

Mexico has made significant progress in space regulation but still faces many challenges, such as the need to establish a National Space Development Law, increase investment in the sector in both the civil and military sectors, articulate the "quadruple helix" around a Mexican space policy and a real Mexican space program with a long-term vision, strengthen the industry supply chain, and develop specialized human talent and national capabilities to drive Mexico's space development. Nevertheless, space regulation offers great opportunities, and the national space sector has the potential to become an engine of innovation, growth, and economic development. While space regulation in Mexico is at an important stage of development and consolidation, and the significant progress made so far is promising, much remains to be done to consolidate the country as a relevant player in the global space arena.

As can be seen, it is necessary that in the coming years, under the Sheinbaum administration (2024–2030), space regulation in Mexico continues to strengthen a solid and comprehensive regulatory framework that will allow increased investment in the sector and develop new applications of space technologies, among many other purposes described here. To achieve these objectives, it is essential to have a long-term vision, a Mexican space program (Romero Vázquez 2024b, c; 2025b, c, d, e) that is both real and realistic and a coherent and comprehensive Mexican space policy with the commitment of all the actors involved: public, private, academic, and organized civil society, the "quadruple helix."

References

Programa Nacional de Actividades Espaciales (PNAE) 2020 – 2024, Avances y Resultados 2021, SCT. https://www.gob.mx/cms/uploads/attachment/file/735889/09_PI_AEM_AyR21.pdf. https://www.gob.mx/aem/documentos/programa-nacional-de-actividades-espaciales-2020-2024

Altamirano AL (2024) "Se espera pronta aprobacion de Ley espacial", portal Aviacion 21, August 30. https://a21.com.mx/aeroespacial/2024/08/30/se-espera-pronta-aprobacion-de-ley-espacial

Aviación 21 (2025) "Presenta ATDT Programa Espacial Mexicano en la Feria Aeroespacial México 2025", abril 28, en https://a21.com.mx/aeroespacial/2025/04/28/presenta-atdt-programa-espacial-mexicano-en-la-feria-aeroespacial-mexico-2025-2/

Diario Oficial de la Federacion (2011) Acuerdo mediante el cual se dan a conocer las Lineas Generales de la Política Espacial de Mexico, July 13. https://dof.gob.mx/nota_detalle.php%3Fcodigo%3D5200730%26fecha%3D13/07/2011&print=true

Diario Oficial de la Federación (DOF) (2025) "Decreto por el que se reforman, adicionan y derogan diversas disposiciones de la Ley Orgánica de la Administración Pública Federal", noviembre 28, en https://dof.gob.mx/nota_detalle.php?codigo=5744005&fecha=28/11/2024#gsc.tab=0

Gobierno de Mexico (2010) Decreto por el que se expide la Ley que Crea la Agencia Espacial Mexicana, Diario Oficial de la Federacion (DOF), 30-07-2010, Camara de Diputados del H. Congreso de la Union, https://www.gob.mx/aem/documentos/ley-que-crea-la-agencia-espacial-mexicana

Gobierno de Mexico (2018) "México preside la Comision para la Utilizacion del Espacio Exterior con Fines Pacificos (COPUOS) de la ONU y la Cumbre UNISPACE+50", press release AEM. https://www.gob.mx/aem/prensa/mexico-preside-la-comision-para-la-utilizacion-del-espacio-exterior-con-fines-pacificos-copuos-de-la-onu-y-la-cumbre-unispace-50-164077?idiom=fr

Gobierno de Mexico (2021) "Registro de Objetos Lanzados al espacio activos y no activos", Agencia Espacial Mexicana (AEM), February 5. https://www.gob.mx/aem/documentos/registro-de-objetos-lanzados-al-espacio-activos-y-no-activos

Gobierno de Mexico (2022) "Instrumentos internacionales firmados con agencias espaciales". AEM, December 13. https://www.gob.mx/aem/documentos/instrumentos-internacionales

Gobierno de Mexico (2023a) "Buscan instalar industria espacial europea en Mexico", AEM, Press release 165-2023, September 20. https://www.gob.mx/aem/prensa/buscan-instalar-industria-espacial-europea-en-mexico-345580?idiom=es

Gobierno de Mexico (2023b) "Proyecto satelital *Constelacion AztechSat* concluye primera fase y es reconocido por NASA", AEM, April 28. https://www.gob.mx/aem/es/articulos/proyecto-satelital-constelacion-aztechsat-concluye-primera-fase-y-es-reconocido-por-nasa?idiom=es

Gobierno de Mexico (2024) "Participa México ante la ONU en foros de alto nivel en materia espacial", Comunicado AEM 078-2024, julio 8, 2024. https://www.gob.mx/aem/prensa/participa-mexico-ante-la-onu-en-foros-de-alto-nivel-en-materia-espacial-370461?idiom=es

Gobierno de Mexico (2025) "IV Encuentro de las Agencias Espaciales de los países membros de la IILA", junio 4. https://www.gob.mx/aem/galerias/iv-encuentro-de-las-agencias-espaciales-

de-los-paises-miembros-de-la-iila and "IV Encuentro de Agencias Espaciales de los países miembros de la Organizacion Internacional Italo-Latinoamericana– IILA en colaboracion con la Agencia Espacial Italiana – ASI". https://iila.org/es/37850/
Gobierno de Mexico, AEM (2012) "Plan de Orbita: Mapa de Ruta de la Industria Espacial Mexicana 2013" AEM, August 5. https://www.gob.mx/aem/documentos/plan-de-orbita-mapa-de-ruta-de-la-industria-espacial-mexicana-2013
Gobierno de Mexico, AEM (2023) "Aprueba Camara de Diputados reforma constitucional en materia espacial", abril 11, 2023, https://www.gob.mx/aem/articulos/aprueba-camara-de-diputados-reforma-constitucional-en-materia-espacial-331196
Gobierno de Mexico, Agencia Espacial Mexicana (2011) "Antecedentes de la AEM", July 13. https://www.gob.mx/aem/acciones-y-programas/antecedentes-de-la-aem
Gobierno de Mexico Embajada de Mexico en Estados Unidos, Secretaría de Relaciones Exteriores (SRE) (2021) ≤Que es Artemisa? https://embamex.sre.gob.mx/eua/index.php/es/2016-04-09-20-40-51/cooperacion-y-educacion/educacion/1925-artemisa
Gobierno de México, Secretaria de Economía (2019) Manifestación de uso y usuario final y sus modificaciones para obtener el permiso previo de exportación de armas convencionales, sus partes y componentes, bienes de uso dual, software y tecnologías relacionadas. https://www.gob.mx/se/acciones-y-programas/se-03-080-manifestacion-de-uso-y-usuario-final-para-obtener-elpermiso-previo-de-exportacion-de-armas-convencionales-bienes-de-uso-dual
LINX ICN UNAM (2023) Colmena la mision mas ambiciosa de LINX. https://linx.nucleares.unam.mx/colmena/
NASA (2024) The Artemis Accords. https://www.nasa.gov/artemis-accords/
Navarrete S (2020) "FEMIA y AEM: Lanzamiento de la Industria espacial mexicana", Mexico Aerospace, November 17. https://mexicoaerospace.com.mx/noticias/femia-y-aem-lanzamiento-de-la-industria-espacial-mexicana
Romero Vázquez (2023a) "La Reforma Constitucional en Materia Espacial en México: Hacia un Marco Legal para el Desarrollo Espacial de México" Boletin del Observatorio Juridico Aeroespacial, N°. 11, June 2023, pages. 20-23, ISSN-e 2792-4114, Asociacion Española de Derecho Aeronautico y Espacial (AEDAE). https://aedae-aeroespacial.org/boletin-11-junio-2023/
Romero Vázquez (2023b) "Hacia un programa espacial mexicano", November 9. https://a21.com.mx/index.php/cafe-espacial/2023/11/09/hacia-un-programa-espacial-mexicano; "De la coheteria experimental hacia un puerto espacial en México", July 6. https://a21.com.mx/cafe-espacial/2023/07/06/de-la-coheteria-experimental-hacia-un-puerto-espacial-en-mexico; "Construir una industria espacial relevante en la era NewSpace" June 22. https://a21.com.mx/cafe-espacial/2023/06/22/construir-una-industria-espacial-relevante-en-la-era-new-space; "2023 y el sector espacial en México, desafios y oportunidades", January 5. https://a21.com.mx/index.php/cafe-espacial/2023/01/05/2023-y-el-sector-espacial-en-mexico-desafios-y-oportunidades and "2024 desafios y oportunidades para México en el sector espacial" January 4. https://a21.com.mx/cafe-espacial/2024/01/04/2024-desafios-y-oportunidades-para-mexico-en-el-sector-espacial
Romero Vázquez (2024a) "Mision Colmena, Mexico en la Nueva Carrera Espacial", enero 19. https://a21.com.mx/opinion/2024/01/19/mision-colmena-mexico-en-la-nueva-carrera-espacial/
Romero Vázquez (2024b) "Política Espacial de México, la necesaria evolución de las Líneas Generales de Política Espacial", noviembre 29, en https://a21.com.mx/opinion/2024/11/29/politica-espacial-de-mexico-la-necesaria-evolucion-de-las-lineas-generales-de-politica-espacial/
Romero Vázquez (2024c) "La AEM en la estructura orgánica de la administración Sheinbaum", noviembre 22, en https://a21.com.mx/opinion/2024/11/22/la-aem-en-la-estructura-organica-de-la-administracion-sheinbaum/
Romero Vázquez (2025a) "Mexico y el Regimen de Control de Tecnologia de Misiles", febrero 7. https://a21.com.mx/opinion/2025/02/07/mexico-y-el-regimen-de-control-de-tecnologia-de-misiles-mtcr/

Romero Vázquez (2025b) "Las fallas estructurales del nuevo programa espacial mexicano (PEM) de la ATDT", mayo 30. https://a21.com.mx/opinion/2025/05/30/las-fallas-estructurales-del-nuevo-programa-espacial-mexicano-pem-de-la-atdt/

Romero Vázquez (2025c) "El sector espacial mexicano, perspectivas en la ATDT", febrero 14. https://a21.com.mx/opinion/2025/02/14/el-sector-espacial-mexicano-perspectivas-en-la-atdt/

Romero Vázquez (2025d) "El sector espacial nacional en el segundo piso de la 4T", enero 29, en https://a21.com.mx/opinion/2025/01/29/el-sector-espacial-nacional-en-el-segundo-piso-de-la-4t/

Romero Vázquez (2025e) "2025, punto de inflexión para el sector espacial", enero 3, en https://a21.com.mx/opinion/2025/01/03/2025-punto-de-inflexion-para-el-sector-espacial/

Romero Vázquez (2010) Hacia la formulacion de una política espacial en México. Revista Mexicana de Política Exterior 90:51–103. https://revistadigital.sre.gob.mx/index.php/rmpe/article/view/591. https://revistadigital.sre.gob.mx/index.php/rmpe/article/view/591/563

The Hague Institute for Global Justice (2023) Sergio Camacho. https://thehagueinstituteforglobaljustice.org/portfolio/sergio-camacho/

United Nations Office for Outer Space Affairs (2017) International space law: United Nations Instruments, Space Law Treaties and Principles, United Nations, New York. https://www.unoosa.org/oosa/en/ourwork/spacelaw/treaties.html

Paraguay

Hebe Romero

Contents

H. Romero (✉)
Universidad Nacional de Asunción (UNA), Asunción, Paraguay

I. Grosner (ed.), *Space Regulation in Latin America*, Space Regulations Library 11, https://doi.org/10.1007/978-3-032-05828-7_7

Abstract In 2021, Paraguay entered the space sector by launching its first satellite, GuaraniSat-1, developed under the Paraguayan Space Agency (AEP). This milestone marked Paraguay's transformation into a spacefaring nation. GuaraniSat-1, part of the BIRDS-4 Project, was launched to the International Space Station and later placed into orbit. The creation of GuaraniSat-1 led to the development of national space policies, including the Paraguayan Space Policy, and compliance with international treaties, such as the 1967 Space Treaty. Paraguay has since joined the Committee on the Peaceful Uses of Outer Space (COPUOS) and has been actively participating in international space forums. The country aims to further develop its space capabilities, highlighted by the planning of its second satellite, GuaraniSat-2, and various international collaborations. These achievements underscore Paraguay's commitment to peaceful space exploration, technological innovation, and international cooperation while setting the foundation for future advancements in its space program.

1 Introduction

In 2021, Paraguay achieved a historic milestone by joining the select group of nations with a presence in space. This accomplishment was made possible through an innovative national strategy led by the newly created Paraguayan Space Agency (AEP). Under its flagship initiative, the "Paraguay to Space Project," the country prioritized building space capabilities through strategic local and international partnerships. The effort culminated in GuaraniSat-1, Paraguay's first satellite, whose full life cycle—design, construction, testing, launch, and orbital deployment—was successfully executed. This feat solidified Paraguay's entry into the space age.

On February 20, 2021, GuaraniSat-1, Paraguay's first satellite, was launched into space, specifically to the International Space Station (ISS), and on March 14 of the same year it was put into orbit. It was part of a constellation of nanosatellites (three in total, from Paraguay, Japan, and the Philippines).

In this unique and innovative project, international cooperation was led by the United Nations Office for Outer Space Affairs (UNOOSA), thanks to the fact that the Japan Aerospace Exploration Agency (JAXA) developed the KiboCUBE Program, consisting of the deployment of CubeSat-type nanosatellites installed on the Japanese experimental module (Kibo) of the ISS (from the Kibo arm). It was an opportunity for Paraguay to participate in the BIRDS-4 Project of the Kyushu Institute of Technology (KYUTECH) in Japan.

GuaraniSat-1 was developed in the light of national and international legislation on the regulation of space activities, which broadly describes it as an object with a specific legal space regime.

The first Paraguayan satellite was a milestone and transcended in accordance with the regulations in force in Paraguay and gave rise to other regulations necessary for the proper development of space activities.

2 Topics

This chapter develops the most relevant topics on Paraguay and space activities, Paraguay as a new space nation, its change of status, national legislation, and international treaties related to outer space.

The role of the Paraguayan Space Agency, a public entity with specific objectives and functions, as a regulatory body for space activities in the country is highlighted. The National Development Plan 2030, the Strategic Planning of the Paraguayan Space Agency, international alliances, as well as the importance of international cooperation are pointed out. According to Paraguay's space policy, the activities that are entering into the development of space capabilities and technological and regulatory capabilities are described.

The registration of space objects is another topic, especially in the international arena and on the administrative process in Paraguay, in addition to other topics that translate into the description of activities reflecting the growth of the country in that aspect.

2.1 Which International Space Treaties Has Paraguay Signed as a Party?

The Republic of Paraguay has signed a number of international treaties on outer space and several related treaties, such as telecommunications and others. Table 1 shows which international instruments have been signed and ratified and others to which the Paraguayan state has acceded, in the case of the instruments of the *corpus iuris spatialis*, almost five decades later. This was due to the fact that Paraguay did not include space issues in the government's agenda, without reflecting on the reasons, and rather clear it was over the years of the milestones that marked space history.

After viewing the table of international instruments signed, ratified, and acceded to by the Republic of Paraguay, it is important to point out that the legislative form of making international instruments part of Paraguayan positive law is through the provisions of the National Constitution of the Republic of Paraguay, of June 20, 1992, the Magna Carta of the country, the fundamental and principal law.

Article 137 of the National Constitution establishes the supremacy of the Constitution and the order of priority: "The supreme law of the Republic is the Constitution. This, the treaties, conventions and international agreements approved and ratified, the laws enacted by Congress and other legal provisions of lower hierarchy, sanctioned accordingly, make up national positive law in the order of priority enunciated."

The Ministry of Foreign Affairs has the legal power, through its directorates, to deal with the procedures for the formalization and entry into force of international, bilateral, or multilateral treaties, as well as interinstitutional agreements, ranging

Table 1 Status of ratifications and validity of conventions in the field of space and outer space law

No	Title	Place and date of adoption	Place and date signature (Py)	Paraguayan ratification (law)	Deposit, ratified. Adhesion	Entry into force document	Entry into force Py
1	Treaty on Principles Governing the Activities of States in the Exploration and use of Outer Space, including the Moon and Other Celestial Bodies	London, Moscow, and Washington Jan 27, 1967	No	LAW N° 5740 Nov 18, 2016	Dec 16, 2016	Oct 10, 1967	Dec 16, 2016
2	Agreement on the Rescue of Astronauts, the Return of Astronauts and the Return of Objects Launched into Outer Space	London, Moscow, and Washington Apr 22, 1968	No	LAW N° 7175 Oct 16, 2023	Pending confirmation by the Depositary	Dec 3, 1968	
3	Convention on International Liability for Damage Caused by Space Objects	London, Moscow, and Washington Mar 29, 1972	No	LAW N° 7097 May 29, 2023	Jul 11, 2023	Sept 1, 1972	Jul 11, 2023
4	Convention on Registration of Objects Launched into Outer Space	Nov 12, 1974	No	LAW N°7051 Jan 4, 2023	Pending confirmation by the Depositary	Sept 15, 1976 (Art VIII.3) Depositary: ONU	
5	Agreement Governing the Activities of States on the Moon and Other Celestial Bodies	Dec 5, 1979	No	–	No	Jul 11, 1984 (Art. 19.3) Depositary: ONU	

from negotiation and signing by the plenipotentiaries of Paraguay, to the processes of incorporation, as the case may be, to the national legal system through the approval and sanction of the Congress of the nation by law of the Republic, the promulgation and publication by the executive power, until the entry into force, after the exchange and/or deposit of the instrument of ratification, accession, approval, and/or acceptance, in each case, in compliance with the precepts of Article 141 of the Constitution of the Republic and the Vienna Convention on the Law of Treaties.

The technical guidelines on the law of treaties are contained in the Constitution of the Republic and the Vienna Convention on the Law of Treaties of 1969, as well as in customary practice in this area. These guidelines govern the entire process of negotiation, refinement, application, implementation, denunciation, or termination of treaties, along with their registration and safekeeping by Paraguay.

2.2 *Is Paraguay a Member of COPUOS?*

The Republic of Paraguay has been a full member of the Committee on the Peaceful Uses of Outer Space (COPUOS) since 2018. Previously, Paraguayan diplomatic representatives of the Mission in Austria participated in the sessions of the subcommissions accompanied by the technicians of the scientific and legal area of the Paraguayan Space Agency, a public entity, directly dependent on the Presidency of the Republic of Paraguay.

Likewise, the aforementioned participations took place not only as a full member but also in working groups. It should be noted that the Ambassador of Paraguay, Juan Francisco Facetti, chaired the Subcommittee on Scientific and Technical Affairs of COPUOS, in the period 2022–2024, being the first time that a Paraguayan representative directly assumed the presidency.

2.3 *Has Paraguay Signed the Artemis Accords?*

To date, the Republic of Paraguay has not signed the Artemis Accords. However, at the 2024 COPUOS sessions, representatives of the delegations of the United States and Paraguay, including the minister, president of the Paraguayan Space Agency, met to agree on the procedure for the signing of the Artemis Accords. On the other hand, the Embassy of the United States sent the invitation for Paraguay to sign.

In order to continue with the procedure indicated in the previous topics, the Paraguayan Space Agency will issue a technical and legal opinion regarding the feasibility of signing the Artemis Agreements.

In this regard, both the Law of the Ministry of Foreign Affairs and Law No. 5151/14 of the Paraguayan Space Agency clearly establish the intervention of the Ministry of Foreign Affairs, in cases of signing agreements with the public and private sectors at the international level.

Thus, and in accordance with the procedure for the signing of agreements, conventions, and/or memorandums of understanding (MOUs), since the beginning of the activities of the Paraguayan Space Agency in 2017, to date, almost 100 bilateral instruments have been signed.

2.4 *Can Space Activities Be Classified as Dual Use, or Are They Only for Defense or Civil Purposes?*

In the first place, technologies are necessary for the development of space activities, and these tools allowed the initiation and development of space activities. Such technologies are dual use because the determination of what they will be used for depends on those who develop them or who can make them available for use in the manufacture of nuclear weapons and other nonexplosive uses.

Throughout history, there have been great technological advances applied or used for peaceful or military purposes, that is, for civilian or defense purposes and for military or war purposes.

In the civil scope, there have been technology transfers, driven by research and innovation and, of course, from the objective of the use of said technology. This fact also occurred as a result of the Cold War with significant secrecy, to later give rise to cooperation with a view to the civil, industrial, and academic spheres. Dual-use technological areas are practically all those that can be used for such use, including information technologies, communications, energy, space systems and infrastructures, materials, optics, biotechnology, and unmanned aerial vehicles (UAVs), for example.

However, in accordance with the principles of space law, dual-use space activities should not be established, since outer space must be used for peaceful purposes. However, as indicated at the beginning, it depends on who can develop and dispose of them and on the objectives and unwavering compliance with the precepts for the use of outer space.

Likewise, in the case of Paraguay, it is relevant to note that Paraguay's space policy, among the guidelines, establishes the training and use of space technology, maintaining that the use and application of professional, scientific, and technological knowledge in the aerospace field will be encouraged by entrepreneurs, national public, and private companies, respecting intellectual property rights, in accordance with international agreements.

The Paraguayan Space Agency (AEP) coordinates initiatives to promote the open dissemination of space-derived knowledge and information—when not contrary to national interests—and trains personnel from public and private institutions in its effective application. By leveraging advanced scientific and technological knowledge, these initiatives maximize the use of national and international space resources in various sectors of production and development.

2.5 *Is There a Registry of Space Objects Maintained by the United Nations?*

Significantly, for the determination of the responsibility of States, of international responsibility for their space objects, a mechanism was established in 1962 to assist in COPUOS discussions on the registration of objects launched into outer space.

In 1976, the Convention on Registration of Objects Launched into Outer Space entered into force. States and international intergovernmental organizations that agree to comply with the Convention should establish their own national registries and provide information on their space objects to the Secretary-General for inclusion in the United Nations Register. The Secretary-General delegated responsibility for the maintenance of the Register to the United Nations Office for Outer Space Affairs.

The UNOOSA web platform is available to view the records of space objects, as provided for in the Convention, and is publicly disseminated. There is also an archive of United Nations documents in which these records are recorded. Objects, such as satellites, probes, landers, manned spacecraft, and space station flight elements that are launched into space, are registered, not in their entirety but in a large majority.

This situation arises from the lack of full compliance on the part of the States that have adopted the Convention and also from their own legislation, some of which is weak in terms of its control and effective registration practice.

As for the Republic of Paraguay, in 2023, through Law 7051/2023, it adhered to the provisions. Likewise, in the practical case of the launch and launch into orbit of its first satellite, GuaraniSat-1 (1U nanosatellite, 10 cm × 10 cm × 10 cm), in February and March 2021, respectively, it had not yet adopted the aforementioned Convention in its legislation. However, in 2016 it had already adopted, that is, it acceded to the 1967 Space Treaty, so it complied with the provisions, and taking into account that the registration of space objects is an obligation imposed on States, the Paraguayan Space Agency was in charge of carrying out the procedure for their registration before UNOOSA, through the Embassy and Permanent Mission of Paraguay in Vienna.

GuaraniSat-1 was registered in accordance with the 1967 Space Treaty and by virtue of the provisions of Resolution 1721 B (XVI) of the United Nations General Assembly of December 20, 1961, and the guidelines indicated by UNOOSA and ITU. This resolution urges States launching space objects to provide timely information on the launch so that the United Nations can maintain a public record, as noted above.

Although UNGA Resolution 1721 B (XVI) is not legally binding, as it is a resolution and does not impose obligations on States, the international registration of space objects launched into space was declared mandatory in 1975 with the Registration Convention, at least as far as States that are parties to the Registration Convention are concerned.

For States that are not parties to the Convention, international registration may be made in accordance with that Resolution. The information to be provided is as follows: name of the launching State(s); appropriate designation of the space object or its registration number; date and territory or location of launch; basic orbital parameters, including nodal period, inclination, apogee, and perigee; and the general function of the space object.

The registration form refers to UNGA Resolution 62/101 of 2007, entitled "Recommendations to improve the practice of States and international intergovernmental organizations in registering space objects." Rather, it refers to additional information, e.g., updating its circumstances: change of function, nonfunctional status, change of orbital position, transfer to an orbit for disposal, and changes in the status of its owner, operator, or the space object itself.

Currently, the Convention on the Registration of Objects Launched into Outer Space is already part of the legal system, through Law No. 7051/2023. As a result of this novelty, the Paraguayan Space Agency is carrying out studies and analyses for the preparation of the national regulation for the creation of the registry.

2.6 Does Paraguay Have a National Specific Space Act or Regulations?

The Republic of Paraguay has a law that creates the Paraguayan Space Agency, and this law dates back to 2014.

The Paraguayan Space Policy was approved by Decree No. 1092 of January 7, 2019, and was established as one more tool for the development and national defense of Paraguay. This instrument has principles, objectives, and guidelines.

The principles are related to the training of human resources, the promotion of national development, and the strengthening of the country in the field of space activity and international cooperation.

Specifically, the principle of human talent development focuses on cultivating specialized capabilities through training in space sciences, technologies, and related disciplines at all academic levels.

This perspective is for the management and coordination of the preparation of training plans and programs with the relevant state bodies, especially those related to academia and professions related to the space area. The objective is to promote the national development through the AEP by seeking Paraguay's insertion into the international space community, generating wealth and jobs for the country, as responsible for all the strategic decisions of the Paraguayan space program, taking into account especially as a developing country that activities related to outer space are innovative, research and development.

To maximize the benefits of the space sector and in observance of the principles governing the activities of States in the exploration of outer space—including the Moon and other celestial bodies—as well as the promotion of all activities carried out by civil society related to the exploitation of space resources and outer space. In this regard, the AEP must establish the relevant regulations that enable space activity by persons and public or private entities, which serve the economic, political, social, and cultural development of the country, as well as compliance with the international legal instruments ratified by Paraguay.

The strengthening of the country in the field of space activity, from the point of view that all space activities will be oriented toward the peaceful use of outer space, procedures that will contribute to strengthening national and international cooperation in the event of emergencies declared by the competent bodies under national regulations, will be complied with in accordance with the provisions of international law.

Interinstitutional cooperation is essential for establishing relationships with public science and technology institutions. This collaboration, conducted within each party's respective areas of expertise, aims to develop programs and projects together that promote technological innovation and scientific research.

Through international cooperation, the basis of international statements, the AEP promotes and coordinates efforts to promote international cooperation in the exploration and use of outer space, in search of the exchange of knowledge and technology by society and for its benefit, and for the promotion and strengthening of competitiveness and innovation in space issues. These are fundamental for the present and future of the country's economic and social progress.

Among the objectives, in accordance with the guiding principles, the objectives were established, such as:

- The sustainability of the State
- The development of the productive sector
- Active participation of national companies and entrepreneurs
- Research, development, innovation, and entrepreneurship (R&D+i+E)

Among the guidelines of Paraguay's space policy, the following are described:

- Implementation of international cooperation
- Legal framework
- Infrastructure
- Promotion of development and protection of the population and its property
- Environmental protection
- Scientific dissemination
- Training and use of space technology
- Promotion of industry and commerce
- Generation of indigenous knowledge and resources
- Safety

The Paraguayan Space Policy can be reviewed periodically, and the AEP is in charge of carrying out the revisions and in turn must submit it to the national government for consideration.

2.7 *Does Paraguay Have a Space Agency?*

The Republic of Paraguay has a Paraguayan Space Agency, created by Law No. 5151 of March 26, 2014. The Law has nine articles. The acronym AEP identifies it, being an autarchic entity, with the purpose of understanding, designing, proposing, and executing policies and programs in space and aerospace matters. It is worth mentioning that the AEP is not an autarchic entity currently; it is included as a program of activities within the Presidency of the Republic. In order for it to be a true autarchic entity, that is, to have its own resources, administrative procedures will have to be carried out so that it is really an independent institution in terms of resources.

The AEP does not depend on a ministry or other public institution linked to science and technology as in other countries. Its location as a public entity in the central administration is directly under the administrative and functional dependence of the Presidency of the Republic.

The overall objective of the AEP is to promote and manage the development of national space activities by promoting the technological innovation necessary to achieve and make peaceful use of outer space.

Among the main functions, the following are cited:

- To implement Paraguay's space policy, through the preparation and implementation of the National Program of Space Activities.
- To carry out research tasks leading to the formation of groups that possess the disciplines and techniques necessary for access to space technology and its applications.
- To carry out development tasks in advanced engineering, covering the fields necessary to achieve adequate national space technology.
- To ensure the training and permanent improvement of researchers, professionals, technicians, and suitable personnel, through courses, scholarships, and interaction with universities, state agencies, and other institutions in the country or abroad.
- To provide technical assistance to the State in space matters.
- To generate guidelines, rules, and regulations so that the exploration, use, and exploitation of outer space serve as a tool for the economic, political, social, and cultural development of the country, in the terms, extent, and conditions determined by international agreements, the international legal system, and by reason of the regulatory principles of the sovereignty, security, and integral defense of the nation.
- To promote and develop cooperation agreements with public and private entities of other countries, in accordance with the foreign policy of the Republic and with the due intervention of the Ministry of Foreign Affairs.
- To regulate and supervise the eligibility conditions for the concessions and granting and assignment of licenses for the use of aerospace technology. The process to process a license will be initiated through an administrative procedure.

– To advise the authorities in relation to the treaties and/or conventions, policies, programs, plans, and criteria that govern the matter.

What Are the Resources of the AEP?

(a) The budget items allocated by the General Budget of the Nation. For this purpose, administrative guidelines and regulations are followed so that the Ministry of Economy and Finance can submit to the Honorable National Congress for annual approval. Administrative procedures are carried out 1 year in advance with the presentation of operational plans and an annual contracting plan (for goods and services, in addition to the human resources necessary for the activities of the AEP).
(b) Income from the rights acquired by patents, licenses, and other rights originating in the activities carried out. To date, no services are offered from which income can be obtained nor are regulations established regarding patents or licenses for space activities. The public institution in charge of regulating the electromagnetic spectrum is the National Telecommunications Commission (CONATEL), and it is responsible for this regulation and the collection of licenses. CONATEL is a member of the Board of Directors of the AEP, as will be seen below.
(c) The amounts assigned to it by the application of special laws. With regard to this provision, there are mechanisms to obtain budget increases, through government bonds or other resources.
(d) The amounts awarded to it to carry out research and academic activities. Currently, the AEP applies for research projects, for example, in the research program of the National Council of Science and Technology (CONACYT), these projects are financed through the funds granted by this Institution, which in turn is a member of the Board of Directors of the AEP.
(e) Donations, legacies, and other contributions made by natural, legal, public, private, national, or foreign persons, in accordance with the laws that regulate the matter.

Decision-making in the AEP is in charge of a Board of Directors, made up of the president and 12 members appointed by the following institutions: (1) Ministry of National Defense; (2) Ministry of Foreign Affairs; (3) Ministry of Education and Science; (4) National Council of Science and Technology; (5) National University of Asunción—Faculty of Engineering; (6) National University of Asunción—Faculty of Polytechnics; (7) National University of Asunción—Faculty of Law and Social Sciences, through its Institute of Aeronautical and Space Law; (8) National Telecommunications Commission (CONATEL); (9) Paraguayan Air Force (FAP); (10) National Directorate of Civil Aeronautics (DINAC); (11) Ministry of Information and Communication Technologies (MITIC); and (12) Universidad Católica Nuestra Señora de Asunción, Faculty of Science and Technology.

Of the 12 public institutions, 1 is private. All 12 have the same faculties, as the representatives of these institutions (members of the Board of Directors) are appointed by decree of the executive power.

The term of office is 5 years, and the position is ad honorem, without remuneration from the AEP or from their own institutions whom they represent.

The same law establishes the powers of the Board of Directors, unlike the president of the AEP, who in terms of human resources is exclusively responsible for the appointment, hiring, removal, dismissal, and management of the same.

2.8 What Is the Primary Regulatory Body Responsible for Overseeing Space Activities?

The main regulatory body responsible for overseeing space activities is the Paraguayan Space Agency, as described in detail in the previous topic.

Now, the regulation of the electromagnetic spectrum is established in the National Constitution, and the National Telecommunications Commission (CONATEL) is in charge at the national level, and in turn it is the representative of the Republic of Paraguay to the International Telecommunication Union (ITU).

2.9 What Are the Primary Regulations Governing Space Activities, and How Are Private Companies Performing Space Activities Authorized, Monitored, and Supervised?

The Republic of Paraguay became aware of the imperative need for the use of national space resources, and, therefore, guidelines were defined in Paraguay's space policy, and several guiding principles were considered for the implementation of activities.

Despite the short time and much progress, there are currently no private companies that carry out space activities.

Since 2017, at the beginning of the administrative activities of the Paraguayan Space Agency, workshops, conferences, congresses, and training courses on topics related to the space field have been held, from satellite patch design competitions to the participation of the space law moot court, in all its forms of activities to promote and inspire the entire society from the participation of children and young school students, professional interns, students, and work interns with the production of programs on public television.

Today it is a matter of putting into practice and showing society more and more about the benefits of space to undertake and create the space economy, with commerce and the space industry.

2.10 *Is There Any Effort Toward Capacity Building in the Space Sector, Both in Terms of Technologies and Regulatory Matters?*

The Paraguayan Space Agency is working hard and defining the update of its Institutional Strategic Plan with the vision of being a leading entity in research, development, and innovation in the space sector, providing quality services that guarantee national sovereignty in the space field.

Clearly, it aligns its mission as an agency under the Presidency of the Republic that promotes, manages, and regulates regulations and policies in space and aerospace matters, for technological, socioeconomic, and cultural purposes and for the development of the country.

2.11 *How Does the State Engage in International Cooperation in the Space Sector, Both in Terms of Technologies and Representation in International Organizations? Are There Any Partnerships with Other Latin American Countries?*

The National Development Plan of Paraguay 2030 establishes in one of the axes the insertion of Paraguay in the international context.

In this sense, from the Paraguayan Space Agency, international relations are constantly developed with both the public and private sectors, from academia, companies, and space agencies

At the national level, there are approximately 100 signed interinstitutional cooperation instruments. At the international level strategic alliances have been established with key public and privates entities, including the Mexican Space Agency (AEM); Argentina's National Commission of Space Activities (CONAE), the Japan Aerospace Exploration Agency (JAXA), the Japan International Cooperation Agency (JICA), and the private companies Satellogic, Innova Space, and ArkEdge Space Inc.

The Japan International Cooperation Agency (JICA) and the AEP are carrying out the Space Program Management Project Applied to Socio-Economic Development, with the aim of contributing to the development of national capacities in the space sector and strengthening the country's social, economic, scientific, and technological development. This project seeks to strengthen Paraguay's ability to use space-related technologies and promote decision-making based on geospatial information.

2.12 How Does the Private Sector Conduct Its Activities in the Field of Space Exploration?

The insertion of the private sector in Paraguay in the field of space exploration is still very incipient and practically nonexistent. Although Paraguay's Space Policy establishes guidelines to promote private sector participation, and the AEP Law grants it the authority to act as a promoter of this sector, over its firts 7 years of operations, the Agency's most significant impact has been in the academic field. Its works has succeded in changing the perception of space-related activities from the initial school level through to the professional stage.

Today, children and young people participate in various space-related activities, such as high-altitude ballon (Globo Sonda) launches, satellites communications, and various experiments.

In the private commercial and industrial sector, it does not have the same luck.

2.13 What Are the Plans for Space Activities in Paraguay? Are Manned Flights and Spaceports Being Planned?

It has not yet been analyzed to be part of manned flights nor to establish spaceports in the Paraguayan territory. In the latter case it is not considered due to the issues proper to the construction and installation of a spaceport in Paraguay and due to the geography and physical conditions of the location of the country itself.

2.14 What Are (and Should Be) the Perspectives of Paraguay on Regulatory Matters Related to Space Debris, Militarization and Weaponization of Space, and Exploitation of Space Natural Resources?

Paraguay's perspective on space regulatory matters, particularly regarding space debris, militarization and weaponization of space, and the exploitation of space resources, reflects the country's commitment to peaceful space exploration and international cooperation. These positions are informed by the principles enshrined in both national legislation and international agreements to which Paraguay is a signatory.

Space Debris

Paraguay recognizes the growing global concern over space debris, as it poses significant risks to the sustainability of space activities. Although the country is still in the early stages of its space development, it acknowledges the importance of responsible space behavior. The Paraguayan Space Agency (AEP) is guided by international norms, including the Outer Space Treaty of 1967, to ensure that any objects launched into space from Paraguay are accounted for and managed responsibly. The country is also aware of the need to align with international best practices on space debris mitigation, such as the United Nations Space Debris Mitigation Guidelines, to protect both current and future space assets.

Militarization and Weaponization of Space
Paraguay firmly supports the use of outer space for peaceful purposes, as reflected in both its domestic policies and international commitments. The nation's space policy, as set by the AEP, explicitly states that space activities should be conducted solely for peaceful purposes. Paraguay's stance is aligned with the principles of the Outer Space Treaty, which prohibits the placement of weapons of mass destruction in space and limits military activities in outer space to nonaggressive purposes, such as scientific research and peaceful exploration.

The Paraguayan Space Agency is actively involved in international discussions on the regulation of space activities, participating in forums like the Committee on the Peaceful Uses of Outer Space (COPUOS). Paraguay's growing involvement in these dialogues demonstrates its commitment to ensuring that space remains free from militarization and weaponization. This aligns with the global push to prevent space from becoming an arena for conflict.

Exploitation of Space Natural Resources
While Paraguay has not yet actively engaged in the exploitation of space resources, it is mindful of the potential opportunities and challenges this area presents. The legal and ethical aspects of space resource exploitation, such as mining on celestial bodies like the Moon and asteroids, are currently being debated globally.

As a developing space nation, Paraguay may support the establishment of clear international regulations to ensure that the exploitation of space resources is conducted in an equitable and sustainable manner. The country would likely advocate for inclusive policies that allow emerging space nations to participate in space resource activities without being disadvantaged by more technologically advanced nations.

Paraguay's perspectives on space debris, militarization, weaponization, and resource exploitation are consistent with its broader goal of using space for peaceful purposes and fostering international cooperation. The country's space policies and involvement in international treaties underscore its commitment to maintaining outer space as a domain free from conflict while also addressing the environmental challenges posed by space debris. As Paraguay continues to build its space capabilities, it will likely support regulatory frameworks that promote responsible behavior in space, ensuring that both developed and emerging space nations can benefit from space resources in a fair and sustainable way.

2.15 Other Relevant Topics

Among the functions of the AEP established in the law is not related to the control of airspace. However, it was created as an entity to understand, design, propose, and execute space and aerospace policies and programs, that is, it has intervention to cooperate with DINAC, in terms of regulation and aerospace programs such as educational and scientific projects of balloon sounders.

Budget and infrastructure are two elementary factors for the strengthening of the AEP. Regarding the budget, there are only State resources, but no services are provided that allow them to be collected. Of the State resources, the AEP, which appears as a Program of Activities of the Presidency of the Republic, was assigned 1% of the budget of the executive branch, specifically of the Presidency of the Republic, as it depends functionally and administratively on it, although the future for the following year will be better, thanks to programs based on strategic alliances.

Paraguay grows hand in hand with the Paraguayan Space Agency, with promotes well-being through training in space science and technology, thereby strengthening the country's capabilities.

Balloon Probe

With the aim of motivating young people in high school in the study and development of skills in science, engineering, technology, arts, computer science, meteorology, and mathematics, through scientific and technological activities that range from the planning and definition of a satellite mission, to the post-processing of data after the launch of high-altitude balloons, the AEP carried out the 1st National Competition of Stratospheric Platforms "Balloon Probe," which consisted of devising, defining, designing, integrating, and implementing a payload (mission) to be launched in a balloon probe. Thirteen teams from public and private educational institutions from all over the country participated (100 students and more than 15 teachers/tutors). The winning teams launched their payloads through the probe balloons provided by the Paraguayan Space Agency. As a result, atmospheric data were obtained, including measurements of humidity, internal and external temperature, UV index, and time.

EIRU

The first space plate was developed entirely in Paraguay by the synergy of the government (AEP) and the academy (FP-UNA—FIUNA). The project consisted of the design and implementation of a payload for the Automatic Packet Reporting System (APRS) communication mission nanosatellite BIRDS-X, organized by the Kyushu Institute of Technology (KYUTECH) of Japan, which selected the design of said communications board to integrate the DragonFly satellite. This marked an important milestone for the development of aerospace engineering in Paraguay, being selected among the four best countries.

This project significantly strengthened the AEP's research and development in space telecommunications. The BIRDS-X satellite, which will carry the plate developed in Paraguay, will be put into orbit between the months of January and February 2025.

GuaraniSat-2: Second Paraguayan Satellite

The government of Paraguay, through the AEP, is committed to the development of national space technology. GuaraniSat-2 represents a continuation of the legacy established by GuaraniSat-1, marking a significant milestone as it was developed entirely within Paraguay. This effort is supported by a robust network of international and local partners.

The main objective of GuaraniSat-2 is to design, build, launch, and operate Paraguay's second satellite, promoting project-based learning strategies to increase the country's space capacity and paving the way for a sustainable space program.

The AEP's SpaceLab initiative seeks to significantly advance Paraguay's space capabilities, evidence of the collaborative effort involving prestigious institutions, including the Mexican Space Agency (AEM), the National Autonomous University of Mexico (UNAM), the University of the Republic of Uruguay (UDELAR), the Polytechnic University of Bari, the Astradyne company of Italy, and institutions in Paraguay.

The GuaraniSat-2 mission currently has the following planned objectives for in-orbit demonstration:

1) Testing of components: deployable solar panels and C&DH electronic board.
2) Validation of algorithms: attitude determination and fault-tolerant systems.
3) Evaluation of AEP-developed systems: a COTS Programmable Logic Device.
4) Operation of an Image Classification Unit of automatically select usable images.
5) Scientific data collection: particle radiation readings in the South American electromagnetic anomaly.
6) Communication tests using Long Range (LoRa) and APRS systems.

Innova Space

This is space technology within the reach of Paraguayan youth. The Paraguayan Space Agency (AEP) and Innova Space of Argentina are collaborating on a project with the aim of developing capabilities in applied space sciences, which focused on the implementation of LoRa communication, allowing the transmission of data from Paraguay to the MDQubeSat-2 satellite.

The project involved young people from the Polytechnic College of the Cooperative of Capiatá, who participated in days of technical visits to the headquarters of the AEP-UNA, with training, workshops, and satellite link tests, in coordination with the institutions involved (AEP-FPUNA). As a result successful transmissions were obtained from the terrestrial node to the satellite, four of them with fictitious data and six of them with data from temperature and humidity sensors.

Strategic Alliance: Enhancing Space and Socioeconomic Development in Paraguay Using Space Sciences and Technologies—JICA-AEP

The Paraguayan Space Agency (AEP) and the Japan International Cooperation Agency (JICA), through the interagency cooperation agreement, have initiated the technical cooperation project called "Space Program Management Project Applied to Socio-Economic Development." The project will be financed by JICA, for an amount close to 1,000,000 USD, which will contribute to the development of national skills in the space sector and strengthen the social, economic, scientific, and technological development of the country.

Two working groups for agriculture and livestock and disaster management were established, which made it possible to obtain the first data that will be used in the pilot project. Through the collaboration between the work team composed of technicians from the AEP and Japanese consultants from JICA, the Second Meeting of the Joint Coordination Committee (CCC) was held with several representatives of key ministries and institutions of Paraguay such as the National Emergency Secretariat (SEN), the Ministry of Agriculture and Livestock (MAG), and the National Service for Plant and Seed Quality and Health (SENAVE) for planning project activities. As a result, the implementation structure and content of the activities to be carried out within the framework of this technical cooperation were developed.

GEOLab New Generations: Innovative Remote Sensing Program for Young People in Paraguay

GEOLab New Generations is the first extracurricular remote sensing educational program for middle school students in Paraguay. Currently, there are 30 young people who are part of this educational project, which develops critical, spatial, and geographical thinking skills through meaningful learning, research, Earth observations, GIS, and remote sensing focused on analyzing and solving real problems in disaster risk reduction and climate change with the support of the NASA Disaster Program and Esri Panama.

The curriculum contains the following technical topics: introduction to geographic information systems; introduction to remote sensing; downloading, analyzing, and processing of satellite images; Earth observation applications; configuration and development of GIS tools for data visualization; spatial analytics using the ArcGIS Online system and ArcGIS Pro; spectral and multispectral images; combination of bands; and supervised and unsupervised classification.

GEOLab of the AEP promotes the use of geospatial data to improve decision-making in national institutions. To comply with the agreements established with the National Emergency Secretariat (SEN), the Ministry of Environment and Sustainable Development, the National Institute of Statistics, and the National Service of Plant and Seed Quality and Health (SENAVE), among others, GEOLab collaborates with these institutions by providing training workshops, technical assistance, as well as value-added products to promote the use of geospatial data for improved decision-making. During the period from August 2023 to June 2024, a total of 40 products, including thematic maps and various technical reports, were delivered at the request of these institutions.

This collaboration also contemplates strengthening the capacities of human capital, for which five trainings and a field trip were carried out with SENAVE with the aim of transferring knowledge and basic skills in the reduction of disaster risks related to fires, floods, and droughts, to promote the implementation of geospatial technology within the supervision processes of their programs and projects.

Atlas of GEOLab 2023

The AEP, through GEOLab, established a monitoring program for the creation of products, in which six university interns were integrated in charge of supervising various spectral indices using satellite data and geographic information systems (GIS) tools. As a result of this initiative, the "Atlas of GEOLab 2023" was produced, an exhaustive compilation of the main maps produced during the year. This atlas includes more than 100 thematic maps covering both the monitoring plan and other projects carried out.

The "Atlas of GEOLab 2023" is a set of thematic maps with methodologies applied to obtain them, the data sources used, and the corresponding credits. As a result of the daily research work, an internal manual was developed that compiles the methodologies used for the preparation of maps related to spectral indices and temporal analyses, which serves as a technical guide and reference for future research and projects in the field of Earth observation and geographic information systems.

AEP as NASA's Global Partner for the NASA Space Apps Challenge for the Third Consecutive Year

The Paraguayan Space Agency (AEP) through GEOLab was selected for the third consecutive year as "NASA Global Partner" for the NASA Space Apps Challenge Asunción 2023. This event was held on October 7 and 8 in person. The challenge brought together 96 participants and 15 teams from Paraguay and Panama, representing various disciplines to address challenges related to space exploration and aerospace technology. The event promoted the use of geospatial data and interest in science and technology.

The importance of this competence is evidenced in results. The young Paraguayan, Luciano Santiviago, was the winner in the "Best Narrative" category globally among more than 30,000 participants, a recognition that was given to the young student and the local organization of the event for Paraguay (AEP), in June of this year at NASA's Headquarters in Washington DC.

Space Law

Young university students from the law degree participated in the tests of the Manfred Lachs Space Law Moot Court Competition, in the city of Bogotá, Colombia, in 2019 and 2020 (face-to-face and virtual). This initiative arose from the General Directorate of Legal and International Affairs of the Paraguayan Space Agency, which was in charge of preparing the students so that they can participate. In addition, this was a magnificent first participation of Paraguay in the rounds of tests for Latin America to be qualified to participate in the annual international competition. Paraguay participated as a member judge of the mock court in the official competition that took place in Punta Cana, Dominican Republic, in 2022.

Volunteering

With the beginning of the activities of the AEP, many children and young people aroused their interest in joining or participating in various activities and even being available in case their collaboration is needed. There is a list of true enthusiasts in the space ecosystem of Paraguay, and for that reason volunteering was given, taking into account that national legislation allows this type of activities under these rules (voluntary collaboration according to the skills of the volunteer and without established schedules).

Internships

Over the years of its administrative life, the AEP was initially classified as a reference of great level for students who want to prepare or get a space abroad in an academic institution, and as it is multidisciplinary, the letters of support or references granted by the AEP are highly valued by young people and professionals.

There are already a large number of interns who took advantage of their educational programs to go through the AEP, from high school students to professionals. The AEP enabled the paid internship program for final-year students of the career related to space for 1 year. It also enabled international and unpaid virtual internships for professionals specializing in aeronautical and space law, under an agreement with the Ibero-American Institute of Aeronautical and Space Law and the Distance University of Madrid (UDIMA). This enables and positions both parties to provide preparation in the areas of space law and policy.

Dictionary of Spatial Terms in Guarani and Braille

In the Republic of Paraguay there are two official languages, Spanish and Guaraní, an indigenous language.[1] For this reason, we worked with the National Secretariat of Linguistics to agree on a dictionary in Guaraní of spatial terms, that is, words for use in the spatial field. In addition, we worked with specialists to have a Braille dictionary.

Magazine

In 2021, the AEP published a digital magazine, in the year of the beginning of Paraguay's space age, a significant milestone for an emerging country in space matters.

The magazine has 50 articles on various topics, all of them linked to space. It brought together distinguished authorities, such as ambassadors, scientists, and researchers, including the AEP's own specialized officials in the field. As a positive legacy, the most relevant topics developed by the AEP and countless activities carried out to share with the Paraguayan society and the world demostrate the tireless effort for Paraguay to daily harness the benefits of outer space.

Educational and Cultural Programs on Public TV

Another attraction for the general population is the edition of public television programs, with the collaboration of Paraguay TV. The format went from general presentations and interviews with referents of the national and international space. Through this TV show, they seek to provide a technical and detailed look at the agency's ongoing initiatives. "Espacio Py" will cover topics related to the development of satellites, scientific research, international cooperation in the space field,

[1] In Paraguay, officially bilingual, more than 87% of the population speaks Guaraní, a language of oral tradition that has been transmitted from generation to generation for 500 years, without losing its strength, despite the use of *jopara*, the combination of Guarani and Spanish.

and the impact of space technology in key areas such as Earth observation and space engineering.

Through "Espacio Py," the AEP reinforces its commitment to transparency and scientific dissemination, bringing the public closer to the advances that position Paraguay on the international space scene.

Logos of the Paraguayan Space Agency

2017–2023

2023–2028

3 Final Remarks

Paraguay's entry into the space sector through the successful launch of its first satellite, GuaraniSat-1, marks a pivotal moment in the country's technological and scientific development. The Paraguayan Space Agency (AEP) has played a crucial role in this achievement, fostering international cooperation and establishing the regulatory framework needed for future space endeavors. By aligning with global space treaties and developing a comprehensive space policy, Paraguay is positioning itself as an emerging player in the peaceful exploration of space.

The country's commitment to space research and innovation is further demonstrated by its continued projects, such as the development of GuaraniSat-2 and participation in international space initiatives. Paraguay's focus on building national capabilities, supported by strategic international alliances, ensures that its space program will contribute to technological growth, economic development, and global cooperation. The journey from GuaraniSat-1 to future projects symbolizes Paraguay's dedication to advancing its space ambitions and securing its place in the global space community.

References

Online Document

Law 5151 (2014) Paraguayan Space Agency. https://www.bacn.gov.py/leyes-paraguayas/4652/ley-n-5151-de-agencia-espacial-del-Paraguay

Law 5740 (2016) Treaty on principles governing the activities of states in the exploration and use of outer space, including the moon and other celestial bodies. https://www.bacn.gov.py/archivos/8267/Ley+5740.pdf

Law 7051 (2023) Convention on Registration of Objects Launched into Outer Space. https://www.bacn.gov.py/archivos/11250/Ley+7051.pdf

Law 7097 (2023) Convention on International Liability for Damage caused by Space Objects. https://www.bacn.gov.py/archivos/11572/LEY7097.pdf

Law 7175 (2023) Agreement on the rescue of astronauts, the return of astronaut and the return of objects launched into outer space. https://www.bacn.gov.py/archivos/11991/LEY7175.pdf

National Constitution of the Republic of Paraguay (1992). https://www.bacn.gov.py/archivos/9580/CONSTITUCION_ORIGINAL_FIRMADA.pdf

Uruguay

Mariana García

Contents

M. García (✉)
CIDA-E: Centro de Investigación y Difusión Aeronáutico y Espacial, Montevideo, Uruguay
e-mail: cidae@dinacia.gub.uy

I. Grosner (ed.), *Space Regulation in Latin America*, Space Regulations Library 11, https://doi.org/10.1007/978-3-032-05828-7_8

Abstract The document analyzes the development of space regulations in Uruguay, highlighting the country's history and evolution of space governance. Since the creation of CIDA-E: *Centro de Investigación y Difusión Aeronáutico y Espacial* (Aeronautical and Space Research and Diffusion Center) in 1974, Uruguay has played an active role in space diplomacy, participating in international agreements and organizing relevant events. The Uruguayan space industry has grown, driven by companies such as Satellogic and software and artificial intelligence start-ups. The potential of Uruguay to develop a spaceport is mentioned in this document, given its strategic geographic position and institutional stability. The country has progressed in regulating space activities to attract investments and encourage innovation. In short, Uruguay is positioned as a relevant player thanks to the democratization of space, with the development of adequate sector regulation being key.

1 Introduction

The space sector's development in Uruguay is in process, driven by the need to adapt to the demands of international law and by the growing interest in participating in the economy based on outer space. Uruguay has been a signatory to important international space treaties and is taking steps to establish a regulatory framework that encourages the participation of the private sector, ensuring compliance with its international obligations. The creation of a space agency and the implementation of specific policies are today's main priorities.

Reviewing its evolution, in 1974, the Aeronautical and Space Research and Diffusion Center (CIDA-E) was created within the Uruguayan Air Force, one of the first governmental organizations in the world specialized in space issues, being formalized in 1975 by Uruguayan Decree 607/975.

On the other hand, it should be noted that Uruguay has been the venue for important space events. In this regard, in 1996, the Third Space Conference of the Americas was held, co-organized by the Ministry of Foreign Affairs and CIDA-E.

In May 2018, the Global Conference on Space Applications (GLAC 2018) was held in Montevideo. It was co-organized by the International Astronautical Federation (IAF) and CIDA-E, as the center has been a member of the IAF since 1985.

In 2024, together with IILA, CIDA-E organized the first International Seminar on Space Law in Montevideo.

2 Topics

2.1 Which International Space Treaties Has Uruguay Signed as a Party?

Thanks to the pioneering work of CIDA-E, Uruguay has ratified the five international conventions of UNOOSA between 1968 and 1981.

- The Outer Space Treaty (Approved by the General Assembly in 1966): Treaty on Principles Governing the Activities of States in the Exploration and Use of Outer Space, including the Moon and Other Celestial Bodies. Ratified in Uruguay by Law No. 13,854 of 04/06/1970[1]
- Rescue Agreement (Approved by the General Assembly 1967): Agreement on the Rescue of Astronauts, the Return of Astronauts and the Return of Objects Launched into Outer Space. Ratified in Uruguay by Law 13,685 of 17/09/1968[2]
- The Liability Convention (Approved by the General Assembly 1971): Convention on International Liability for Damage Caused by Space Objects. Ratified in Uruguay by Law 14,545 of 22/07/1976[3]
- Registration Convention (Approved by the General Assembly 1974): Convention on registering objects launched into outer space. Ratified in Uruguay by Law 14,675 of 01/07/1977[4]
- Moon Agreement (Approved by the General Assembly in 1979): Agreement Governing the Activities of States on the Moon and Other Celestial Bodies. Ratified in Uruguay by Law 15.169 of 10/08/1981[5]

2.2 Is Uruguay a Member of COPUOS?

Uruguay has been a voting member of the Committee on the Peaceful Uses of Outer Space (COPUOS) since 1981.

[1] https://www.impo.com.uy/bases/leyes-internacional/13854-1970/1.

[2] https://www.impo.com.uy/bases/leyes/13685-1968.

[3] https://www.impo.com.uy/bases/decretos-ley/14545-1976/1.

[4] https://www.impo.com.uy/bases/decretos-ley/14675-1977/1.

[5] https://www.impo.com.uy/bases/decretos-ley-internacional/15169-1981/1.

2.3 Has Uruguay Signed the Artemis Accords?

Uruguay is the 36th country to sign the Artemis Accords, reaffirming its commitment to international space diplomacy. The Artemis Accords not only represent a framework for cooperation in lunar exploration but also reflect our shared values of transparency, interoperability, and the responsible use of space.

Also, under consideration (as of the date of this article) is the signing of a collaboration agreement with the Chinese Deep Space Exploration Laboratory (DSEL), also in relation to the exploration of our natural satellite.

Both agreements aim to strengthen space diplomacy and develop guidelines that will govern future generations in lunar exploration.

This collaboration reinforces our value as a neutral and conciliatory country that trusts in international cooperation as an essential pillar for progress in space exploration.

2.4 Can Space Activities Be Classified as Dual Use, or Are They Only for Defense or Civil Purposes?

In Uruguay, space activities are classified mainly for civil and research purposes. However, the dual-use potential of space technologies is recognized, which requires adequate regulation to avoid the militarization of space and ensure that activities are peaceful and oriented toward sustainable development.

In this regard, the bill for creating a space division within the Uruguayan Air Force (FAU) is being promoted. This responds to the need for a specific body to address defense issues, where the technical capabilities related to space applications that the military institution requires to fulfill its mission are gathered and generated. The regulation considered those matters of greatest interest to the defense, such as intelligence, surveillance, recognition, management of emergency situations, and security of space operations, reserving them to the scope of its competence in the interest of the State. It is currently under consideration by Parliament.

2.5 Is There a Registry of Space Objects Maintained by the United Nations?

The Uruguayan project of the Decree of the National Registry of Objects Launched into Space aims to begin filling the existing legal gap at the internal level in our country. It complies with the international agreements signed by our country. However, it has not yet been approved by the Executive Branch.

It should be noted that despite our country not having a national body with space registry competence, the National Innovation Agency (ANII) carries out this work and fully complies by registering under the United Nations.

2.6 Does Uruguay Have a National Specific Space Act or Regulations?

Space Legislation and Governance in Uruguay
Uruguay is currently developing a regulatory framework that will provide the country with guidelines for establishing space institutions and regulations.

In 2021, the creation of the first level of governance was promoted: the National Space Policy Board.

National Decree 71/2022[6] allowed the creation of a Space Policy Board, which was approved by the Executive Branch and published on March 7, 2022. This interministerial body comprises permanent members, advisory members, and occasional members, allowing flexibility for its integration according to the subject to be considered and discussed. This is the body currently responsible for supervising and regulating space activities.

Through Article 3 in the said Decree, the Executive Branch conferred on the Board the following duties: (a) Advise the Executive Branch on all matters related to establishing a space policy and its execution. (b) Evaluate compliance with the rules governing space services by those who use them and propose the modification or adoption of the relevant legal and regulatory rules to the Executive Branch. (c) Issue opinions on issues within its field that are raised. (d) Facilitate and coordinate the research and use of space science and technology activities of public and private institutions or organizations. (e) Promote the execution of multilateral or bilateral space cooperation agreements with space agencies or other similar public or private national or foreign organizations. (f) Ensure compliance with the international treaties that regulate outer space, signed and ratified by the country. (g) Promote the training of national technicians for the best use of space technology. (h) Develop space projects. (i) Assign competent organizations to control, supervise, and register space activities. (j) Authorize the performance of any space activity, understood as such the construction, processing of space data, launching, operation, orientation, and reentry of space objects in and from outer space, as well as other related activities. (k) Issue any waiver, revocation, suspension, or declaration of expiration of authorizations or concessions for space services. (l) Propose to the Executive Branch the designation of national representatives and delegations to international organizations specialized in the matter. (m) Give instructions to representatives or delegates of the Republic, who must attend national or international events or meetings related to the space activity. (n) Carry out the control and supervision of the

[6] https://www.impo.com.uy/bases/decretos-originales/71-2022/1.

activities of the Republic and eventually sanction violations of the rules that regulate space activity.

There are also a series of complementary rules for space activity, which are expressed below.

Spectrum Management Effective radio frequency spectrum management is essential for satellite communication and data transmission. Every government must establish processes for allocating, coordinating, and monitoring the spectrum to avoid interference and allow efficient use of the spectrum by satellite operators. In this manner, on February 21, 2001, the Communications Services Regulatory Unit (URSEC)[7] was created as a decentralized body of the Executive Branch. On July 9, 2020, its legal nature was changed, becoming a decentralized State legal entity (decentralized service), directed by a Board of Directors made up of three members. The law established URSEC's main tasks, which are regulating and controlling activities and sectors related to telecommunications.[8]

Intellectual Property Rights A solid legal framework is a must to promote innovation and protect intellectual property.

Intellectual property is a technical legal instrument that has been defined as the most important tool for helping innovation so creators can control their products, negotiate, and obtain economic benefits from it.

In Uruguay, copyright is guaranteed by the constitution and special laws that recognize the author's right of ownership over the production of its invention, science, or art. On the other hand, the registration of patents for inventions is an exclusive right granted by the government to the owner of an invention susceptible to industrial applications.

Patents grant rights in the country in which they were registered. Therefore, each invention must be presented in the different countries where it seeks protection, which makes implementation difficult, especially for start-ups. For this reason, Uruguay recently joined the Patent Cooperation Treaty[9] (PCT) signed in Washington on June 19, 1970, which facilitates the possibility of filing patents internationally, standardizing requirements, and extending the filing period in the different member countries.

Data Protection and Privacy Since satellites collect and transmit data, it is essential to establish standards to safeguard the protection and privacy of data. In this regard, the Personal Data Protection and Habeas Data Action Law[10] and its regulatory decrees will be applied depending on the potential of the data collected by each

[7] Ley 17.296 de 21 de febrero de 2001.

[8] https://www.gub.uy/unidad-reguladora-servicios-comunicaciones/institucional/creacion-evolucion-historica.

[9] Ley 20.299 de fecha 21 de junio de 2024.

[10] Ley 18.331 de fecha 11 de agosto de 2008.

satellite to affect privacy. In such cases, the databases that involve personal data must be registered with an agency created to protect confidential information.

Investment Promotion[11] Uruguay's political and macroeconomic stability, as well as the incentive regimes that the country has generated together with access to the region through the Mercado Comun del Sur (MERCOSUR) agreement and other bilateral agreements, has the potential to directly benefit the space industry. Since 1998, the law for the promotion and protection of investments has established the legal framework for its application in national territory, whether by national or foreign investors. The law divides tax incentives into those of a general nature and those of a specific nature regarding investments, particularly granting tax exemption and VAT refunds on purchases.

This law has evolved through regulatory decrees with different options adapted to different specific activities. In this sense, for example, R&D companies governed by private law have been promoted, being able to obtain tax credits.[12] Similarly, as applicable to the software industry, the income derived from software development activities and the services linked to it is exempt from IRAE tax (tax on income from economic activities).

Exemption from Customs Duties In this area, we can mention the free trade zone regimes (ZZFF), which have been declared of national interest to achieve a series of economic and social objectives such as job creation, promoting activities with high technological content, promoting decentralization, and developing international trade, which is materialized through a preferential tax regime with broad exemptions. There are currently 12 ZZFF in the country distributed in the cities of Canelones, Colonia, Colonia Suiza, Florida, Fray Bentos, Libertad, Montevideo, Nueva Helvecia, Nueva Palmira, Punta Pereira, and Rivera. In general terms, users enjoy the right to a total exemption from national taxes, with the exception of special contributions to social security.[13] In the same sense, through Law No. 19,784, industrial parks (PIs) and scientific-technological parks (PCTs) were declared to be of national interest, defined as that public or private portion of land authorized by the Executive Branch, equipped with the infrastructure for carrying out industrial, service and training activities, research, and innovation. The PIs have the objective of installing and operating manufacturing and service industries, while the PCTs have the objective of installing knowledge and innovation centers, as well as innovative companies.

[11] Guía del Inversor Uruguay XXI file:///C:/Users/garci/Downloads/Reg%C3%ADmenes%20promocionales%20para%20la%20inversi%C3%B3n-PDF.pdf.

[12] Ley N° 19.739, Decreto N° 407/019.

[13] Ley N° 15.921 y modificativas, y Decreto N° 309/018.

2.7 Does Uruguay Have a Space Agency?

Lastly, there is the bill for the constitution of the Uruguayan Space Agency, planned as a decentralized body within the Presidency of the Republic, which will act with technical autonomy.

Its objective will be to direct, coordinate, and implement the Republic's space policy originating from the National Space Policy Board and its related instruments and formulate the National Space Plan, its dependent programs, and its projects. It will promote the development of the space sector in Uruguay with an emphasis on its inhabitants' economic, social, and cultural development. It is worth clarifying that at the time of this work, the bill is under consideration by the Uruguayan Parliament.

This law will also constitute our first space law since its articles include key definitions for the space legal system, such as the determination of a space object and the limit our country takes for space jurisdiction. To this end, the latest recommendations of the United Nations General Assembly on national legislation were considered.

From an administrative point of view, this law aims to ensure coherence and transparency in the authorization and supervision of space activities.

2.8 What Is the Primary Regulatory Body Responsible for Overseeing Space Activities?

The National Space Policy Board is the body that currently allows the country to develop in space matters, respond to the demands of the private sector, and represent the country abroad.

However, the main regulatory body in Uruguay will be the future Uruguayan Space Agency, which will be responsible for supervising all space activities in the country. This agency will work closely with the current National Space Policy Board and other national and international bodies to ensure compliance with space regulations.

2.9 What Are the Primary Regulations Governing Space Activities, and How Are Private Companies Performing Space Activities Authorized, Monitored, and Supervised?

Space regulations in Uruguay are under development, focusing on the authorization, monitoring, and supervision of activities performed by private companies. Implementing these regulations is essential to ensure that space activities are carried out in a safe and transparent manner, facilitating the growth of the private sector in the space industry.

2.10 *Is There Any Effort Toward Capacity Building in the Space Sector, Both in Terms of Technologies and Regulatory Matters?*

Uruguay has been promoting significant efforts in capacity building in the space sector, both technologically and regulatorily. These efforts include collaboration with academic and technological institutions and participation in international initiatives that allow the country to develop a robust space infrastructure.

Satellite Industry

Regarding technology and training, in 2014, Uruguay launched a college-grade satellite called ANTELSAT to train students in space technologies and develop skills in communications and aerospace engineering. The satellite, which was developed by the Faculty of Engineering of the University of the Republic and sponsored by the State-owned telecommunications provider ANTEL, was the first State satellite.

Years later, because of the arrival of nanosatellites, which are those small structures usually in the form of a cube that does not exceed 10 × 10 × 10 cm and that can be scalable through a set of several blocks of similar dimensions, the miniaturization of electronic components was now possible and with very good capacities. This technological change allowed the satellite industry to leap exponentially, as satellite development costs decreased dramatically.

With this concept in mind, the Argentine company Satellogic, dedicated to Earth observation (EO), established itself in Uruguay in 2015. In 2016, they launched the first commercial satellites developed in Uruguayan territory, where their integration and manufacturing plant is located.

Thanks to the satellites launched by Satellogic, the number of satellites manufactured in the country and sent into space exceeds 50, becoming the leading provider of high-resolution satellite imagery offering rapid integration and scalable manufacturing of EO satellites. Their low-Earth-orbit (LEO) satellite constellation and product platform deliver geospatial data at low costs, making Earth observation data accessible and affordable for better global coverage.

In the software industry, Uruguay has Latin America's highest per capita software export rate. In this area, we find, for example, the company Digital Sense, a start-up that develops software for processing satellite images.

Following these successful experiences, the Argentine start-up Epic Aerospace was established in 2019; they build orbital transfer vehicles (OTV). Their LEO line of spacecraft is the simplest and most cost-effective way to deploy anything into low Earth orbit, from one-off demonstration missions to full constellations with precise orbital spreading. Their geostationary orbit (GEO) line spacecraft provide complete insertion services, taking satellites from the drop-off Geostationary Transfer Orbit (GTO) to their precise slot in GEO.

We also find SpaceAI within the industry, which creates groundbreaking distributed-edge supercomputers and ground stations. The NIO CubeSat is a cutting-edge distributed-edge supercomputer and ground station. This compact yet powerful device connects the network to the real world, enhancing unmanned systems, robotics, the Internet of Things (IoT), and space Internet capabilities. Their groundbreaking technology is designed to revolutionize data processing and connectivity on the ground and in space.

Another good example is TLON Space, which is now looking at Uruguay as its next launch location. Their unique approach and engineering creativity allow them to substantially miniaturize their launch vehicle. This has resulted in a significant mass reduction while maintaining commercial viability, a milestone that has not been possible until now. "Aventura I" is on track to become the lightest orbital rocket in the world. At a full weight of 500 kg, it can insert an approximate 10-kg payload into a circular 250-km Sun-synchronous orbit (SSO). All companies are examples of civil use of space technologies.

2.11 How Does Uruguay Engage in International Cooperation in the Space Sector, Both in Terms of Technologies and Representation in International Organizations? Are There Any Partnerships with Other Latin American Countries?

Uruguay became a full member and shareholder of the International Telecommunications Satellite Organization (INTELSAT) in 1981.

More recently, Uruguay has participated in Italo-Latin American Institute (IILA) space agency meetings and will be an Ibero-American Space Agency Network associate member.

It is also considering joining the Latin American and Caribbean Space Agency (ALCE).

2.12 How Does the Private Sector Conduct Its Activities in the Field of Space Exploration?

The private sector in Uruguay, led by companies such as Satellogic, plays a crucial role in space exploration. These companies are developing advanced software and artificial intelligence technologies, positioning Uruguay as a center of innovation in the region.

2.13 What Are the Plans for Space Activities in Uruguay? Are Manned Flights and Spaceports Being Planned?

Even today, for some people in Latin America, the idea of our countries' participation in space activities seems like science fiction, but this is no longer the case.

Data obtained from space satellites are increasingly used in our daily lives, and for this to happen, it is necessary to transport these space objects to their destination in orbit. In the current commercial space era or New Space, the business world demands new places to carry out these launches.

Therefore, States have taken on a different role, abandoning the role of leading actors to play the role of promoter and supervisor. This role is fundamental in the development of the space sector and consistent with the obligations acquired from the international corpus juris, especially Articles VI and VIII of the Outer Space Treaty.

Thus, the object of space law is now focused on the construction of different organizational architectures at a national level, which vary according to the space policy of each country, from space agencies, ministries of science and technology, specialized commissions, etc., in charge of the difficult task of regulating commercial space activities. Regarding planning the regulation and licensing of spaceports for Uruguay, it is taken into account that spaceports are currently transitioning, given that low Earth orbits are increasingly commercialized. Private companies are competing to offer this service and need space to launch.

The United States currently has 12 spaceports whose license is granted by the Federal Aviation Administration (FAA).

The licensing process is a standard method a State uses to authorize and regulate nongovernmental space activities at a national level. The license requirements include scientific, technical, environmental, safety, and financial criteria. Regarding spaceports, there is no definition at the level of international regulations, but in general terms, it can be said that any site or place has the capacity to carry out a launch.

In Uruguay, through Decree 71/022 for the Creation of the National Space Policy Board, the Executive Branch granted this body, in Article 3, sufficient authority to act as the competent body for the development of the national regulatory framework in the field of commercial suborbital transportation.

Regarding location, Uruguay presents notable regional advantages for conducting launches, with an extensive coastal strip and a favorable orientation toward the east. The value proposition for launching small satellites from our country includes launches to polar and equatorial orbits from the same point. This is complemented by attributes of institutional solidity, socioeconomic stability, ease of doing business, tax incentives, world-class telecommunications, and a dynamic innovation ecosystem.

Simultaneously, significant interest has emerged in the private sector regarding rocket launch projects to transport small satellites into space. Recognizing this opportunity, the Uruguayan State has evaluated the technical and legal feasibility of a spaceport in our territory. As a result of this study, the regulation of this activity, in its various phases, is currently in progress to provide a solid framework for investments, guaranteeing the State's interests with appropriate oversight while aiming to maintain dynamic processes for interested companies.

2.14 What Are (and Should Be) the Perspectives of Uruguay on Regulatory Matters Related to Space Debris, Militarization and Weaponization of Space, and Exploitation of Space Natural Resources?

Uruguay maintains a firm stance against the militarization of space and advocates for its peaceful use. The country is also committed to regulating space debris and exploiting natural resources in space, promoting a sustainable and responsible approach in these areas.

In reference to this, the diplomatic mission of Uruguay in Vienna participated in the 67th session of the United Nations Committee on the Peaceful Uses of Outer Space (COPUOS), held in June 2024, where Uruguay cosponsored the "Lisbon Declaration on Outer Space Activities" presentation by Portugal on the Management and Sustainability of Space Activities that constitute the contributions of the space field for the next Future Summit. A series of preparatory events were held to consult with Member States in a collaborative effort to achieve this declaration. This decision by Uruguay underlines our firm commitment to the sustainable and responsible management of space activities.

The Lisbon Declaration establishes principles and guidelines that are fundamental for creating international standards that will govern space activities in the future. Just as the COPUOS conventions, ratified by Uruguay, defined the regulations that govern our current activities, this declaration seeks to establish a framework that allows for the responsible and sustainable use of space in the coming decades.

By adhering to this declaration, Uruguay reaffirms its commitment to the following principles:

1. Protection of the space environment: Minimize the generation of space debris and promote the cleanup of existing debris.
2. Peaceful use of space: Promote international cooperation to ensure that space is used exclusively for peaceful purposes.
3. Equitable access to space: Ensure that all nations, regardless of their level of development, can benefit from the use of space.
4. Responsible for innovation: Promote innovation and technological development that contribute to the sustainability of space.

Adherence to the Lisbon Declaration is a significant step in this direction, and Uruguay is proud to be part of this collective effort.

2.15 Other Relevant Topics

Topics of Interest and Future Plans

Among the possible lines of work are attracting new actors, including fundamental companies in the space industry, and seeking international prospecting through investment attraction agencies.

At the same time, actions are carried out to raise awareness in the local industry about the opportunities in the space sector. In this regard, it is important to have suppliers of the technologies and components necessary for this industry, carry out actions to attract and develop businesses it in the country, have a catalog of regional suppliers, or facilitate the import processes.

Access to talent should be included in a complementary manner, emphasizing training programs within the academy on future challenges and outlining an agenda of specific actions with this focus. On the other hand, talent from abroad is attracted, exposing the excellent living conditions in the country.

Work is also being done in the country to promote innovative start-ups, making access to financing for developing ideas or their acceleration possible.

In this sense and as an example, Microsoft chose Uruguay to establish the first and only AI Co-Innovation Lab in the southern hemisphere, and the first and only in, being only the third one outside the United States (since today there are only two in Shanghai, China, and Munich, Germany). This laboratory will help solve various technological challenges for organizations in the region and obtain guidance and recommendations from experts to materialize the full potential of artificial intelligence and the Internet of Things.

Also recently, at the government level, Uruguay Innovation Hub was established, a national program seeking to propel Uruguay to the forefront of the knowledge economy. It focuses on consolidating the local innovation ecosystem, through the implementation of instruments and the development of initiatives that promote collaboration and synergies between the various actors in the ecosystem. It seeks to promote and accelerate ventures in high-growth sectors such as advanced technologies, green technologies, and biotechnology, as well as position the country as a benchmark in the search and resolution of global problems through innovation.

Both initiatives align with the Uruguayan government's vision to become an innovation center for the region, positioning the country as a facilitator of innovation and development.

3 Final Remarks

Aware that the space sector is an ecosystem very similar in its general description to other high-tech sectors such as artificial intelligence, biotechnology, or cybersecurity and that ultimately, all these industries find great potential for expansion in international trade, helping with their dynamism to improve performance in other sectors (spillover), it is understood that their treatment is a priority and a complementary must.

This innovative industry development phenomenon ultimately underlines and complements the possibilities of establishing a space cluster in our country.

Implementing a solid legal framework in national space law is essential to promoting the sector's expansion in Uruguay and, consequently, the country's economic and technological growth.

Creating the Uruguayan Space Agency will allow space activities to be aligned with international standards, promoting space activities. In addition, the regulation and licensing of spaceports and other related activities have the potential to attract foreign and national investments, together with existing promotion policies, leading to Uruguay's participation in the global space economy.

This approach will not only position the country as a relevant player in the space industry but will also generate employment opportunities, promote education and research in key areas, and strengthen the ecosystem of technological start-ups.

MIX
Papier aus verantwortungsvollen Quellen
Paper from responsible sources
FSC® C105338

If you have any concerns about our products,
you can contact us on
ProductSafety@springernature.com

In case Publisher is established outside the EU,
the EU authorized representative is:
Springer Nature Customer Service Center GmbH
Europaplatz 3, 69115 Heidelberg, Germany

Printed by Libri Plureos GmbH
in Hamburg, Germany